Family and The State of Theory

Family and
The State of Theory

DAVID CHEAL

UNIVERSITY OF TORONTO PRESS
Toronto   Buffalo

First published in North America in 1991 by
University of Toronto Press
Toronto Buffalo

ISBN 0–8020–5994–5 (cloth)
ISBN 0–8020–6928–2 (paper)

Typeset in Times 10/12 by Columns Design and Production
Services Ltd, Reading, England
Printed and bound in Great Britain by Billing and Sons Ltd,
Worcester

Canadian Cataloguing in Publication Data

Cheal, David J.
  Family and the state of theory.
Includes bibliographical references and index.
ISBN 0–8020–5994–5 (cloth)   ISBN 0–8020–6928–2 (pbk.)
1. Family.   2. Family – Research.   I. Title.
HQ728.C54 1991   306.85   C91–094102–5

For Viv
lover, wife, friend

CONTENTS

Acknowledgements   ix

Introduction   x

Chapter 1 Family theory after the Big Bang   **1**
   Standard theory of the family   3
   From convergence to divergence   6
   Feminist theory   9
   Out of order   11
   From positivism to post-positivism   14
   Contemporary contradictions   18
   Notes   23

**Chapter 2 Progress and decline: Modernism and
anti-modernism**   **25**
   Social science and modernity   26
   Modernism and the idea of progress   30
   Family changes: Progress or decline?   37
   Anti-modernism and the idea of decline   40
   The limits to anti-modernism   45
   Notes   47

**Chapter 3 System and liberation: Dialectics of modernity,
division I**   **49**
   Power over life   52
   Family policy   55
   The politics of reproduction   57
   The medical model and family interventions   60

Family systems theories   64
Family conservation and familial conservatism   72
Beyond bounded systems   75
Notes   79

**Chapter 4 Private and public: Dialectics of modernity,
division II**   **81**
The private family   86
Capital, class and labour   91
The family and the state   106
Beyond private/public dualism   111
Notes   116

**Chapter 5 The one and the many: Modernity and
post-modernity**   **119**
Family changes revisited: Standardization or
diversification?   120
Rethinking what we study   125
Individualization   132
Something is happening   141
The post-modern family?   145
Notes   150

**Chapter 6 Conclusion: The instabilities of post-modern
social theory**   **153**
From polarization to pluralization   155
In search of the future   159
The instability of analytical categories   162
The fuzziness of 'schools of thought'   163
Notes   165

References   167

Author index   197

Subject index   202

ACKNOWLEDGEMENTS

Preparation of this book was assisted by a study leave from the University of Winnipeg. The author gratefully acknowledges permission to use material from the following sources: Chapter 2 in *Marriage and the Family in Canada Today*, ed. G.N. Ramu, Prentice-Hall Canada Inc.; Chapter 3 in *Family and Marriage*, ed. K. Ishwaran (Wall and Thompson); *Habits of the Heart*, Robert Bellah *et al.*, copyright 1985 The Regents of the University of California; *Acta Sociologica*, vol. 32 (1989), p. 174, Universitetsforlaget (Norwegian University Press), Oslo.

The author also wishes to acknowledge the understanding and support extended by the Social Sciences and Humanities Research Council of Canada, whose acceptance of research rescheduling made writing this book possible. Secretarial services were provided by Lesley Murphy. Her unfailing commitment to meeting deadlines, and her dedication to producing a manuscript of high quality, were vital assets for prompt publication in a rapidly changing field.

INTRODUCTION

A number of influential theories about family life are brought together in this book, in order for them to be examined in relation to one another. In this way the following pages provide a broad introduction to concepts and issues in family theorizing. Further, an overarching conceptual framework is provided that is intended to help students understand why different theories exist, and to provide them with a positive orientation towards theoretical pluralism.

Students of family and marriage are often puzzled by the conflicting images of family life that are presented in sociology. Their confusion is not surprising, as family theorists are probably more divided now than they have been at any other time. Sociologists often interpret the meanings and significances of family processes in different ways, and they have drawn contradictory conclusions about the nature of family living and about its future. Making sense of that diversity of opinion is a matter of some importance. It is closely bound up with larger changes that are underway in our understanding of sociological theory as the codification of sociological knowledge.

The position adopted in this book is that sociological knowledge is an aspect of contemporary culture. This approach to the interpretation of knowledge encompasses two well-known points of view that are often thought to be alternatives. One approach to knowledge, associated especially with positivism and standard sociological theory, conceives of knowledge as a set of propositions. This leads naturally to a concern with the methods of reasoning by which propositions are produced, and with the methods for providing proof by which propositions are validated and made publicly available. A second approach, associated especially with Marxism and the sociology of knowledge, conceives of knowledge as the subjective outcome of social structures. This leads to a concern with the social determination of ideas and ideology.

These two problematics of knowledge are both important, and they receive some attention in this book. However, their significance for present purposes lies in the way in which they are both located within a broader account of the social organization of knowledge. The key idea underlying the account of sociological theory provided in this book is that knowledge is considered to be a special kind of cultural activity. Knowledge is that dimension of culture which deals with competent intersubjective signification or, in other words competent discourse. The various contents of knowledge may be distinguished by the different kinds of discourse that take place concerning them. To put the same point in a different way, different discourses express different knowledges.

The existence of a number of competing theories in sociology has sometimes been defined as a 'crisis', in so far as it is thought to impede the universal integration of social scientific knowledge. However, when sociological knowledge is considered as a form of culture, the issue of theoretical diversity in sociology is better redefined as an instance of the much larger question of cultural pluralism in contemporary social life. It is from this point of view that the present book has been written. The thesis of cultural pluralism provides the main theme that links the chapters together, and it provides the motivation for taking issues of theoretical diversity seriously. How we deal with theoretical pluralism within sociology is an index of how we deal with cultural pluralism in contemporary society in general. The question of how we choose to live and work, in the face of sociological and other pluralisms, is important for all our futures.

The task of making sense of the diversity that exists in family theory today is a special challenge for the current generation of students. It is not enough for students to be exposed to only a minor fraction of the many kinds of theory which are being developed. Any narrowing of the sociological imagination is to be regretted, for whatever reasons it occurs. It reduces our ability to understand how people with different sociological backgrounds from our own think, as well as limiting our capacities to talk to them effectively, or even to recognize that they exist. In an increasingly interdependent world, this is a disturbing thought. Living as we do in complex pluralistic societies, there is always something useful to be learned from encounters with ideas that are different from our own.

Courses and textbooks, even handbooks, are inevitably selective since it is not possible to cover everything. However, a survey of reviews of family theories published in different countries quickly reveals that the process of selection is not random. For example, American sociologists of the family rarely mention Marxism, which has had a considerable influence on the sociology of the family in Britain and, especially, in Canada. At the same time, British and other European family theorists do not often pay much attention to exchange theory, which has a wide following in the United States in one version or another. These obvious contrasts between national traditions are only the tip of the iceberg of intellectual selectivity in family studies. Within national sociologies too, presentations of the field are often slanted towards one style of theorizing rather than another.

The present book can hardly be expected to overcome these massive limitations in sociological knowledge. What it does do is suggest how we might begin to trace the networks of sociological theories that criss-cross the English-speaking world, and that link us to wider communities of social thought. In the course of doing so, some attention will be paid to the 'national question' in sociology. It should be apparent that no approach to this question can be completely satisfactory from every point of view, particularly where nationalistic and linguistic sensitivities are involved. The following brief remarks on that point may be useful, in order to avoid any potential misunderstandings about what this book does, and does not, set out to do.

Despite significant national differences, such as those mentioned above, sociology is an international discipline and it draws much of its strength from this fact. The core of sociology as a discipline is constituted by its relations with world-wide processes of modernization, such as urbanization, industrialization and the struggles for emancipation of oppressed and disadvantaged groups. This book locates the sociology of the family within these global processes and should therefore be suitable for wide usage.

Of course this study is constrained by the conditions of its production: the literature cited is exclusively in the English language and the sources discussed, as well as the illustrations used, are drawn mainly from the American, British and English Canadian social science communities, with which the author is most familiar. However, there are also significant references to authors and issues from the Scandinavian and Continental European countries, as well as Australia.

Clearly, national emphases in this book are not equal. More references are made to the works of American social scientists than to those of any other single national group. At the same time, it must be said that American reflections upon the state of family theory have only recently been informed in a serious way by the sociology of knowledge, and they have yet to be adequately integrated with current work in the cultural sciences. The conceptual framework within which particular theories are analysed here is, therefore, more European than American.

The manner in which I have set about the task of describing the various theories differs from that of most American accounts of family studies. It merits a brief comment here so that the reader can better judge its value. To begin with, the point of view from which this book is written is that the most important divisions in social theory are best understood as consequences of the contradictory nature of social life itself. The argument to be presented here is that there exists today a variety of social contradictions, all of which can be seen as consequences of the general process of modernization. Sociological theories of family life are the results of human reflection upon that process, which is described as a general feature of *modernity*.

The value of the sociological conceptualization of modernity for this book is as a meta-theory: that is to say, it is a theory that can account for the characteristics of other theories. It does three things that are very important in establishing the grounds for my subject matter. First, it provides descriptions of the contents of particular theories. It does this by identifying what are the key concepts in a theory, and by translating those concepts into the common terms of a general discourse. The initial problem for any comparative analysis of theories is that of conceptual abstraction – of finding a sufficiently general form of discourse within which a variety of concepts can be shown to have definite relations of similarity and difference. Second, the theory of modernity gives explanations for the existence of particular theories: that is to say, it accounts for the origins of theories within given intellectual, social or historical contexts. Finally, it accounts for the existence of sociology itself. The sociology of the family is a highly specialized form of knowledge. It is argued here that as such it must be viewed as a result of cultural production in specifically modern societies.

The concept of modernity is used in two ways in this book. First, the concept of modernity is applied to history, in order to show how modern social organization produces contrasting, and often competing, types of sociological theories. This theme is taken up in Chapters 3 and 4, which are concerned with two dialectics of modernity. Chapter 3 deals with the opposition between theories of system equilibrium and theories of liberation. Chapter 4 deals with the contrasting experiences that are derived from differentiated domains of public and private life.

Second, the concept of modernity is presented as being itself a cultural construct in history. It is an aspect of that world view which is referred to here as modernism. The modernist world view has possessed enormous prestige and power, not only in everyday life but, perhaps especially, in the social sciences. Nevertheless, it is in fact only one of several possible world views. The modern world view is contested, in whole or in part, by anti-modernists and by post-modernists. Anti-modernist approaches, which are described in Chapter 2, have a long history and display recurring features that are by now well known. Post-modernism, which is discussed in Chapters 5 and 6, on the other hand, is an emergent phenomenon whose outlines are not yet entirely clear, even to its advocates. Post-modern theories have not yet given rise to a substantial body of literature in the sociology of the family. In the discussions of post-modernism we therefore begin to test the limits of existing theories, in order to explore the implications of new ways of thinking.

It is appropriate to close this Introduction, and to open the book itself, on that tentative and forward-looking note. The only thing we can be sure of in family sociology, and in family life, is that families and family theories will continue to change, in ways that are not completely predictable from our inherited knowledge of the past.

CHAPTER 1

FAMILY THEORY AFTER THE BIG BANG

Theories of the problems and strengths in families are important issues studied by sociologists today. Serious questions are asked about the possibilities and directions of change in families, and the nature of family life is thought about and debated in the most thorough fashion. The prominent social theorist Anthony Giddens has remarked that 'The study of the family used to seem to many one of the dullest of endeavours. Now it appears as one of the most provocative and involving' (Giddens, 1987b:23). In this book we are going to find out why Giddens, and many other sociologists who were previously uninterested in family studies, today find the sociology of the family both exciting and demanding.[1]

One of the reasons why the sociology of the family is so challenging now is because there are many different, and often conflicting, views about family life. We will examine the nature of those differences, and we will consider what their implications are for sociology and for understanding family life. In order to do this we must first examine how the principal controversies in the sociology of the family came into existence, and how they are connected to larger issues in the history of sociology.

The history of sociology is important not so much for what it tells us about the past as for what it can tell us about the present, and for what it may tell us about the future. By briefly tracing the main lines of development of the sociology of the family we will be in a better position to find out where family sociology is going, and what we can expect from it. This will be the main task of this chapter.

The recent history of sociology is one of great dissension. This has been especially evident in the sociology of the family. Indeed, it has often been said that the sociology of the family was in crisis during the decades of the 1970s and the 1980s. The dimensions of that crisis were carefully observed, and the major issues of debate have been thoughtfully described (Liljeström, 1986). However, students of the family are often unsure about what this situation means for the family field as a discipline. Jetse Sprey has recently stated that:

> The connection between the perceived aims of knowing and its methodological and theoretical aspects indeed seems vital to our understanding of where we are going as a discipline. It would be helpful to know, for instance, *why*, at this point, our field attracts groups with differing interests and to what extent such a continuous but changing heterogeneity is a factor in its survival. (Sprey, 1990:12)

These are important questions. They justify taking a close look at developments in one of the most dynamic areas of sociology today.

We will begin by describing some of the changes that have occurred in the sociology of the family during the past three decades. These will be illustrated by focusing upon the feminist challenge to earlier approaches in social theory. The fact that feminism is selected for special emphasis here does not mean that it has been the only significant new approach in the period under review. Rather, it is because feminist scholarship has constituted a particularly rich medium for the development and circulation of ideas of many kinds. Feminist scholars have provided a global forum within which new ideas have been rapidly exchanged. Unlike much social research, which focuses on narrowly defined problems with a view to national policy recommendations, feminist studies have been at the leading edge of international communications. Also, feminists have subjected marriage and other social institutions to the most profound questioning. In so doing they have explored practically all of the existing theoretical possibilities in western sociology. The most creative intellectual traditions – such as phenomenology, Marxism, symbolic interactionism and post-structuralism – were sooner or later all reflected in feminist analyses of family life, and they were in turn transformed by it. The recent history of the sociology of the family is of course much more than the history of feminism;

however, it is above all in the history of feminist influence upon theories of family relationships that the major directions of change today can be discerned.

Recent changes in the sociology of the family have involved a great upheaval in the nature of theorizing about family life. At the same time, dramatic shifts have been occurring in families themselves. Both events have caused a great deal of confusion, and their conjunction has made it necessary to sort out a lot of previously unexamined ideas (Scanzoni *et al.*, 1989). Nostalgia for a time when life was simpler is a common response to such disorienting change, in family life and in professional life. One result is that people often find it comforting to think of a past when family values were strong, and when everyone knew the value of family living. The decade of the 1950s is a common reference point for such nostalgia.

Standard theory of the family

The nostalgic feelings for family life as it existed in the 1950s that are found today among some sociologists are strengthened by an image of unity and certainty in sociological theory, which also existed at that time. It is necessary to examine what happened to that unity, and to see why it is that we can never go back to it. Nostalgia for a lost paradise is comforting, but it is no guide to the present.

It has been said that the decade of the 1950s was the 'golden age' of the nuclear family. That decade was also dominated intellectually by a kind of sociological analysis which supported nuclear family living (Goldthorpe, 1987). This type of sociological analysis was developed mainly in the United States by theorists such as Talcott Parsons and William J. Goode. Mullins called this approach 'standard American sociology', because its domination of the American discipline in a formative period of growth meant that it had deep and lasting effects (Mullins, 1973). It established patterns for sociological education which are still followed today. The influence of standard American sociology also extended far outside the United States, since its rise coincided with the high point of American prestige in the period immediately after the Second World War. In recognition of that international dimension we may refer to this type of sociology simply as *standard sociological theory* (Cheal, 1989a; 1989b).

In the standard theory of family life the family is believed to be an adaptive unit which mediates between the individual and society. Defined in this way, the family is held to meet the needs of individuals for personal growth and development, and for physical and emotional integrity. An early, and very influential, version of standard sociological theory was *structural functionalism*. That approach maintains that any major social institution must ensure the well-being not only of individuals, but also of the society upon which those individuals depend. Thus, families are believed to perform essential functions (or 'functional prerequisites') for family members, and for society. Kingsley Davis (1948) argued that the existence of family groups is to be accounted for by the ways in which they meet society's needs for the continuous replacement of its members. In his view, the four main social functions of the family are the reproduction, maintenance, social placement and socialization of the young. Later sociological discussions narrowed the definition of family functionality somewhat, but throughout the 1950s and early 1960s the structural functionalist argument remained much the same. The family was considered to be a universal institution because it fulfilled universal functional prerequisites for the survival of human societies (Reiss, 1965).

If the structural functional argument is correct, then the smooth functioning of families must be vital for the success of any society. According to Goode, the failure of the family to perform adequately 'means that the goals of the larger society may not be attained effectively' (Goode, 1964:5). It follows that in a normally functioning society, when the structure of the society changes the forms of family life will be reshaped, so as to ensure that societal needs continue to be met. Standard sociological theorists have therefore been most interested in the 'fit' between family and society (Harris, 1983). They claim that in the modern western societies families have adapted to meet the needs of an industrial economy. The dominant family type produced by this process of social evolution has sometimes been described as the 'conjugal family' (since it is founded upon the marriage relationship) and sometimes as the 'nuclear family' (since it is a minimal social group). This type of family group is a small unit that Goode hypothesized fits the needs of industrial organization, such as a high level of labour mobility (Goode, 1963).

The principal architect of the sociological model of the 'isolated nuclear family' was the prominent structural functionalist sociologist Talcott Parsons. He claimed that the conjugal or nuclear family is the only type of family that does not conflict with the requirements of an industrial economy (Parsons, 1964). Consisting of husband, wife and children (if any), it is small enough to be highly mobile. Furthermore, the obligations of family members to kin outside the nuclear family are held to be separated from occupational commitments, and thus individuals are relatively free from kinship pressures at work (Parsons, 1949). Parsons described the American kinship system as consisting of interlocking conjugal families (Parsons, 1943). In the conjugal family the tie between husband and wife is the central family relationship. Because of the overwhelming importance of that relationship, descent ties (that is, ties through parents and children) are relatively de-emphasized. According to Parsons, that under-emphasis makes it difficult for solidary kinship groups to form. Each conjugal family, Parsons claimed, usually lives as an independent nuclear family household (Parsons, 1943; 1971a).

Parsons argued that the nuclear family household has two main functions in modern industrial society. They are the socialization of children and the 'personality stabilization' (or 'tension management') of adults. He thought that in all other respects the functional importance of the family was in decline, since many of its traditional functions had been taken over by other social structures. In particular, Parsons stated that the modern nuclear family was no longer engaged in much economic production (Parsons, 1955).

According to Parsons (1949), in middle-class families resources are provided by the employment of the husband/father, while the wife/mother stays at home to look after the emotional needs of family members. Parsons thought that this differentiation of the sex roles was necessary, because otherwise competition for occupational status between spouses would undermine the solidarity of the marriage relationship. He therefore described the husband/father as the 'instrumental leader' of the normal family, and the wife/mother as its 'expressive leader'. The particular tasks assigned to the sexes are, in Parsons's opinion, due to the primacy of the relationship between a small child and its mother (1955). The special nature of that relationship, he claimed, is a consequence of the unique responsibility of women for bearing and nursing children.

Although Parsons's ideas about gender relationships are now rather old, not to say old-fashioned, they are still sometimes perceived as having a subterranean influence in sex roles theorizing, where they have encountered considerable opposition (Beechey, 1978; Edgell, 1980; Thorne, 1982). Critics of standard sociological theory have followed a variety of approaches, but they are agreed on one thing: standard family models are believed to have paid insufficient attention to the real diversity of experiences in family life, including the increase in numbers of single-parent families. Parsonian images of married family life have been especially criticized for being governed by a rigid, exaggerated and oversimplified view of marital interaction in general, and women's experiences in particular (Laws, 1971; Oakley, 1974; Beechey, 1978).

Interest in standard sociological theory, especially in its Parsonian form, declined sharply in the late 1960s and during the 1970s. Nationally and internationally its prestige had reached a low point by the early 1980s (Mullins, 1983; Brym with Fox, 1989). That fall from grace was no doubt partly due to the documentation of contemporary demographic changes, which suggested that the nuclear family was becoming of lesser importance as a locus of primary relationships (Kobrin, 1976; Davids, 1980; Glick, 1984). However, the theoretical implications of that discovery were relatively minor, compared with the argument that standard theorists had been slow to identify problems created by normal family life itself (D.H.J. Morgan, 1975; Barrett and McIntosh, 1982).

From convergence to divergence

It is convenient, though somewhat misleading, to describe the decline of standard sociological theory as the dissolution of an 'orthodox consensus', as Giddens has done (Giddens, 1979; 1987b). The extent of agreement about the family and related matters was indeed significant in the 1950s and early 1960s, but it should not be exaggerated. For one thing, it appears that the image of consensus in American sociology was stronger among scholars working outside the United States than it was for American sociologists themselves (Himmelstrand, 1986). In fact, notable differences of opinion existed in American sociology, even when the influence of standard sociological theory was at its height.[2] A swirl of controversy has always surrounded Parsons's work, for example, including claims that he was misunderstood by many of his critics (Harris, 1983; Skolnick, 1983).

The principal characteristic of American family theory after the Second World War was in fact not so much consensus as convergence. It was widely believed that an unscientific state of confusion about ideas could gradually be overcome through the careful comparison of propositions, and by standardizing the terms employed in them. The phrase that is most often used to describe deliberate efforts at theoretical convergence in the sociology of the family is *theory systematization*. A variety of strategies for theory systematization have been proposed, some of which are more ambitious than others (Burr, Hill *et al.*, 1979). One of the more limited proposals was Hill and Hansen's early suggestion for conceptual integration. They proposed that the integration of ideas within theoretical approaches should be increased by ordering concepts in terms of their levels of generality and abstraction (Hill and Hansen, 1960). Later, more ambitious arguments were made for theory building as a cumulative enterprise (Burr, 1973). From that point of view, the barriers between theoretical approaches were seen as distracting scholars from the work of refining concepts for research use. The logical outcome of that conclusion was the goal of theory unification.

The strongest and most influential call for theory unification was made by Reuben Hill. He called for 'an all-purpose general family framework which could be understood and used by representatives of all the many disciplines working in the arena of family study' (Hill, 1966:23). This was to be achieved by the interdefining of existing concepts and by the development of new bridging concepts. Such concepts would allow theorists to translate the terms employed in one theoretical approach into the language of another. Hill's goal of a unitary theory attracted increasing support from sociologists of the family in the late 1960s and the early 1970s. However, its implicit assumption of common experiences of family life for men and for women was undercut by new ideas that emerged at the same time. The result was a dramatic enlargement of perspective in family theorizing by the late 1970s, which was sometimes accompanied by a sense of a loss of direction (Harris, 1979; Vanier Institute of the Family, 1981).

In the early 1970s it could be claimed in good conscience that the sociology of the family had entered a phase of systematic theory building (Broderick, 1971; Burr, 1973). It was thought that theory construction techniques, such as the 'specification of hypotheses', would result in an increasingly integrated set of propositions about the family. Theory building therefore seemed to offer the prospect of a steadily expanding and cumulative body of knowledge about marriage and family life. Unfortunately, it is no longer possible to believe in that trouble-free view of family theory.

In the mid-1970s the sociology of the family went through a Big Bang in which feminism played a conspicuous part, through, among other things, notable original contributions from outside the United States (D. Smith, 1973). That explosion blew the field apart, and the separate pieces have been flying off in different directions ever since. As expected, there was indeed a rush of theorizing about family issues in the 1970s. However, only a portion of this growth resulted from the application of theory construction techniques. At the same time as the established theoretical traditions were being refined, new types of theory were emerging. Those theories did not build on earlier work in the sociology of the family, and they asked new kinds of questions (Hamilton, 1978).

One problem that had proved to be particularly troublesome was the assumption in standard sociological theory that there is a universal core to family life, which can be given an objective definition as *the family*. The difficulty with this concept that initially attracted the most attention concerned its application in structural functionalism. It became apparent that a variety of structures, some of which are referred to by familial terms and some of which are not, could conceivably fulfil a given functional prerequisite (Weigert and Thomas, 1971). And if that were so, then the possibility had to be considered that *the family* might not be a universal institution after all (Collier, *et al.*, 1982). As a result of this realization, sociological attention shifted in the 1970s to the study of forms of living that were not circumscribed by the standard theory of the family.

By the mid-1970s it was clear that three decades of theoretical convergence had exacted a heavy price. That price was the omission of issues and theories which did not fit the image of the family favoured in standard sociological theory (D.H.J. Morgan, 1975). It came to be understood that the conceptual frameworks which were first elaborated in the 1950s had been potentially complementary, or at least were capable of peaceful coexistence, because they all had one thing in common: they had either ignored or played down conflicts in relations between family members and in relations between family theorists. This was not true of some of the new approaches that began to emerge during the 1960s, and most especially it was not true of feminism.

Feminist theory

Feminism is not only an academic school of thought, it is also a broad movement for change. Supported by a variety of groups and networks, its advocates have made public issues out of women's private problems, including domestic violence, childcare and the financial difficulties of dependent wives. It is thought by many feminists that these problems are affected by the social organization of family life.

Heidi Hartmann has criticized most family research for being committed to a view of the family as an active social unit, or 'agent' (1981a). The underlying concept of the family in the standard sociological approach is that of a unified interest group. In Hartmann's view this concept is erroneous, and it should be replaced by a model of the family as a 'location' in which production and redistribution of resources are carried out. As such, the family 'is a location where people with different activities and interests in these processes often come into conflict with one another' (Hartmann, 1981a:368). Family members are therefore described as using familial structures in different ways. In so doing, they act not only as members of families but also as members of gender categories.

The allocation of tasks among family members is seen by feminists as taking the principal form of a sexual division of labour (Mackintosh, 1981). Although this division of labour may appear to be an equal pooling of contributions within the family economy, women are typically described as giving much but receiving less in return (Delphy, 1976; Hartmann, 1981a). That unequal process of exchange is theorized as an aspect of the internal stratification of family life, in which men receive superior benefits to those of women (Delphy, 1979; 1984). The familial division of labour is therefore held to be a form of oppression (Barrett, 1980; Barrett and McIntosh, 1982). Feminist sociologists emphasize that oppression within the family is shaped by a ramified system of social control, whose power is based on the collusion of men against women in a variety of social institutions (Smart and Smart, 1978). That system of social control is referred to as *patriarchy* (Coward, 1983; Walby, 1990).

The central contribution of feminist theory to the sociology of the family is to describe women's oppression in marriage as a consequence of patriarchal relations. Processes of control and domination are thought to come into play wherever men and women interact. The most subtle forms of social control are cultural influences upon images of self. Through their socialization into differentiated sex roles, men and women experience themselves as being different from the other sex. Those experiences are described by feminists as being rationalized in ideologies, which assert that there are natural causes for observed differences in behaviour between the sexes. Common ideas that are claimed to have an ideological foundation include the assumption that heterosexual marriage is the natural basis for family life (Thorne, 1982; Ferguson, 1989).

The family itself is sometimes identified by feminists as an ideological construct (Barrett, 1980). That is to say, it is thought to be a system of ideas that has been created and carried by particular social groups, whose interests it serves. Family life as we know it is therefore studied as the outcome of an historical process of the social construction of reality (Hall, 1979; Nicholson, 1986). In this way the critique of familial ideology paves the way for structural analyses of the social causation of contemporary family life.

In macro-structural theories of family life, men's relations with women are thought to take the principal form of male control over the production of people for social positions, in biological and social reproduction (B. Fox, 1988). This patriarchal system is thought to include the social construction of women's desires to nurture and care for children. For example, O'Brien (1981) argues that the origin of patriarchy lies in the process of sexual reproduction. She suggests that the 'alienation of the male seed' in sexual intercourse creates for men a deep uncertainty about biological paternity. Since men's biological relationships to the particular children of particular women are unclear, the resulting uncertainty can be removed only by an enforced social agreement. Individual men assert their rights to certain children by claiming to have rights over their mothers. According to O'Brien, the legitimacy of those rights is sustained by an elaborate ideology of male supremacy.

Out of order

Feminist theorists such as O'Brien have raised deeply political questions about the most personal and intimate matters. It is therefore not surprising that their assertions have met with a wide variety of responses, ranging from elation to confusion and anger. The nature and causation of family life have consequently been hotly debated not only between feminists and non-feminists, but also among feminists themselves. There are considerable differences of opinion, for example between liberal feminists, radical feminists and socialist feminists. In all these diverging streams of thought the social organization of family life has been a subject of intense interest. One result of this interest is that public policies concerning family issues are now often politically controversial in a way that would have been unthinkable in the 1950s (Land, 1983; Graham, 1984; Land and Rose, 1985; Glendinning and Millar, 1987).

Issues of social policy and social theory have always been closely linked, and it is not surprising that 'the war over the family' was carried into the heart of sociology (B. Berger and P. Berger, 1983). Responding to this challenge, feminist scholars showed how social policies are affected by assumptions about the family which are rarely questioned in standard sociological theory (Eichler, 1985; 1987; 1988).

Feminist theorists worked hard throughout the 1970s and the 1980s to introduce new ways of thinking about family life into family studies. As a result, Barrie Thorne was able to claim that 'By pursuing the implications of gender as a basic category of analysis, feminists have made important contributions to family theory' (Thorne, 1982:10). It is common these days for feminist contributions to family studies to receive favourable acknowledgment from senior scholars (Adams, 1988; Komarovsky, 1988). However, that was not always the case in past years. For example, in their review of developments in American family theory during the 1970s Holman and Burr failed to acknowledge feminist scholarship, to the extent that they did not even list it as a peripheral approach (Holman and Burr, 1980). Instead, they complained that the massive literature on sex roles would have 'more illumination as the heat subsides' (Holman and Burr, 1980:734).

Despite the niggardly attitude towards feminism, the review of the 1970s by Holman and Burr did mark a watershed in American family studies. In it they stated in unambiguous terms their conclusion that a general theory of the family was both impossible and undesirable. In Canada the Vanier Institute of the Family arrived at a similar conclusion, and it sent out an appeal for recognition of the multiple meanings of family life (Vanier Institute of the Family, 1981). It was, in fact, too late by then for appeals and directives from authoritative sources to have much effect. Social theorists in Britain and elsewhere were already striking out in a variety of new directions that were to shape family studies in the 1980s (D.H.J. Morgan, 1979).

As the decade of the 1980s unfolded, it became apparent that one consequence of opening the gates to new ideas would be a proliferation of theoretical approaches to family life (Osmond, 1987). Among these approaches are claims for the invention of new programmes of family studies (Beutler et al., 1989). Ambitious attempts to lay down fresh foundations for the sociology of the family can be expected, but on present evidence they are unlikely to attract a large following. The reason for this is that at the same time as new ideas about intimate relationships were being introduced into family studies, the very basis for theorizing about family life was shifting. That shift makes the possibility of a new movement toward theoretical unity increasingly unlikely.

Some theorists working in the feminist tradition have argued that if we really want to understand family life we must 'deconstruct' (Barrett and McIntosh, 1982) or 'decompose' (Thorne, 1982) the concept of *the family* itself. What they mean by this is that the concept of a family unit should be dissolved, so that instead of studying the family we would study underlying structures such as the sex/gender system. Margrit Eichler, for example, holds that one reason why sociological theory 'lags behind reality' is that it is still dominated by what she calls 'the monolithic model of the family' (1981b:368). According to Eichler, standard concepts of the family are monolithic in the sense that they assume the congruence, or correlation, of activities such as emotional involvement, procreation, socialization and economic support. In reality, she claims, these activities are often carried out independently of one another, and thus outside of family groups as they are conventionally defined. Eichler therefore recommends that we adopt a (multi)dimensional model of familial interaction, in which the degree of congruence between the different dimensions is taken to be an empirical question.

The critical re-evaluation of monolithic sociological models, such as Weber's ideal type of bureaucracy, has been a minor social science industry for several decades. Perhaps the only thing that is truly surprising about the present situation is that this conceptual revolution took so long to catch up to family studies. Some feminist theorists argue that the reason why we have continued to think about 'the family' as an active social unit is because of the ideological aura of sanctity that surrounds family life in capitalist societies (Barrett and McIntosh, 1982; Wearing, 1984). In this connection Rapp has claimed that 'the concept of family is a socially necessary illusion' (1978:281). Since the concept of 'the family' has in fact been the basis for scientific family studies, Rapp's claim that it is all an illusion strikes at the very heart of the programme of family social science.

From positivism to post-positivism

The modern sociology of the family was founded in the United States in the belief that following scientific procedures would produce effective techniques with which to control and improve family relations (Mowrer, 1932; Broderick, 1988). The emphasis on social control required developing an ability to predict the outcomes of family processes, through the objective study of behaviour. This idea of social research, known as *positivism*, involves the scientific observer in developing a detached, value-free view of his or her subject matter. The discovery of objective laws is thought to depend upon pure reason, and therefore the scientific mind must be freed from disturbing passions and prejudices.

It was recognized quite early in the history of the social sciences that objectivity would be difficult to achieve in sensitive areas such as the study of family life. Nevertheless, Mowrer felt that by the early 1930s a few social scientists had reached the point where 'they can approach the whole network of human relations in family life without the emotional colorings of the past' (Mowrer, 1932:25). Belief in the wisdom of the dispassionate scientific observer remained the dominant view in the sociology of the family for the next half century (Thomas and Wilcox, 1987). It continues to be an influential ideal today, as Bert Adams has recently reminded us (Adams, 1988).

The idea of a value-free family science was appealing because it promised advances in human knowledge on a scale unknown in previous centuries. The key to this process would be the discovery of laws describing the forces that determine social behaviour. General laws, such as are produced in the natural sciences, possess the capacity to predict many things, due to the fact that they are highly abstract. The production of social scientific laws, therefore, involves abstracting from the whole of human experience general elements, whose continuity and strong effects make them significant predictors of attitudes and behaviour. Special attention is paid by social scientists to selected independent variables such as sex, generational order and family income. Positivist theorizing consists mainly of formulating hypotheses about relationships between these independent variables, and dependent attitudinal and behavioural variables.

Testing such hypotheses remains the dominant ideal in family research in the United States, although according to Nye it is an ideal which is followed less often than we might expect (Nye, 1988).

One of the principles of positivism is that knowledge is cumulative, in the sense that scientists come to agree about the status of new knowledge, and about its relevance as the basis for new work (J. Turner, 1989). It follows from this idea that the scientific process does not end with the testing of hypotheses: once hypotheses have been verified, they may be given the status of propositions that deserve to be integrated into a larger body of accepted knowledge. An important idea here is that findings in earlier periods do not lose their relevance, in so far as they are thought to have laid the foundations for later achievements that would not otherwise have been possible. This belief has sometimes given rise to the explicit goal of making inventories of propositions, in order that theorists can consciously reflect upon the accumulated body of knowledge. In this way, it is thought, theorists might derive more abstract propositions that merit consideration as general laws.

The 'inventorying' of propositions was very popular among American family scientists when the influence of positivism was at its height (Goode *et al.*, 1971; Burr, Hill *et al.*, 1979). However, under present conditions of theoretical crisis there is little to be gained from this that could possibly justify the amount of work involved, because the criteria according to which propositions might be evaluated and ordered are themselves in flux. Feminist theorists, for example, have criticised positivist methods in the social sciences for what is claimed to be their sexist bias (J. Stacey and Thorne, 1985). In the face of such critiques, any inventory that included propositions derived from research conducted according to positivist methods clearly could not provide a consensual picture of the state of family theory today. The current prospects for programmatic unification through new syntheses of family studies would therefore seem to be unpromising (cf. Burr, 1989).

In recent years positivism has been called into question by scholars working within a variety of intellectual traditions (Thomas and Wilcox, 1987). We will focus here on some of the feminist critiques of positivism, which are particularly influential in current rethinking of the relations between family life and social theory. Feminist thinkers have argued that, despite its claims of scientific objectivity, positivist sociology is not value-free. They claim that in the past sociologists failed to describe women's oppression within the family, because the procedures and assumptions employed were faulty and because they were unconsciously biased towards masculine points of view (Eichler, 1981a; 1988).

Arguably, the most influential statement about bias in family research was made by Jessie Bernard. She observed that in every marital union there are two marriages – his and hers (Bernard, 1972). Men and women experience marriage in different ways, and they often report their experiences differently. According to Bernard, husbands tend to report having more power in relation to their marriage partners than they have in reality, whereas wives tend to report having less power than they really do. Bernard stated that the over-reporting and under-reporting of marital power is due to cultural expectations of gender inequalities, which men and women have learned.

The significance of Bernard's point about the two marriages is not simply that it is hard to obtain accurate results in survey research. It is, rather, that certain distortions in social science data are socially produced. Data which are most likely to be lost concern the less prominent members of society, such as women. Therefore, one of the goals of feminists working in the social sciences is to render visible women's experiences that are not well represented in the classical theories (M. Stacey, 1981). Those experiences have included the labour of housework, which for many years was not taken seriously as a subject for investigation by male sociologists (Oakley, 1974).

Feminists who explored the invisibility of women's lives arrived at two conclusions that have significant implications for contemporary sociological practice. One conclusion is that the experiences of female subjects should be taken seriously by researchers, and women should be encouraged to speak freely about their interpretations of social life. The other is that the distinct ideas of female researchers and male researchers should be recognized as two potentially very different forms of knowledge. Both those recommendations involve paying close attention to subjective factors in social research.

One of the 'new' ideas in the social sciences is the recognition that all concepts employed in social theory are derived from the commonsense knowledge which social actors employ in daily life. Feminists claim that the commonsense ideas of men are dominant, or hegemonic, because men dominate the public discourse in our society (D. Smith, 1987). It is argued that hypothesis testing is likely to reinforce this bias, and that research methods such as unstructured interviews must be employed, in which women's suppressed interpretations of their experiences can be elicited. Those interpretations are then refined by the social scientist into theoretically useful concepts, which may be used to challenge previous theories (Currie, 1988).

In an extension of the male hegemony argument, it is pointed out that the privileged position historically given to male speakers is also there in the social sciences, most of whose practitioners have been men (D. Smith, 1974; 1975; M. Stacey, 1981). It is further suggested that male philosophies are different from those of women (with men being more concerned with power and control, for example), and that this is reflected in the characteristic concerns of the social sciences (Hartsock, 1983). The important conclusion drawn from this line of argument is that science is not neutral (Sydie, 1987). Feminists therefore claim that women in the social sciences must be given resources and intellectual space with and in which to develop female perspectives on human behaviour, without being limited by existing theories.

Whether or not we agree with that conclusion, it is important to recognize what its consequences are when it is taken seriously by a large number of people. Sociological knowledge today is most unlikely to take the form of a unitary theory. Rather, social theory will consist at a minimum of what Margrit Eichler and Jean Lapointe refer to as a 'dual perspective', provided by male and female viewpoints (Eichler and Lapointe, 1985). Eichler and Lapointe express the hope that eventually social scientists will have an effectively integrated vision of social reality, and they believe that some men and women who have been influenced by feminist research are able to combine male and female perspectives. However, they expect divergence rather than convergence of views at this time, as they do not think it is possible for all researchers even to attempt a dual perspective. Realistically, they suggest, researchers will have to make deliberate efforts to identify their own points of view and to relate their findings to what has been produced from the other viewpoint (Eichler and Lapointe, 1985:19).

Attention to the different points of view that exist among social scientists is a principal feature of *post-positivist* sociology (Thomas and Wilcox, 1987). Assumptions of scientific objectivity are thereby called into question, as it seems that beliefs about what is true are always relative to some viewpoint or other. As a result, the interpretation of contrasting viewpoints and the analysis of their effects upon social theorizing are now recognized as being of great importance. That recognition has sometimes provoked a feeling of profound unease. One observer of the contemporary scene in family studies has noted: 'In the face of this new-found diversity and complexity in the family researcher's purview, there is manifest methodological restiveness and growing theoretical doubt' (Edwards, 1989:817). We must now begin to consider what the common dimensions of that theoretical doubt are, in order to gain a better understanding of the state of family theory today.

Contemporary contradictions

From a narrowly scientific point of view, a theory is a set of propositions that describes a set of observations. The number of propositions in a theory is usually much smaller than the number of observations to which the theory can be applied, and so theories summarize and organize what we know about the world. Theories in this narrow sense of the term are sometimes referred to as 'models', because they are intended to provide an immediate image of something that has been identified from experience. The Parsonian model of the structurally isolated nuclear family is a well-known example.

There is also a wider aspect to theorizing. This concerns the ways in which a model and the experiences to which it is applied are *both* shaped by underlying ways of thinking. Theories in this sense (otherwise known as theoretical approaches or theoretical perspectives) affect the process of theorizing in a number of ways. First, theoretical approaches provide us with concepts which we use in analysing and communicating our observations of social life. The key concepts in theory models are usually derived from these conceptual frameworks. Second, theoretical approaches suggest the kinds of question we should be asking, and hence direct our attention to certain kinds of event rather than others. Third, they provide us with ways of answering questions, in the form of orienting assumptions and guides to observation. Fourth, they help us to interpret what we observe, and thus they structure the process of perception. And fifth, theoretical approaches involve value-judgments about what social scientific knowledge is for, and how it should be applied in social affairs.

Theoretical approaches to the study of family life clearly have profound effects upon the nature of what we judge to be valid social scientific knowledge. For this reason they deserve our careful attention (Ehrlich, 1971). For instance, theoretical approaches may employ value-judgments that have as their sources radical or conservative ideologies, as has often been the case in recent debates about gender, marriage and the family (Targ, 1981). An important corollary of this point is that, through the effects of ideologies upon theoretical approaches, family social science is open to influences from the larger society. Social scientists themselves are social beings, and they have social experiences that shape their views about the world. Those experiences change over time, in so far as the groups in which social scientists are located are subject to external pressures and demands. Considered as a type of cultural activity, the social sciences are obviously an element *in* society. They are, therefore, a product of social organization like other social institutions. No matter how scientific sociological knowledge may be, it is inevitably affected by the conditions under which it is produced (Münch, 1989). Robert Bellah and his colleagues have recently emphasized this point by noting that:

> Social science is not a disembodied cognitive enterprise. It is a tradition, or set of traditions, deeply rooted in the philosophical and humanistic (and, to more than a small extent, the religious) history of the West. Social science makes assumptions about the nature of persons, the nature of society, and the relation between persons and society. It also, whether it admits it or not, makes assumptions about good persons and a good society and considers

> how far these conceptions are embodied in our actual society. Becoming conscious of the cultural roots of these assumptions would remind the social scientist that these assumptions are contestable and that the choice of assumptions involves controversies that lie deep in the history of Western thought. (Bellah *et al.*, 1985:301)

Social scientific models, such as concepts of 'the family', are commonly derived from folk models (that is, lay or commonsense theories), which we all use to interpret our everyday social experiences. The choices and conflicts that we face in daily living require us to articulate our own point of view about social issues, to ourselves and to others. This involves us in categorizing social objects, such as 'marriage' or 'parenting', in order to describe the consequences which we believe that they have for interaction. When these categories become objects of attention in discussions and debates they acquire common meanings within a shared way of talking, or *discourse*. Discourses about family experiences provide a rich source of ideas for social scientists, whose theories are therefore extensions of lived social practices.

The implications of this state of affairs for the process of theory development have sometimes been misunderstood. Whether it is acknowledged or not, *all* studies of contemporary family life emerge from the conditions of our present social existence. They are therefore affected by the fragmentary experiences and perspectives which that existence produces. Some of those experiences are contradictory, in the sense that they involve contact with social forces which pull in different directions.

Insightful analyses of contemporary contradictions of family life have been undertaken by the Swedish sociologist Edmund Dahlström (1989), and by others. We may use their work as the starting point from which to develop a conceptual framework for the description of trends in theorizing about family issues. There would appear to be four major contradictions in the western societies that have deeply affected how people think about family life today. Those contradictions will be described briefly here. Expanded discussions of them will be presented in the remainder of the book, where each contradiction will be the basis for a separate chapter.

The first social contradiction to be taken up in the following pages is that between what Dahlström refers to as the 'patriarchal heritage' of traditional family structures, and reformist ideals for improving the possibilities for personal development. Consequences arising from this contradiction have sometimes included inter-generational conflicts. However, there can be no doubt that at present its most visible outcome is controversy over the nature of relations between husbands and wives. Pressures for altered family responsibilities by many women, and the reluctance of many men to make the requisite adjustments, have resulted in an unstable process of change in contemporary families. This particular contradiction has generated much friction in marital relationships in recent years, as well as divisions and disjunctions in family theorizing that were noted earlier in this chapter. In Chapter 2, theoretical oppositions arising from projects for the enrichment of life experiences on the one hand, and family traditions on the other hand, will be discussed. They will be identified as manifestations of the general conflict between *modernism* and *anti-modernism*, which is present to varying degrees in every western society.

There is a related contradiction that has influenced the formation of family theories, which is taken up in Chapter 3. Inso-far as people are prepared to reconsider traditional ways of doing things and to alter family arrangements, the question arises of how much change is to be preferred, and how that change should be brought about. This issue takes its most dramatic form in contrasting perspectives on divorce. Is the breaking of marriage ties, and the break-up of families, to be seen as a problem with serious economic, social and psychological consequences? Or is it instead to be seen as a rational choice, in circumstances when emancipation from crippling social constraints cannot be achieved in any other way? As Dahlström (1989:45) points out, the answers given to those questions depend in part upon which family relationships are the particular focus of attention. A concern with children's lives tends to be associated with an interest in relational simplicity and interactional stability in families, which is believed to provide the emotional security needed for the psycho-social development of children. On the other hand, a concern with adult lives is often associated with a focus on the liberating effects of relational experimentation and interactional innovation.

The contradiction between goals of security and experimentation, or between *system* and *liberation* (as I will refer to them
below), is not only grounded in different practical interests and
social programmes. It is also shaped by contrasting ideologies.
Stabilization of families is often a special concern of the family
professions, such as marriage counselling. The dominant
ideological themes advanced by family practitioners are therapeutic
relationship management, and gradual change. On the other
hand, radical feminists and socialists are more favourably
disposed towards revolutionary social transformations. Their
ideologies are more likely to encourage radical breaks with
existing social structures.

In Chapter 4 we turn to a different social contradiction. This is
the contradiction between private and public spheres of action.
Dahlström identifies two salient dimensions of this contradiction.
One he refers to as the contrast between bureaucratic culture and
primary-group culture. The former is impersonal and rule-
governed, and motivates performance through financial incen-
tives; the latter is personal and intimate, and relies upon moral
commitments. The second contrast described by Dahlström is
that between production and reproduction. The production of
goods and services, that is to say, is carried out largely in public
organizations, which in a capitalist society are profit seeking and
therefore oriented toward cost reduction. The reproduction of
human beings, on the other hand, is carried out privately and
often involves making personal sacrifices. The financial costs of
this essential activity are born largely by individuals, rather than
by public institutions. These two contrasting principles of social
organization have been subjects of great sociological interest in
recent years, and they have stimulated much new family theory.

Finally, there is a fourth social contradiction that is rapidly
emerging as a major issue in social theory. That is the disjunction
between the idealization of one type of family, and the reality
that there are many types of family which arrange their lives in
quite different ways. The cultural ideal of one type of family is
called by Scanzoni *et al.* (1989) the 'standard package', or the
'benchmark family'. It will be described in Chapter 5 as the
consequence of a *modern* idea, namely that human progress
follows one path, which must be the same for everyone. In
contrast, *post-modern* theories hold that social life is heavily

pluralistic. It is therefore claimed that assumptions of diversity and multiformity, rather than of normality and uniformity, should be the starting point for social theory.

The last contradiction, between the cultural idealization of the 'one' and the social construction of 'the many', continues to be strongly felt in the sociology of the family. It reminds us of the extent to which sociology is an element within the very cultures that sociologists study in their capacities as social scientists. This point is made in a number of places, and we return to it in the final chapter.

Notes

1. Giddens (1987a) has suggested three reasons why the study of family life is challenging for sociologists today. First, there is new information about families in the past, which forces sociologists to reconsider their models of social evolution; second, there are controversies about family life raised by new theoretical approaches, especially feminism; and third, there are the uncertainties and risks associated with changing family forms. In this book we will be especially concerned with the last two factors. For an illustrative discussion of the first factor see Mitterauer and Sieder (1982).
2. Several interesting comparative analyses of family theories were conducted in earlier decades, and some of their achievements were not sufficiently appreciated at the time. In particular, Reuben Hill and Donald Hansen conducted a major review of family studies in the 1950s, in which they identified five conceptual frameworks. They were: the interactional approach, the structure-function approach, the situational approach, the institutional approach and the developmental approach (Hill and Hansen, 1960). Hill and Hansen's classification of conceptual frameworks aroused a great deal of interest among social scientists in the United States, and it stimulated a series of reviews on developments in American family theory (Christensen, 1964; Nye and Berardo, 1966; Broderick, 1971; Holman and Burr, 1980). Not surprisingly the lapse of time has made the contemporary relevance of Hill and Hansen's original classification increasingly tenuous. The most durable contribution made by Hill and Hansen was to point out that any particular theoretical approach could be understood in terms of certain general properties of social theory, which were visualized as overarching dimensions of analysis. The

principal dimensions which Hill and Hansen identified were: structure, process, time and space. Interestingly, the last two dimensions received little attention then, but they have gained new recognition in more recent years, largely owing to the influential work of Giddens (1979). Orientations toward time will figure prominently among the themes to be discussed in Chapters 2 and 6.

CHAPTER 2

PROGRESS AND DECLINE: MODERNISM AND ANTI-MODERNISM

Culturally grounded assumptions are not easy to uncover, or to describe, because in everyday life we do not ordinarily need to think about them or to discuss them. One of the goals of post-positivist family theory is, therefore, to gain a better understanding of the cultural assumptions in different theoretical approaches, and the effects that they have upon the forms of theory models. It follows from this that analyses are needed of the origins of theoretical approaches to family life in particular social contexts and in particular historical periods (Berardo and Shehan, 1984; Elder, 1984; Boss et al., forthcoming).

The pursuit of answers to questions about the social origins of theoretical approaches leads to another, much larger, question. This concerns the purposes for which social scientific knowledge is sought and by which the production and distribution of social scientific knowledge is legitimated. We must ask ourselves what part theories of family life play in the social life of the societies that produce them. With this last question we arrive at an issue that is now recognized to be of great importance for social theory: the role of social scientific knowledge in the self-creation of modern societies.

Pre-modern societies are often referred to as traditional societies, because in them most social action was guided by the authority of tradition. Family life was for the most part not a cause of conscious reflection, still less of deliberate analysis and investigation. Under normal conditions there was no reason for families to be identified as problems. Customary behaviour was produced by following rules of conduct between categories of kin that were taken for granted, and it covered most of life's eventualities. In traditional communities, such as those still found today in rural India, for example, family structures are believed to be permanently fixed by such immutable forces as human nature and divine power (Dhruvarajan, 1988).

In modern societies, on the other hand, family life is often perceived to be a problem for one reason or another. At the end of the nineteenth century and the beginning of the twentieth century, for example, there was a great deal of public concern about the connection between parental alcoholism and the neglect of children. Problems that are currently of concern include the spread of sexually transmitted diseases, the large numbers of children who live in poverty, the moral dilemmas posed by new reproductive technologies, and the lack of good, affordable daycare for children of working mothers. It is here that family experts enter into modern culture (Bernardes, 1988; Höhn and Lüscher, 1988). Sociologists and other social scientists are expected to provide data about the dimensions of family problems, and analyses of their causes that will permit informed policy making (Shkilnyk, 1984; Edelman, 1987; Beaujot, 1988). It is understood that this task usually involves describing shifts in familial attitudes and behaviour, considered as features of the larger social changes characteristic of a modern society (Davis, 1985; Kiernan, 1988; Boh *et al.*, 1989; Joshi, 1989; Thornton, 1989).

Social science and modernity

Modern society, and the place of sociology in it, are so much a part of our experience today that we consider their existence to be normal. We take it for granted that modern society is an environment within which we can pursue complex projects of invention and discovery. We are rarely required to think about what it means to be 'modern', or about how the modern world came into existence. None the less it is obvious that modern societies are different from traditional societies, and that modern societies are the results of an historical process. This process, which is sometimes referred to as modernization, produced the type of social organization known today as *modernity*.

Modernity is generally understood to consist of a culture that favours the invention of certain kinds of social structure, namely those which bring about continuous transformations in social life. Such structures include, for example, the market economy, the nation state, the mass media and science. The ultimate justification for the ceaseless change brought about by these social inventions is thought to be the improvement of the human condition, or *progress*. Historically, the idea of progress has had revolutionary consequences. It means believing that things tomorrow can always be better than they are today, which in turn means being prepared to overturn the existing order of things in order to make way for progress. It means, in other words, being prepared to break with tradition.

The principal distinguishing feature of modernity is its orientation towards change. In the modern attitude, the present is designated as a field of activity that is subject to deliberate management. The systematic management (or planning) of daily life is made possible by the application of reason to human affairs. It is believed that through applying the powers of reason the natural environment can be controlled, human co-operation can be achieved, and individual actions can be directed towards the fulfilment of values. The application of reason to these tasks produces differentiated structures for solving different kinds of problem. Among these structures are the forms of enquiry and communication known collectively as *science*.

Modern conduct is rational conduct, in the sense that ordered relations are established between goals and the means for achieving them. Modern conduct is also rational in the sense that concordant relations are believed to exist between present goals and their horizons of past and future. Naturally it only makes sense to create plans for achieving genuinely new goals if the present is not determined by the past. This autonomy from inherited institutions, which is defined as the freedom to begin anew, is one of the most powerful ideas in modernity. Similarly, the planned creation of new lines of activity is worthwhile only if the future is believed to be an open field of opportunities. This does not mean that success is thought to be guaranteed, but it does mean that it must be a possibility. In the modern world view the image of the future is not something to be feared, as a presentiment of disaster. Rather, it consists of a set of challenges that are held to be manageable, and that are thought to contain the potential for progressive change. A relevant example of this idea is the concept of 'marriage enrichment' (Mace, 1986). The marriage enrichment movement is a response to current high expectations about marriage, facilitated by learned interaction techniques. The goal here is the improvement of marriage through 'continuous growth'.

Modern culture, in the sense outlined here, is usually credited as having been ushered in by the Enlightenment of the eighteenth century. At that time the belief was also established that reflexive social thought, or social theory, could make a useful contribution to the rational organization of human affairs (Badham, 1986). Historically that idea did not come easily, and its tenure is by no means assured today. It implies the contested belief that human beings can create their own social arrangements and control their own moral beings through reason, rather than through divine intervention. Secularization and the expansion of the social sciences are closely linked in the process of modernization. Summarizing the effects of the Enlightenment, Badham states (1986:11):

> It was during this period that faith in divine revelation, and the authority of the Church as interpreters of God's will, were increasingly undermined by this new confidence in the ability of human reason to provide an understanding of the world and a guide for human conduct. Similarly, the understanding of history as the chronicle of the fall of man from God's grace, with spiritual salvation only attainable in the next world, was largely replaced by a belief in human perfectibility and the increasing faith in man's power and ability to use his new-found knowledge to improve mankind's estate. The importance of these two assumptions should not be underestimated. Without the faith in reason, social theory could not be regarded as playing any important role in society. Without the belief in the possibility of progress, whatever reason's ability to understand the nature of society, social theory would not be able to fulfil any positive role in improving upon man's fate.

Giddens confirms that: 'Sociology has its origins in the coming of modernity – in the dissolution of the traditional world and the consolidation of the modern' (Giddens, 1987b:15). He therefore concludes that the very existence of sociology is 'bound up with the "project of modernity"' (1987b:26). The result of this tight linkage is that most sociological approaches to social life are recognizably modern.

In the first place, it is commonly understood that the ambition of sociologists is 'to influence for the better the human condition' (Giddens, 1987b:17). In order to achieve that goal, social life is treated as an object of reflection and manipulation. This is evident in sociology's early positivism. The nineteenth-century application of the methods of the natural sciences to the study of social behaviour was an extension of the power of reason, which had proved to be so beneficial for human progress in other areas. The second modern feature of sociology is its choice of subject matter for investigation. Unlike anthropology, for example, which took up the study of traditional worlds from a comparative point of view (i.e. by comparison with modern societies), sociology took as its subject matter modernity itself. As Giddens states, in sociology the 'prime field of study is the social world brought about by the advent of modernity' (1987b:vii–viii).

The study of modernity takes two principal forms in sociology. Firstly, it is the business of sociology to keep track of the constant changes and surprises generated by modern institutions. This 'tracking' can be, and often is, purely descriptive. Such non-theoretical or pre-theoretical research is often labelled pejoratively as 'empiricist', but its place in sociology deserves to be recognized.[1]

Secondly modernity is studied in sociology through the analysis of the causes of contemporary conditions, with a view to their eventual improvement. The means proposed for the improvement of social conditions may be the administration of social programmes that are to be implemented by agencies of the state, or the retailing of expertise to clients by consultants and therapists, or the expansion of self-knowledge through mass education. In all cases the essential point to note is that social theory is linked to the practice of human progress, directly or indirectly. It is inherent in modernity that the analysis of social relations is part of the experience of constantly forging and reforging social life, in order to bring about that state of permanent transformation which Touraine (1977) refers to as 'the self-production of society'. Giddens notes that this involves sociology in the 'tensed zone of transition between diagnosis and prognosis' (1987b:17). The tension in this zone is sometimes expressed in criticisms of the influence exerted by professionals trained in the social sciences (Carlson, 1988; Kooistra, 1989). Reasons for such tension will be examined in the remainder of this chapter, and in the following two chapters.

The tensions that exist in sociology are among the reasons for current theoretical doubts. It often happens that two groups have conflicting ideas about how they think both society and their academic discipline ought to develop. As a result, each of them acts in ways which limit the opportunities for success of the other. These limitations to the production of knowledge are in-stitutionalized within universities – in different evaluations of professional competences, in competing claims for teaching resources, and in specialized academic departments and research centres.[2] In these respects, too, social theory has practical consequences for modern institutions, which in turn effect the development of social research.[3] All of this adds to doubts about the possibility of restoring convergent theorizing as a practical goal for the social sciences (B. Turner, 1989). Nevertheless, the *ideal* of theoretical convergence remains firmly entrenched in many places, as an element in the modern idea of progress.

Modernism and the idea of progress

Sociology has been described as having two principal interests, in so far as it is engaged in the study of modernity. These are the tracking or charting of social change, and the diagnosis and prognosis of conditions affecting human performance. It might be thought that the first of those interests can be separated from social theory, in research that is purely descriptive. However, this is not so. The choice of events to be charted, and the ways in which change is measured and interpreted, always reflect some-body's assumptions about what it is that we need to know about the modern world, and why we want to know it.

As soon as social scientists move beyond the simple presenta-tion of raw data on events, and attempt to summarize processes of change, they are involved in detecting and analysing trends. Trend lines may show that the frequency of some situations is increasing (e.g. divorce), while the frequency of others is decreasing (e.g. poverty among the elderly). From the modern point of view such trends are not innocent 'facts'. They are read as evidence of the present generation's successes, or failures, in realizing the expectations of progress held by their own and previous generations. This being so the interpretation of trends is influenced by the investigator's own preconceived ideas about what kinds of change are most desirable and so judged to be progressive, and what changes are considered to be undesirable and retrogressive (e.g. Fletcher, 1988). The effects of such assumptions upon sociological theorizing are visible in the work of Talcott Parsons.

Parsons's sociology was distinctive in the early post-Second World War period, not because he was a structural functionalist (as so many other sociologists were at that time), but because he was unfailingly modernist in his approach. Modernism is a self-conscious commitment to, and advocacy of, the world-changing potential of modernity. As Habermas defines it, modernism is a 'radicalized consciousness of modernity which free(s) itself from all specific historical ties' (1981:4). Parsons's modernism was expressed in his admiration for contemporary western institutions in general, and for the contemporary American way of life that he knew in particular. Parsons was largely uncritical of modern American institutions, and he did little to suggest that they might have fundamental limitations.

Parsons's principled commitment to the project of modernity is most evident in his evolutionary theory of societies. His general theory of social evolution is not often discussed by sociologists of the family, and it is therefore worth pointing out the reason for describing it here. Parsons's evolutionary theory shows just how fundamental concepts of modernity are for theories of family life. As a matter of fact, Parsons elaborated a full-blown evolutionary theory only after he had already published his most significant papers on family and kinship. Nevertheless, he often drew upon his early conclusions about the family in his later theorizing. In his treatment of family issues there is a consistency of themes in Parsons's diverse writings that justifies considering them as one body of theory.

Parsons claimed that there is a universal evolutionary direction to social change. That claim is invariably linked to modernist assumptions about human progress, as it is in the otherwise very different work of Marx and Engels. The criterion of evolutionary change that is adopted is always some presumed *improvement* of condition, which is believed to lead towards *superior* forms of social existence (Wallerstein, 1988). Parsons himself indirectly acknowledged this point in his statement that the abstract processes of structural change which he identified to-gether 'constitute "progressive" evolution to higher system levels' (1971b:26). It is, therefore, not at all surprising to find that in Parsons's (1966) classification of stages of evolution, the highest stage is that which he identifies as 'modern'.

For Parsons the directional criterion of evolution is the 'enhancement of adaptive capacity'. He was somewhat vague about what this concept meant, but it is perhaps best understood as an increase in capacity to control and benefit from a great variety of situations. Parsons theorized that enhanced adaptive capacity in social systems is the result of four interconnected processes of change. They are: differentiation, adaptive upgrad-ing, integration and value generalization. The details of these processes need not concern us too much, but brief definitions are necessary.

First, *differentiation* is a type of splitting or separation of a previously undivided unit. The new units created by this process differ from the earlier unit by being more specialized in the functions they perform. The two new units differ from each other, since they are structured in such a way that each of them can perform unique functions that the other unit cannot. Second, *adaptive upgrading* refers to an increase in efficiency, as a result of which the total performance of social functions is now 'better' than it was before. Third, *integration* is the process of coordinating the specialized activities of the different social units. And fourth, *value generalization* is a cultural change through which increased structural complexity is made understandable and acceptable. By comparison with the first three factors, Parsons had little to say about value generalization in relation to family changes. We shall therefore ignore it for present purposes.

Parsons liked to illustrate the nature of evolutionary change by citing the emergence of both the modern nuclear family and the modern 'employing organization' (i.e. wage labour) from the diffusely organized traditional peasant household (1971b:26;

1977:275–6). This process is first of all described by Parsons as a process of differentiation. According to Parsons:

> the kinship-organized household in predominantly peasant societies is *both* the unit of residence and the primary unit of agricultural production. In certain societies, however, most productive work is performed in specialized units, such as workshops, factories, or offices manned by people who are *also* members of family households. Thus two sets of roles and collectivities have become differentiated, and their functions separated. (1966:22).

Parsons insisted that the differentiation of the nuclear family household from economic production was not simply a loss of function. Rather, it was a process of specialization, as a result of which the household 'may well perform its other functions better than in its earlier form' (Parsons, 1966:22). In other words, Parsons was prepared to believe that adaptive upgrading had occurred in family life, and that in certain respects the modern family must be considered as superior to earlier (and alternative) family forms. Since economically productive activity had been removed from the home, adult family members are now able to devote more time and attention to the emotional quality of their relationships, as well as to the learning experiences of their children. Parsons therefore concluded that: 'These developments enhance the significance of the family as provider of a secure emotional base for its members' participation in society' (1971b:100–1).

As specialized social units, modern families are engaged in transactions with other specialized units, such as the economic organizations in which family members are employed. These relations have the potential for creating friction and conflict. For example, the claims of family life and employment combined may make excessive demands upon individuals' resources of time and energy. Parsons assumed that competitive obligations would be carefully adjudicated so that they could be made manageable for individuals. From the perspective of the larger society he labelled this process integration, since 'the producing and household collectivities must be coordinated within the broader system' (Parsons, 1966:22).

Parsons's sociological theory was ambitious and challenging. It has had major effects upon the development of sociology, both positively and negatively. Positively, Parsons insisted that micro-processes such as family interactions must be theorized in relation to macro-structures such as societies, and in the contexts of long-run historical changes. Negatively, Parsons's generalizations about family life were often seriously oversimplified because they were parochial, reflecting narrow experiences of gender, class, race and nationality. Inevitably, that resulted in Parsons drawing some conclusions which have not stood up well to empirical investigation, or to the passage of time (Lenero-Otero, 1977; Lee, 1980; Elliot, 1986). For example, there are as yet very few signs of positive integration of the demands which are made upon employed wives by the occupational structures of industrial societies and by traditional gender roles in the family (Williams, 1988). This is the case not only in capitalist societies but, interestingly, also in state socialist societies such as the previous German Democratic Republic (East Germany). The past emphasis in the latter on central planning of socio-economic conditions included notable supports for women with children. However, those supports did not completely alleviate the double burden of commitments to work and family, which were felt especially by women but also by men. Rueschemeyer notes that even under such relatively favourable conditions of modernization, 'the uncoordinated demands of workplace and family can add up to a crushing burden' (1988:362).

Underlying all of the specific difficulties with Parsons's propositions is his characteristically modernist assumption that anything identified as 'modern' is somehow fundamentally different from, and superior to, what existed in the past. Parsons was especially strongly committed to the idea that America was evolving in ways that were highly favourable to the realization of the highest ideals, understood as derivations of Judaeo-Christian morality. In the event, Parsons's faith in American institutions to deliver the good life to everybody proved to be unjustified. It was above all else this failure that eventually led to the decline in popularity of his theories.

Parsons did not pay enough attention to the contradictory nature of modernity. Rapid changes in one area, such as female employment, may be accompanied by little or no change in other areas, such as the division of domestic tasks. The achievements due to one set of changes, then, can be undercut or limited by the lack of supporting change in other areas. Even more paradoxical, the same events can have consequences that are both 'good' and 'bad', with no evident direction. European sociologists, for example, have attributed both increasing intimacy and emotional satisfaction in marriage *and* increased frequency of divorce to a greater emphasis upon individual well-being and personal autonomy (Liljeström, 1986). This trend of the 'individualization' of relationships is described as a further development of the process of differentiation in social systems, to be expected from the continuous pressure for enhanced functioning in modern social life (Höhn and Lüscher, 1988; Nave-Herz, 1989).

At some level, Parsons was aware that highly specialized functioning of the modern family might have negative side effects. He noted that in so far as 'the breadwinner' is 'usually the adult male', the strains of providing emotional support would fall most heavily upon the housewife (Parsons, 1971b:100–1). However, Parsons himself never made this insight a central part of his description of family life, or of his theoretical framework. It is in the nature of modernity that modernists such as Parsons assume their ways of living are superior to those of previous generations. Parsons's beliefs about family life undoubtedly seemed to him to be perfectly modern at the time, although today many people would think of them as naïve and antiquated. The latter judgment, too, is a reflection of modernity, since the substance of what counts as modern changes subtly with the passing years, as new achievements are recorded and new challenges are revealed.

Current modern ideas include a new appreciation of the limited progress that has been achieved in the everyday lives of many women. In sociology this idea has resulted in a critical reassessment of Parsons's structural functionalist theories about the family. Feminists have articulated women's submerged experiences, described alternative family forms, traced gender divisions as sources of power and conflict within families, and developed a more complex understanding of the relationship of families to other institutions. In so doing they have argued that, while instrumental and expressive tasks have to be accomplished in a family system, these specialized *tasks* do not have to be performed within specialized *roles*. Boss and Thorne (1989) have been particularly critical of Parsonian assumptions about the identification of women with expressive roles. They state that in so far as Parsonian assumptions are upheld, women more than men will have difficulty setting limits to care-giving tasks. Women can be overwhelmed by tasks of caring for husband, children, parents and in-laws when they are exclusively prescribed the job of tending to human and social connections, as they may feel that any suffering or friction is their fault. Boss and Thorne point out that since many women care-givers also work for money, they have a heavier burden than Parsons envisaged.

In an influential critique of Talcott Parsons, David Morgan (1975) pointed out, in keeping with Merton's (1957) more balanced structural functionalism, that it was necessary to describe not only the functions performed by families but also their disfunctions. He argued that while family structures might help to ensure the success of the society as a whole, they could also hinder the successful adaptation of individual members. In particular, he suggested that the successful functioning of the 'breadwinner' family was often at the expense of the educational and occupational aspirations of women.

Morgan's analysis was an important transition point in sociological theorizing about families, especially in Britain. He concluded that the structural functional concepts of 'function' and 'disfunction' were in the end inadequate because they implied that while positive functioning was normal, negative functioning was abnormal and therefore theoretically residual. Instead, he argued, what was needed was an analysis of family life in terms of its contradictions. He showed that opposing principles of social organization create tensions, which may be released in overt conflict. An important consequence of this analysis of family contradictions is that it then becomes possible to describe intimate violence as a predictable outcome of mainstream family life.

Awareness of the contradictory nature of family processes, including 'love-hate' relationships, has grown enormously in recent years along with a general increase in sensitivity to the many contradictions in modern life (Dahlström, 1989). As a result, the easy sense of optimism about family progress that existed after the Second World War has often been replaced by doubt and questioning, and sometimes by pessimism. This negativism has been reflected in general social theory, and in the sociology of the family.

Family changes: Progress or decline?

Today the opinion of social scientists concerning the direction of changes in family life is unclear. Furthermore, their views are often contradictory, being torn between optimism and pessimism. In North America this has taken the form of a reassessment of the image of the family as a 'social support system' that is often held among those making policy for social service agencies. Now families are viewed more ambivalently, as potentially both providers of supports and neglectful and harmful (Perlman and Rook, 1987). Similarly, Höhn and Lüscher (1988) have noted a growth of ambivalent assessments about family life in the former Federal Republic of Germany (West Germany). Although the freedoms of individualized life-styles are often highly praised, there is also concern that some people may experience a loss of attachment and spontaneous solidarity. In Germany, and in every other western society, the inspection of statistical trends for evidence that will either confirm or deny doubts about family progress is a major research activity at this time (Nissel, 1982; R. Nelson and Skidmore, 1983; Davis, 1985; 1988; Burch, 1987; Kerber, 1987; Voydanoff and Majka, 1988).

From a sociology of knowledge perspective, it is interesting to note that social scientific worrying about families is not a new state of affairs (Lasch, 1977). It was also a serious preoccupation of social scientists in earlier periods of disruptive change, such as during the Great Depression that occurred between the two world wars (Elder, 1984). For example, Ernest Mowrer opened his volume on *The Family: Its Organization and Disorganization*, published in the early 1930s, with the following observation:

> No problem in modern life so challenges the attention of thoughtful students of society as does the family crisis, if one may interpret the tenor of recent writings upon the subject. One group heralds the present situation as the beginning of a new day in which all the old restraints of family mores will be thrown aside; the other group is alarmed lest the most treasured of institutions may disappear to bring havoc upon modern civilization. Both, however, agree that the family in America is at a turning of the way. (1932:3).

Mowrer's words from approximately sixty years ago sound very familiar. They could have been written just yesterday. Even more striking is Mowrer's description of the different groups that greeted evidence of changing mores in the 1930s with either joy or alarm. The most optimistic groups, Mowrer reported, were the socialists and the feminists (1932:8–9). 'Socialistic writers', he said, 'indict the present family as an outlived social heritage and a conservator of the present capitalistic system.' On the other hand, he stated, 'The feminists criticize the present-day family because the responsibilities of the home fall upon the woman and so limit her activities'. Both groups, Mowrer pointed out, had adopted radical programmes that 'idealize the future'. At the other extreme were the conservative groups, some of which asserted that what was needed was reinforcement of the teachings of Christianity and control by the churches. Mowrer stated that these groups 'attempt to give new life to the family forms of the past . . . They look toward reinforcing the forms of an earlier age which to them embody the ideal elements of family life' (1932:5).

The divisions of opinion about family life that Mowrer described in the 1930s were soon put aside, and later buried and forgotten, when the world was plunged into total warfare that demanded maximum response from civilian populations as well as from the armed forces. When the war ended, public attention was focused on issues of national and international reconstruction. Privately, millions of ordinary people wanted only to re-establish a 'normal life' for themselves. If, in retrospect, that desire was expressed in ways of living, and in sociological theories, that now seem to us to be stereotypical and perhaps politically suspect, it nevertheless deserves the respect of any good sociologist as a very human response to profound disturbances.

Beginning in the 1960s, old questions about public morality and private choices were raised in new social movements. University students were among the earliest and most active participants in those movements. They quickly had an enormous influence upon a social scientific community that was experiencing unprecedented growth in numbers, resources and influence. Feminism was one of those movements. As we saw in Chapter 1, the revival of feminism made family issues controversial once again.

In the 1930s, and again in the decades after the 1960s, we find that the social sciences are influenced by radical and conservative social movements that are opposed, but for which family change is a common focus of attention. Those social movements share a fascination with modernity as a seemingly relentless force for change, affecting all traditional practices. Where they differ is in their reactions to the nature of change. Berman (1982:15) describes the modern experience of change in the following way: 'To be modern is to find ourselves in an environment that promises us adventure, power, joy, growth, transformation of ourselves and the world – and, at the same time, that threatens to destroy everything we have, everything we know, everything we are.' This double-sidedness is one of the characteristics of modernity that makes sociology a field of social and intellectual tension. The interplay of cultural expectations between promise and threat is not only played out in everyday life. In social theory it takes the form of conflict between modernism and anti-modernism.

The impact of modernity on the family has been a persistent cause of concern and controversy among social scientists. Marriage and the family are sometimes perceived as part of the traditional social order that is gradually being disintegrated by such powerful developments as secularization, individualism, permissiveness and female employment (Katz and Briger, 1988). Contemporary modernists typically respond to news about the dissolution of social forms with equanimity, and sometimes with joy. Chilman (1983) reports her personal feelings of delight at the beginning of the 1970s, when she and other 1960s pioneers of 'alternative family lifestyles' discovered evidence of a broad cultural change among others away from narrow convention. The 1970s was indeed the decade in which it became acceptable, and even respectable, to explore – in person, in field research, and in print – alternatives to monogamy, sexual fidelity and marriage (Libby and Whitehurst, 1973; 1977). Some of the 1970s sense of excitement at investigating previously illegitimate frontiers of intimacy carried over into the 1980s (Richardson, 1985; Lawson, 1988). However, its place in public consciousness (and on library bookshelves) did not go unchallenged for long. As Chilman (1983) also reports, anxieties about the consequences of loosening moral codes prompted the formation of 'pro-family' movements, whose concerns were echoed by some social scientists.

Anti-modernism and the idea of decline

In opposition to modernist beliefs of continuous progress, anti-modernists argue that the family is in decline. They claim that institutional supports for marriage and inter-generational ties are failing. It is their perception that, as a result, families are disintegrating and family life is less highly valued. The most explicit proponent of this thesis in sociology in recent years is David Popenoe (1988). He insists that there is a long- term trend in the weakening of families in modern societies, and that this trend could possibly lead to the 'death of the family'. Popenoe suggests that this process is furthest advanced in the most modern societies, such as Sweden, and that it is proceeding in the same direction, but at a slower pace, in more traditional societies such as the United States.

Popenoe identifies five aspects of family decline (1988:8–9). First, he claims that relationships between family members are becoming deinstitutionalized: ties of economic interdependence are becoming weaker, and there is less effective control over individual members. Second, he thinks that the family is becoming less effective in carrying out its traditional functions of procreation, childcare, child socialization and the control of sexuality. Third, Popenoe states that the family is losing power over its members to other groups, especially the state. Fourth, he says that families are decreasing in size, and they are becoming increasingly unstable. Fifth, he believes that the family as a unit is now valued less than the individual.

Popenoe attributes the immediate causes of this complex and cumulative trend of family decline to underlying processes of modernization. He believes that in the second half of the twentieth century (which he refers to as 'late modernization'), the principal cause of decline is the idea of progress as self-fulfilment, which creates a situation of unchecked individualism (Popenoe, 1988:329). He claims that if this trend is not reversed, its effects will include the decline of families as mediating structures between the individual and society. In his opinion the decline of the family contributes to the decline of community, and it is therefore seen as part of a larger social crisis.

The effects of modernization on family life are often experienced as social crises in societies such as Israel, which contain a large traditional sector as well as a powerful modern one (Katz and Briger, 1988). Popenoe has argued that even in a country as wealthy and progressive as the United States, there is still a powerful current of family traditionalism. In such countries, the clash of opposing forces of modernization and traditionalism may give rise to movements to 'save' the family. Pro-family movements are often anti-modern, in the sense that they seek to slow down the pace of change in family life and to achieve a reconciliation between new possibilities for living and valued traditions. In France, for example, public opinion concerning family issues is divided between a reformism that is mainly concerned with individual happiness, and a conservatism that values group reproduction and the family arrangements defined in the Napoleonic Code (Roussel and Théry, 1988). Anti-modern reactions to post-Second World War social attitudes and social policies affecting family life are also strong in Canada and America. The most visible expressions of anti-modernism there have been the movements of the (largely Protestant) 'Moral Majority' in the United States, and the (largely Roman Catholic) anti-abortion 'Pro-Life' protestors there and in Canada (Hadden, 1983; McDaniel, 1988). Members of both movements insist that the family is the basic unit of social life, in opposition to what they define as individualistic hedonism. Their concerns have been echoed by family scientists who have argued for a greater appreciation of the 'role of spiritual influences' in the lives of people (Thomas and Henry, 1985).

Social movements of many kinds have influenced the development of sociology, in part because sociologists themselves have personal values that affect their work (Popenoe, 1988:vii–viii). At any given time, there are a number of complex interactions going on between ideological themes and social theories (D.H.J. Morgan, 1985). The influence of the New Christian Right in America upon the formulation of family issues in the social sciences is an instructive illustration of this point.

Sociologists seek to contribute to social progress by providing information that will lead to improved understandings of contemporary social life. In order to have that effect, it is of course necessary for sociologists first to produce statements that are recognized as the results of following sound procedures for the collection and analysis of data. However, sociological knowledge cannot have its intended effect upon social behaviour unless it is taken up and used in the pursuit of *non-scientific* interests. Political groups, social movements and corporations will naturally use sociological knowledge only if doing so is likely to make a difference to the probability of achieving their goals. The sociologist who wishes to be useful, and to gain public recognition for the discipline of sociology, is therefore constrained to some degree by the political realities of his or her time and place (Genov, 1989). G.L. Fox's prescription for new directions to be taken by the sociology of the family in the United States in the early 1980s illustrates how this process can work. Fox recommended that the concerns of a 'reactionary family protectionism' should be taken seriously and responded to, because to ignore them would be to risk becoming politically irrelevant (1981:261).

Many people in North America have for some time now been troubled by apparent contradictions between individualistic models of progress, symbolized by images of 'freedom', and the moral obligations imposed by collective existence in groups such as families. Culturally distinctive anti-modernist responses to this situation include a long-running interest among white, middle-class Americans in the extent and causes of premarital (mainly adolescent) 'sexual permissiveness'. This interest has provoked a substantial body of research, as well as sustained efforts at theoretical integration (Reiss and Miller, 1979). The motivation for much of this interest lies in the challenge that modern life-styles pose to traditional (i.e. pre-modern) Christian morality (Hargrove, 1983). It is not surprising, therefore, that the extent to which religious involvement has been a controlling factor in adolescent sexuality continues to be a focus of attention in this theoretical tradition (Thornton and Camburn, 1989).

The continuing undercurrent of anti-modernist reaction in America, which is reflected in social scientific studies of sexual permissiveness, was articulated by the religious sociologist Robert Bellah and his associates. They state that by examining the dilemmas of individualism and commitment they hope to recover the insights of 'biblical tradition' (Bellah *et al.*, 1985). Bellah *et al.* are concerned with the weakening of motivational commitments to collective purposes of families, communities and the nation. They believe that this has brought America and the world to 'the very brink of disaster, not only from international conflict but from the internal incoherence of our own society' (Bellah *et al.*, 1985:284). Today's challenge, as they see it, is how to 'reverse the slide toward the abyss'.

Bellah *et al.* describe the cause of general decline as the unchecked growth of individualism, 'inside the family as well as outside it' (1985:90). Outside the family, utilitarian individualism is the ethos of a dominant market economy. Inside the family, individual autonomy first appeared as the 'expressive individualism' of freely chosen love matches. More recently, individualism has manifested itself within family life in the form of an individualized modern project of personal growth. That project is an open-ended quest, which does not reach an automatic conclusion in commitment and emotional bonds. Rather, commitments may be seen as expendable and therefore as temporary stepping stones, in a life-long goal of 'finding oneself'. The problem with this new ideology of self-knowledge and self- realization, Bellah *et al.* state, is that it has dropped the traditional sense of obligation to others that was derived from socially binding moral codes. The danger here, for those like Bellah who value the security of traditional marriage, is that 'lasting relationships' that are merely personal preferences may not last.

Bellah *et al.* suggest that Americans have lost a sense of the continuity of time, and therefore of history and tradition, both public and private. They claim that 'the meaning of one's life for most Americans is to become one's own person, almost to give birth to oneself' (Bellah *et al.*, 1985:82). That sense of creating one's life anew is supported by a general 'amnesia', in which middle-class white Americans forget where they came from, how they became what they are today and, most importantly, who helped them along the way. The result, Bellah *et al.* conclude, is a widespread 'inability to think positively about family continuity' (1985:82).

The American attitude towards social time described by Bellah (namely that it is a perpetual self-renewing present) is immediately recognizable as a full-blown symptom of the culture of modernity defined earlier in this chapter. In fact, Bellah *et al.* explicitly state their belief that the underlying cause of declining continuity in inter-generational and marital ties is modernity itself. The weakening of commitments is for them only 'the latest phase of that process of separation and individuation that modernity seems to entail' (Bellah *et al.*, 1985:275). Bellah *et al.* have therefore set out to search for a 'a way out of the impasse of modernity' (1985:277). This leads them to recommend combining contemporary knowledge with the traditions received from the past, preserved by 'communities of memory' such as the churches.

The argument advanced here is similar to that employed by Parsons in his account of modern society, although the conclusion reached is not the same. For both Bellah and Parsons the main world-shaping principle of change has been differentiation. It is this that brings into existence new and unique structures, and it is also responsible for individualism. Parsons nevertheless assumed that the disintegrative process of differentiation – the breaking apart of older and more comprehensive social units – would in the end always be counteracted by forces of integration, since otherwise no society could survive. Clearly it never occurred to Parsons to question seriously the capacity of America to survive and prosper. Bellah *et al.* are less sanguine. They do not appear to believe that progress and survival are inevitable, and they seriously doubt whether the modern integrative recipe of 'full, open, honest communication' can overcome the disintegrative effects of individualism.

The tension between individualism and integration, between autonomy and community, has become a highly charged battlefield in recent ideological struggles between the traditionalists of the New Christian Right and feminists (Cohen and Katzenstein, 1988). The historical reasons for this, as seen from the perspective of conservative ideologists, are clearly visible in the description of family life provided by Bellah *et al.* (1985:88 espec.). Social participation in the nineteenth century is described as being divided into a male sphere of employment and a 'woman's sphere' of domesticity and nurturance. That social division in turn gave rise to a cultural separation, between 'the self-aggrandizing individualism of the men' and 'female familial morality'. The female culture of familial morality was then, as it still is now, seen as a positive force for good in a corruptible world. In particular, within an open, voluntaristic society family life could find a secure foundation only in a moral order of love.

Since men were, as noted, unreliable moral beings, the key to family life was necessarily the 'unselfish love' of a wife and mother for her husband and children.

The politically important consequence of the conservative view of history is .that, since the 'moral superiority' of women is the most visible example of a code that is different from political economy, any undermining of the ideology of 'woman's sphere' must threaten the very basis of moral order. That point of view is expressed indirectly by Bellah *et al.* in the following way: 'There is anxiety, not without foundation, among some of the opponents of feminism, that the equality of women could result in complete loss of the human qualities long associated with "woman's sphere"' (1985:111). It goes without saying that such anxiety fuels anti-modernist suspicions about modernity.

The limits to anti-modernism

The questions about modernism and anti-modernism that have been raised in this chapter may, at first sight, have seemed to cover ground that is very different from the developments in sociological theory reported in Chapter 1. However, both chapters in fact deal with the same two issues. Those issues are as follows:

1. The sources of different sociological theories about family life in fundamentally different theoretical approaches, or paradigms as they are sometimes called.
2. The pivotal position occupied by assumptions about the status of women in family life for the most active, influential and contested lines of family theory today.

These two issues are so fundamental for understanding contemporary family theory that they deserve some additional comment here.

The first point that should be made is that analyses of the position of women within the contemporary sociology of the family are not important simply because of feminist interventions in family studies. Feminist politicization and the reactions to it are themselves consequences of social structural factors that can be described sociologically. Those factors need to be well understood, and integrated explicitly into family theory. In particular, the practical and symbolic values attached to women in the multiple contradictions of modernity are central to theories of change in contemporary family life. The general point has been expressed by Lynda Glennon in the following way:

> A case can be made that feminism is at the center of the subjective and structural crises of modernity. While all people must confront, to a greater or lesser degree, the ambivalences and ambiguities engendered by modernity, the 'woman question' combines these confrontations in multiple ways. (Glennon, 1979:171)

The exploration of these multiple confrontations that was begun in this chapter will be extended in the following two chapters.

The second point to be made here is that the permanent existence of theoretical pluralism has to be taken very seriously. It is necessary to make this point in opposition to those voices that are once again calling for theory unification and a new synthesis in sociology (Giddens, 1987b; Fararo, 1989). In a later chapter I will show that the project of theory unification is in fact a predictable consequence of the ideology of progress. Unification is therefore itself to be understood as an element in the cultural package that has been referred to here as modernity. This means that the efforts by modernists towards constructing a new synthesis in sociological theory are not likely to be integrated with the work of those who criticize modernity, namely the anti-modernists and the post-modernists. For anti-modernists, participation in the project of theory unification would mean having to separate completely their religious beliefs and values from scientific practice, and being prepared to ignore or even completely transform sacred traditions. The typical presuppositions of modern sociology, and of modern culture in general, are not easily reconciled with traditionalism.

In this chapter we have seen how Bellah and his associates hope to revitalize traditional emphases and concerns as topics in the sociology of the family. Yet, curiously, the result is an equivocal traditionalism. Their equivocations indicate the reasons why anti-modernism can never be the dominant approach in sociology.

Bellah *et al.* do not want to restore a social order that existed in the past (1985:283). Nor are they seeking to return to the harmony of a traditional society (Bellah *et al.*, 1985:296). This is just as well, because neither option is a realistic possibility. The forces for change in the modern world are simply too powerful to be reversed or frozen. In the last analysis, anti-modernism can only be reactive. It exists only in a negative relation to the transformations of modernity, which are constant. The best that anti-modernists can hope for is either to prolong the life spans of selected traditions for a little longer, or to invent new ways of incorporating elements from the past into contemporary ways of living.[4] Either way, anti-modernists cannot in the end entirely avoid working within the new and changing forms of modern life.

A new form of family interaction that is discussed at some length by Bellah *et al.* is the self-conscious mutual analysis by couples of their marital behaviour. That practice often relies upon the modern social technology of marital therapy. Therapeutic interactive techniques are used to improve communication in couples, thus enabling partners to work out solutions to difficulties in their relationships. The social theory of marital and family therapy has a distinct history, which is quite separate from the classical sociological literature (Kaslow, 1987). However, sociologists of the family are increasingly realizing that understandings of family therapy need to be incorporated into any theory that claims to deal with contemporary family issues (D.H.J. Morgan, 1985). Family therapy is both a significant social experience for a number of people today, *and* a body of scientific theory about social relationships. That is to say, it is a perfect example of the modern phenomenon of reflexive social thought for the purpose of rational organization of human affairs. It is a dimension of modernity that will be of special interest to us in the next chapter.

Notes

1. Although empiricist research is not directly relevant to our interests here, its popularity in family social science should be noted. In the empiricist view of the social sciences, knowledge is believed to emerge from the inspection of data. The collection and classification of data

are therefore its principal research activities. Empiricist research can
contribute to theory development, if statements in the form of
propositions about relationships between variables are later developed to describe the data. Much early work in the sociology of the
family followed this inductive strategy of theory development. Its
characteristic difficulties include uncertainty in determining which
aspects of the data are worth theorizing about. This is sometimes
accompanied by an unmanageable eclecticism of concepts. Difficulties
may also arise in deciding what a theory produced in this manner can
be expected to achieve, and in establishing the nature of its
relationships to other theories. Examples of all of these problems can
be found in the history of family life cycle models (Hill and Rodgers,
1964; Hill and Mattessich, 1979; Nock, 1979; Mattessich and Hill,
1987).
2. For a successful attempt to mediate contrasting approaches to the
   study of family issues, which would otherwise have been made more
   rigid by the effects of academic specialization, see Dornbusch and
   Strober (1988:esp. preface).
3. A locally influential example of the process of academic specialization
   in family studies is the attempt to establish within the American
   university system a new discipline, sometimes referred to as famology
   (Burr and Leigh, 1983) or *familogy* (Burr, Herrin *et al.*, 1988). It
   appears that one of the consequences of the familogy programme, if it
   is successful, would probably be to insulate American family scientists
   from the individualist and radical approaches that are found among
   many sociologists, and that are more often encountered in secular as
   opposed to religious world views (Burr, Herrin *et al.*, 1988; Beutler *et
   al.*, 1989). D.H.J. Morgan states that proposals for the development
   of this new discipline may take family theorizing 'even further from
   the mainstream of social theoretical concerns' (1985:299).
4. On the 'invention of tradition' as a general process in modern culture
   see Hobsbawm (1983), and as an element specifically in family
   relationships see Cheal (1988a:77–81).

CHAPTER 3

SYSTEM AND LIBERATION: DIALECTICS OF MODERNITY, DIVISION I

Within the western societies, the continuing hegemony of modernism over anti-modernism would seem to be secure. But this does not mean that those societies themselves are stable. Rather, social life in our societies is an unstable amalgam of conflicting influences. So too is our social theory. As we have seen, this includes deep divisions between modernists and anti-modernists, whose effects upon sociology are felt especially in the sociology of the family. Current divisions also include the results of contradictions within and between modern institutions, to which we now turn.

Most divisions of opinion in sociology do not arise from questioning the possibility or desirability of progress, but from different interpretations of the means by which progress can be achieved. Underlying many of the differences here are two opposed theories of modernity. On one side is the idea that progress is the result of gradual change in established structures of collective organization. It follows from this point of view that sociological knowledge should be of the kind that can be used to improve the existing social system, including its component sub-systems such as families. That idea has had a considerable influence in the social sciences, although it has often been incorporated into family science in ways that obscure its origins. Broderick has noted that, contrary to the impression created by current emphases on research and conceptual clarification, the constitution adopted by the National Council on Family Relations (NCFR) at its first meeting in 1939 included the statement that the organization's purpose was 'to advance the cultural values that are now principally secured through family relations, for the advantage of the individual and the strength of the Nation' (Broderick, 1988:581). Dissenting from that point of view is the alternative idea that progress comes from the creative powers of individuals, which must be released from all artificial constraints of culture and state regulation. In sociology this idea is expressed in critical accounts of the flaws in systems of power and the oppressive nature of the dominant social order. Feminist critical theory, in particular, links general analyses of domination to specific concerns about women's roles in families (Marshall, 1988).

The existence of these contradictory tendencies in social theory is well known, through discussions of 'consensus v. conflict theories'. In the sociology of the family that division is reflected in carefully drawn distinctions between conservative, mainstream theories and alternative, radical-critical theories (Osmond, 1987). There is much evidence to support this dualistic image of family theory. Polarization of opinions has often been the most visible of the changes that have occurred in family studies during the past two decades (Cheal, 1989a). The purpose of this chapter is to show how the relationships between these two opposed theoretical positions continue to influence the sociology of the family today, in ways that have become increasingly subtle and complex. In order to do this we must first say something about the nature of modern culture, and we need to consider the various roles that family theories play within it.

The self-production of modern societies is the result of constant interaction between the carriers of different ideologies. This includes ideologies about families. Agents for these different principles of social organization interact with one another (albeit often indirectly), in relations of mutual influence. The stakes in these relationships are the collective opinions of large numbers of people, who can be mobilized to work for change once progressive goals are identified. The role of sociology in this process is to provide a forum for articulating, exchanging, clarifying and testing the veracity of ideas about social change. Sociology today constitutes one of the principal arenas within which the circulation of such ideas takes place. As the family sociologist Ira Reiss has observed: 'Sociology and other social sciences offer a comprehensive perspective on the competing ideologies and an overview of the social scene that is not available elsewhere' (1981:282).

The particular dialectic of modernity to be examined in this chapter arises from the contradiction between mechanisms for managing change on one side, which are intended to guarantee behavioural predictability in unstable environments, and on the other side liberating programmes of free experimentation. The fact that there is indeed a choice to be made here has been demonstrated for everyday life by Askham's (1984) study of marriage in Aberdeen, Scotland. Marriage, today, Askham concludes, is in many ways a balancing act between stability-maintaining and identity-upholding behaviours. On the one hand, most individuals value stable intimate relationships within the home, particularly where children are involved. On the other hand, they also value identity development, which may require the exploration of highly individual experiences.

At the collective level, these contradictory tendencies have produced ideologies that are promoted by different kinds of group. One emphasis leads to ideologies for social equilibrium and relational control that include a strong commitment to ideas of the unity and continuity of the family, or *familism*. Mormonism is an important example of an intensely familistic ideology today (J. Smith, 1985). Its influence can often be detected in strong and distinctive interests in the family unit among social scientists based in Utah.

In contrast to familistic ideologies, there are the ideologies of personal pleasure-seeking and emotional autonomy. It might be thought that these emphases would lead directly to the throwing off of all restraints, and to the breaking of family ties. That is, of course, what the anti-modernists fear is happening in many places today. However, the historical process of family change appears to be more complex than that. The possibility must be considered that the decline of traditional social orders has been replaced not by random individual choice, but by new and more subtle forms of control. Contemporary discussions of the history of sexuality illustrate this point of view.

We begin with the cultural division referred to in the previous chapter, between traditional order and modern possibilities for gratification. Reiss (1981) has suggested that in contemporary America this division is expressed in two conflicting ideologies, which he calls the traditional-romantic and the modern-naturalistic. Traditional-romantic ideologies focus upon the production of correct behaviour that reinforces existing social roles. Spontaneous sexuality is therefore distrusted, because it may lead to the formation of socially disapproved relationships that would disrupt family and kinship ties. The sexuality of women is particularly feared. It is subjected to the special controls of a sexual 'double standard' that consists of male freedom and female restriction. The key principle of social organization here is male dominance, through which men control the sexual, reproductive and status uses of women's bodies. In modern-naturalistic ideologies, on the other hand, the emphasis is on open, reciprocal enjoyment of physical pleasure and emotional intimacy. These ideologies presuppose equalitarian relationships between men and women, and they encourage the exploration of a variety of erotic behaviours.

Tensions between the carriers of traditional-romantic and modern-naturalistic ideologies often occur today, as part of the larger struggle between anti-modernism and modernism that was described in Chapter 2. Modern-naturalistic ideologies have tended to prevail most of the time, to varying degrees in different places and in different groups. We might suppose, therefore, that the history of sexuality in the western societies could be described quite simply as one of increasing freedom from social and psychological repression. However, the French philosopher-historian Michel Foucault insisted that this is not so. His arguments are interesting in themselves, and they provide a broad perspective from which to view some important recent developments in theorizing about systems of power.

Power over life

The work of Foucault has not always been considered in the context of the sociology of the family. However, some of his descriptions of the 'disciplines' that are applied to the human body clearly relate to issues in family studies. Foucault pointed out that although traditional social controls may be in decline, as in the case of marriage alliances between lineages, this does not mean that modern family life is without direction (1978:106–7). Rather, he argued it is the case that one 'apparatus' of direction is gradually being supplanted by another. The apparatus that is being displaced he termed the 'deployment of alliance'. Its features are: the centrality of kinship ties, the definition of links between marriage partners in terms of their social statuses, the transmission of names and possessions between statuses, and the determination of lines of property transmission by legal statutes. From the eighteenth century onward, Foucault believed, a different apparatus came into existence, which was initially superimposed upon the previous one. This he referred to as the 'deployment of sexuality'. Here life forces are both stimulated *and* channelled, by exploiting the capacities of the human body for sensation and pleasure. Although Foucault seems to have believed that sexuality is emerging as the dominant force in everyday life today, he nevertheless felt that the deployment of sexuality and the deployment of alliance are closely interrelated within the contemporary family. On the one hand the legal basis of marriage provides a permanent support for sexuality, and on the other hand sexuality provides an 'economy of pleasure' that intensifies the bonds of marriage (Foucault, 1978:108).

Foucault stressed the great significance for modern familial culture of the invention of social and psychiatric technologies that are intended to enhance human performance. All technologies offer techniques as solutions to certain classes of problem, such as how to stabilize a marriage that might otherwise fail. According to Foucault, these technologies include abundant discourses about sexuality, which have proliferated since the eighteenth century. All techniques, including studied sexual practices, involve the careful regulation of behaviour.[1] In this way intimate and private arrangements may become subject to definite constraints. Reiss (1986) has illustrated this point with reference to the identification of 'premature ejaculation' as a 'sexual dysfunction' (see e.g. Jehu, 1980a). He argues that ideas about early ejaculation, and its recommended treatment by the 'squeeze technique', are best understood not in terms of concepts of sexual health, but in terms of conformity to a normative ideal of equalitarian sexual gratification found in contemporary western societies. The conclusion he draws from this is that 'the judgment that premature ejaculation is a problem that requires therapy is culturally based' (Reiss, 1986:130).

Foucault observed that, beginning in the seventeenth century, the European societies developed new dispositions toward exercising power over life, including sexuality. Life processes became objects of conscious attention, as well as objects of deliberate manipulation, in so far as they could be controlled. Foucault traced the origins of this development to the expansion of capitalism, which he stated 'would not have been possible without the controlled insertion of bodies into the machinery of production and the adjustment of the phenomena of population to economic processes' (1978:141). Furthermore, capitalism encourages (or, as Foucault would say, it 'incites') the optimization of life forces and life skills, though only in ways that do not make them more difficult to govern. Foucault claimed that this process began among the owners of industry, in response to their personal needs for increased performance in competitive economic relations and in political conflicts. Later, the benefits of body hygiene, longevity and healthy children were extended to other classes, whose productivity became a critical factor in advanced capitalist economies. Here Foucault identified the emergence of a recognizably modern project which acquired enormous importance in the twentieth century, namely, 'that of the indefinite extension of strength, vigor, health, and life' (Foucault, 1978:125). This project was to have profound effects upon the social organization of family practices (Donzelot, 1979; Paterson, 1988).

Foucault insisted that the project of transforming life itself is deeply enmeshed in power relationships, and is therefore part of a generalized power over life or 'bio-power', as he also termed it. This power, he pointed out, evolved in two basic forms, both of which have significant implications for contemporary families. One form of bio-power is concerned with the control of the body's biological and psychological life forces. Here the focus is upon integrating individuals efficiently into the economic, political and social systems in which they are called upon to play their part. This form of power over life Foucault referred to as the *anatomo-politics of the human body*. The other form of power over life focuses on the demographic characteristics of national populations, upon which the strength of nation states depends. The issues here include birth rates, mortality rates, life expectancy and levels of physical and mental well-being. Foucault described the introduction of regulatory measures in these areas as due to a *bio-politics of the population*. Both of the types of politics analysed by Foucault have significant effects upon families today. They have therefore given rise to lively discussions about a variety of social institutions that impinge upon family life, including institutionalized social science (Stark and Flitcraft, 1983; P. Morgan, 1985).

Family policy

The institutional growth of the social sciences, and the expansion of social scientific research, were stimulated by practical interests in acquiring knowledge that might be useful for the purposes of modernization. As a result, the social sciences have been intimately connected to the bio-politics of population, through conducting research on issues such as poverty and health that is of value to the modern state (Wagner, 1989; Wittrock, 1989). The roles that social scientists play in relation to the political, legal and administrative institutions which comprise the modern state are subjects of increasing interest. Whatever those roles may be (and they have taken a variety of forms at different times and in different places), they raise challenging questions about social scientific discourse, and about the connections between knowledge and power (O'Neill, 1986; Gagnon, 1989).

The bio-politics of population has been explicitly recognized as an issue for family theory, mainly under the concept of 'family policy' (Zimmerman, 1988; Ryant, 1989). As defined by Moen and Schorr (1987:795), the term 'family policy' means 'a widely agreed-on set of objectives for families, toward the realization of which the state (and other major social institutions) deliberately shapes programs and policies'. The utility of the concept of family policy is that it increases awareness of how a wide range of government programmes affect, or potentially affect, family life. These days the various levels of government that comprise the modern state have an enormous combined impact upon everyday living. However, their effects upon families are not always taken into account in policy planning by politicians or by government bureaucrats (Garbarino, 1982). The concept of family policy is therefore intended, at a minimum, to focus attention on the need to understand what those effects are. Going one step further, it has been argued that national governments should set up comprehensive programmes to monitor the effects of changes in government policies upon family conditions. This measure is sometimes referred to as 'family impact analysis' (Shera and Willms, 1980; Ory and Leik, 1983). Most ambitious of all, it is suggested that governments should develop a coherent approach to all of the many connections that exist between families and other social institutions (Fogarty and Rodgers, 1982).

Social policy of any kind involves collective intervention in social processes, in order to bring about an improvement in the aggregate relationships of a society. Attitudes towards collective interventions in family life have been most positive in a number of European countries, in particular Belgium, France and Sweden (Fogarty and Rodgers, 1982; Dumon, 1988). In other countries, such as Italy, family policies have been described as implicit and reluctant (Trifiletti, 1989). In the United States, Britain and English-speaking Canada the idea of family policy is usually treated with some suspicion. It is often presented hesitantly, even by its advocates (Wicks, 1983; Bane and Jargowsky, 1988). Perhaps this is due to the highly individualistic cultures of these societies, and to related preferences for market processes rather than organized solutions to problems (Moen and Schorr, 1987:796). Of course, it is not uncommon for right-wing politicians in these countries to adopt 'the family' as a slogan. However, the goal of strengthening family life has often been interpreted by them in practice as meaning the reduction of government 'interference', so that families can be independent and responsible (Eisenstein, 1982; Close, 1989). Under the political conditions that prevailed during the 1980s, there was little incentive in most cases for politically active sociologists to pursue interests they might otherwise have had in defining collective responsibilities for families (though see Barrett and McIntosh, 1982).

It is perhaps not surprising that theoretically oriented family sociologists have expressed little interest in developing an explicit family policy.[2] In fact their reactions to the idea of family policy are often ambivalent, and a lack of sociologists in the field of family policy development has been reported (Dumon, 1988). On the one hand, sociologists see family policy as an opportunity for the application of sociological knowledge. On the other hand, they have learned to be cautious about the uses to which power over others may be put. In this regard Foucault's work has been very influential, directly and indirectly. Sociologists are likely to adopt a somewhat critical position that seeks to uncover underlying power relationships of class or gender, and they often question which groups are being served by political claims to represent the interests of the family. That has led in turn to critical reassessments by sociologists of their own internal uses of concepts such as family policy, which are carefully scrutinized for evidence of linkages to oppressive social structures (Bernardes, 1987). Critical theorizing of this sort has been particularly strong with respect to the form of bio-power that Foucault called the anatomo-politics of the body.

The politics of reproduction

For many sociologists the key question to ask about policies that are applied to the human body is what power relationships they involve. Foucauldian theorists, in particular, hold that the project of modernity is inextricably caught up in power relationships, and that therefore 'power is everywhere', as Foucault put it. Although Foucault's discussions of power are not always easy to interpret, the reason why modernity is saturated with power relationships would seem to be quite clear. The starting point for the project of modernity is the idea that human existence can always be improved upon, through the rational direction of activity. Planning for improvement involves setting goals and standards for human behaviour. In order to set goals for improved practice it is necessary to define performance criteria, and to separate out those situations where the criteria are achieved from those in which they are not. The latter can then be subjected to conscious remedial management.

Definitions of performance criteria for the human body are still being elaborated today. They produce such contemporary concepts as 'sexual adequacy' (Slater, 1984) and 'reproductive competence' (Franklin, 1983). Inevitably, some individuals will be judged adequate or competent, but others will be judged as inadequate and incompetent. For example, it is stated that many men in America today suffer from stress, as a result of their low 'parental competence' relative to increased societal expectations for father involvement in parenting (McBride, 1989). Negative assessments of this sort are used to legitimate educational and therapeutic interventions in people's lives, *for their own good.* This, as Foucault insisted, is a form of power relationship that is missed when power is conceptualized only as repression.

The central characteristic of power in the modern world, Foucault argued, is its close links with knowledge. He symbolized this linkage by the conceptual pairing 'power-knowledge'. In Foucault's theory of modernity the causal relationship between knowledge and power appears to work in both directions, and in practice it is difficult to distinguish one direction from the other. Knowledge of human functioning is the basis for defining standards of normality and pathology, and for the invention of remedial techniques and performance-enhancing aids. It is also the case that the will to acquire knowledge may derive from the desire to dominate others, in which case knowledge must be considered as a 'strategy of power'.

According to Foucault, the deployment of mechanisms of power and knowledge is achieved through discourses, or in other words through ways of describing the world that focus upon particular objects, such as 'sex' or 'motherhood'. These discourses circulate within collectivities, such as the human service professions and the social sciences. A relevant example of this is the discourse of *pro-natalism* that emerged as a significant social force in the 1930s, due to fears of a long-term decline in the birth-rate (Riley, 1983). The language of pro-natalism included unquestioned linkages between concepts of 'woman' and 'mother', and between 'maternity' and 'the family'. In the immediate post-war period the importance of locating maternity within a stable family environment was strengthened by popular psychological writings about the positive consequences of 'attachment' and the negative consequences of 'separation' between mother and child. New anxieties about 'maternal deprivation', which drew upon psychoanalytical research, reinforced beliefs about the proper location of women as mothers within the family – and not working for wages outside the home.

Increased professional and scientific involvements with maternity in this century have also included attention to the physical health of mothers and babies, as well as the process of birth itself. In recent years a number of sociologists, especially feminist sociologists, have been greatly concerned with the effects of medical discourse upon the biological process of birth, and in particular upon the bodies of women. That concern stems from a division of social experience between the home and the hospital (or clinic), which has been socially constructed. The precise way in which the division between family life and medical treatment has been constructed is of general sociological interest, as Talcott Parsons also realized. We will therefore return briefly to a further consideration of Parsons's influential ideas, to see how they have subsequently been modified by awareness of the social inequalities that are generated by systems of power.

In Chapter 2 we noted that structural functional sociologists, such as Parsons, described the process of historical transformation in the western societies as one of progressive 'functional differentiation'. It is thought that specialized social structures are produced that henceforth perform only a limited range of functions, such as infant socialization and emotional stabilization in the case of the modern family. In modern societies each social structure is highly specialized, and it produces only a small number of the requirements for its own existence. As a result, it must depend upon interchanges with other social structures for its continuation. Individuals occupying specialized roles in families are therefore thought to engage in transactions, as a result of which families are linked to other structures in ties of interdependence.

Parsons's analysis of differentiation continues to influence contemporary macro-sociology, as we shall see in the next chapter. However, most sociologists today are likely to add three corrections to the account of differentiation that Parsons provided. First, the dynamic factor in social evolution, and therefore the principal cause of differentiation, is no longer seen as the survival of society through its enhanced adaptive capacity. Rather, the dynamic factor is thought to be a growth-oriented culture, whose dominant principle is competitive expansion at every level, via such goals as profit maximization, status enhancement and the prolongation of life.[3] Second, thanks to the work of the conflict theorists, interactions between individuals occupying specialized roles are not seen only as ties of interdependence. As well, they may be seen as unequal transactions which comprise relations of *dependence* (Collins, 1985). The general consequence of most processes of social differentiation, it seems, is to produce both functional complementarity and structural hierarchy. This means, for example, that interactions between doctors and mothers-to-be should be thought of as being in part power relationships. Third, and here we see the return of feminism in the current rethinking of sociology, it is pointed out that most persons in positions of power, such as doctors, are male. For women patients, interactions with medical practitioners are also gender relationships. They can therefore be analysed as patriarchal relations.

The historical gendering of medical care for women was part of a larger process of the professionalization of medicine, which included the differentiation of medical care away from the home (and a community of women) and into the hospital (and the professional control of men). That process of differentiation has been studied in some detail in the case of childbirth (J. Lewis, 1980). Feminists have been concerned for some time about the implications of the extensive powers over women's bodies that male medical practitioners acquired as a result of these changes (Oakley, 1976; 1980; 1987; Kitzinger, 1978). Oakley reports that in contemporary Britain it is illegal for a woman to give birth without attempting to call for medical help (1979:10). Quoting Foucault, she further argues that it is necessary to consider even voluntary participation in medical interventions, such as antenatal care (i.e. care during pregnancy), as a form of social control that is structured by power relations (Oakley, 1984:252). Murphy-Lawless (1988; 1989), too, has used Foucault's theory of the politics of the body as the basis for a feminist critique of childbirth management in Ireland.

The medical model and family interventions

For the theory of the family, the most important issue in the medicalization of childbirth concerns how the female body became the object of a new kind of discourse, namely medical discourse. Medical discourse has some general characteristics that are worth emphasizing, because it has been widely applied. First, the body is objectified; that is to say, it comes to be seen as a 'thing' that can be studied scientifically, and which can subsequently be professionally manipulated. The body is not usually seen as the property of a person, whose views might then have to be solicited and taken into account, because lay views are thought to be in error as a result of ignorance and folk superstitions. Second, the body is believed to be the source of a wide range of potential problems. These problems can be classified, and their causes delineated, within a stock of expert knowledge. Third, some of the body's problems are invested with an aura of physical or moral danger that may justify intervention 'in the interests of the patient', whether or not the individual has initiated a request for it. Fourth, in so far as the body becomes an object of professional intervention, it is subject to the autonomous institutional forces within which professionals work, such as specialization in technical skills. One of the results of professional specialization is that the body comes to be seen in a fragmented way, and the concepts that are applied to it are defined according to special interests.

The discourse of the medical model has not only been applied to the human body. It has also been applied to many other things, including families. In its extended application, medical discourse is sometimes referred to as the 'clinical model' or the 'medical model'. According to Kelly (1988:263–5), this model is used implicitly whenever families are identified as exhibiting certain pathological characteristics (e.g. chronic poverty) for which specific causes can be identified (e.g. poor work habits). Solutions are then proposed that involve professional or policy interventions (e.g. the introduction of work-for-welfare programmes). Sometimes this medical model is applied overtly to families, as when a socially aware paediatrician talks about 'the family as the patient' (Franklin, 1983), or when a psychiatrist talks about 'healthy families' v. 'dysfunctional families' (Beavers, 1982).

Although it is not always made explicit, the medical model has provided several guiding assumptions for theories of marriage and family therapy. Russell *et al.* (1985), for example, refer to the principal goal of family therapy as 'symptom reduction'. This involves looking beyond the 'presenting problem' itself, in order to arrive at 'diagnoses' of the relationship dynamics that maintain symptoms. D.H.J. Morgan (1985) has referred to the application of the medical model to families by professionals as 'the medicalization of marriage'. That process is still at work today, as we see in Kaslow's description of the theory of scientific marital and family therapy (1987:855):

> For a body of knowledge to be worthy of the appellation *theory*, it must contain all of the following elements:
>
> 1. Explanatory power regarding the *etiology* of the symptom, disorder, or dysfunction.
> 2. Methodology and vocabulary for *diagnostic* assessment of the malady or problem, be it of the identified patient, or of the couple or family system, or both.
> 3. A system for intervening to bring about the desired changes, some format or mapping of the *therapeutic process* during the beginning, middle, and ending phases of therapy, and for any needed follow-up. This system includes a firm grasp of the vital ingredients for bringing about positive change, growth, and healing.
> 4. *Prognostic power*, that is, tools and concepts for predicting outcomes.
> 5. *Evaluative potential*; that is, it must lend itself to being evaluated through psychotherapy process and outcome research.
> 6. *Preventive capability*; that is, because of the changes wrought in the therapy, a more wholesome environment should be produced.

The influence of the medical model upon the sociology of the family is also evident in theories of family stress (Hill, 1949; D. Hansen and Hill, 1964; D. Hansen and Johnson, 1979; Boss, 1987; 1988). Serious family problems are conceptualized as 'crises' that are precipitated by 'stressor events'. The first phase of a crisis is described as a period of family disorganization, in which earlier coping strategies that no longer work are gradually abandoned. Subsequently, the regenerative powers of families are mobilized, and the family is described as entering into a period of reorganization or 'recovery'. From the perspective of the medical model, a 'normal' or 'healthy' family is one that is potentially a self-healing system. Healthy families are thought to use their regenerative powers to respond creatively to disruptive events. As a result, the stressed family is described as finally entering into a new level of reorganization, in which family functioning is once more stabilized. The goal of family researchers here is to identify those conditions, such as problem denial (Boss, 1988), which prevent families from making positive changes.

The medicalization of certain parts of family science has had some important consequences for social theory. Family theories have been adapted to serve the practical concerns and needs of practitioners. One of the ways in which this happens can be seen from sociological research on the human service professions. Recent sociological studies of medical institutions have drawn attention to the significance that professional concepts of 'family' often have for organizational procedures. Gubrium and his colleagues have pointed out that family issues regularly arise in human service organizations such as hospitals (Gubrium and Lynott, 1985; Gubrium, 1987; 1988). A division of responsibilities must be decided between service providers and family members, and the benefit to be derived from the treatment given to patients and clients is believed to be affected by family relationships. The anatomo-politics of caring for the body therefore includes a family discourse, in which the nature of family life is interpreted in relation to organizational purposes (Gubrium and Holstein, 1990). For example, in the case of court recommendations for involuntary mental hospitalization, the discourse about families includes assessments about whether or not individuals have 'any family' to care for them (Holstein, 1988). That in turn may raise questions about which relationships count as 'family', and where precisely a person's 'real family' is to be located.

Social workers trained as family therapists often participate in the process of institutional family definition. This is particularly interesting sociologically, because here we see one of the ways in which family theories shape the forms of modern culture. In Foucault's terms, family theories are part of the knowledge through which certain kinds of power relationship (such as involuntary hospitalization) are constituted. The kinds of theory that are used by family professionals in power-knowledge structures are not likely to be random, and not all theories are equally represented among them. In institutional discourse about the delivery of care to clients, human service professionals have an interest in how families care for their members. 'Real families', it is thought, support their members who have problems. In other words, 'real families' are envisaged as 'support systems', because that is their main practical significance for the purposes of human service organizations. This is no doubt one reason why the models of family life employed by human service practitioners are often derived from theories of families as systems.

Sociologists, too, have long been concerned with the connections between families and human service organizations, because there is a great deal of interest in the ways in which families cope with, or adjust to, the problems that affect them. Old age is often thought of as one such period of adjustment. Sussman, for example, concluded that the family is important to old people because it is 'continuously engaging in linkage activities with bureaucratic organizations on behalf of its elderly members' (1976:221). That linkage has continued to be a topic of interest in studies of coping in old age, conceptualized as 'the interplay between informal and formal care systems' (Chappell, 1989:202). Social gerontologists often visualize families as informal support systems that protect their members and help them to live long and healthy lives (Shanas, 1979). The sociology of aging is in fact one of a number of fields in which the image of the family as a system is firmly established as a major focus for sociological research into family processes.

Family systems theories

A system is a set of interacting elements (the 'parts' of the system), which is capable of maintaining a 'boundary' between itself and the outside world, and which enters into transactions (or 'interchanges') with its environment. These concepts are derived from an interdisciplinary *general systems theory*, which originated in engineering. General systems theorizing was introduced into family studies by family therapists (Kantor and Lehr, 1975; Piotrkowski, 1979), human ecologists and home economists (Paolucci, *et al.* 1977), and the sociologist Reuben

Hill (1971; 1977) and his associates. Hill's contributions in particular had a major influence on the sociology of the family in America.

According to Hill (1971:12), a family is a social system because it has the following characteristics:

> 1) family members occupy various positions which are in a state of interdependence, that is, a change in the behavior of one member leads to a change in the behavior of other members; 2) the family is a relatively closed, boundary-maintaining unit; 3) the family is an equilibrium-seeking and adaptive organization; 4) the family is a task performing unit that meets both the requirements of external agencies in the society, and the internal needs and demands of its members.

Hill saw these four system characteristics as being related in mutually reinforcing ways. In its internal arrangement, the family system is described as consisting of a structure of social positions, or roles. The activities in which individuals engage while occupying these roles include attempts to solve the various problems faced by family members. In time, it is thought, successful solutions to problems become stabilized as normative behaviour. That is to say, the patterns of family life are believed to be supported by a general consensus among the members on what are appropriate and useful ways of acting. These patterns distinguish one family from another, and so they give it 'boundary maintaining qualities'. The extensive communication that takes place within a family's boundaries enables it to maintain its structure. This in turn is a precondition for collective response to stress, and hence for family adaptation to changes in the environment. Cumulatively, the adaptive responses that are achieved through co-operative interaction make it possible for a family to perform the functions that keep it viable. Hill identified six such functions. They are as follows:

1. Physical maintenance of family members through the provision of food, shelter and clothing.
2. Addition of new members through reproduction.
3. Socialization of children for adult roles.
4. Maintenance of order.
5. Maintenance of morale and motivation.
6. Production of goods and services.

The family systems approach has had a wide influence on theories of families, in several disciplines (Garbarino, 1982; Constantine, 1983; D.H.J. Morgan, 1985; Vetere, 1987; Montgomery and Fewer, 1988). The broad appeal of general systems theory is partly due to the scope of its concepts. Its generality enables a wide range of specialists to share a common language, and it therefore facilitates communication among them (Sluzki, 1985). For example, all forms of external influences on families can be conceptualized in the same way, as 'inputs' to the family system. Darling has noted that, because of its generality, 'This approach can provide a framework in which multidisciplinary study can be accomplished and in which various theories and approaches can also be combined' (1987:819). This is particularly valuable, she feels, in fields such as family life education where the 'wholeness of family study' contributes to 'allowing disciplines and professions to work cooperatively rather than in competition with each other' (Darling, 1987:822). That holistic dimension is also likely to be important in settings such as hospitals, where practitioners trained in a wide range of technical specialities must co-operate in the delivery of human services.

Andrews, Bubolz and Paolucci (1980) note that today a myriad of agencies work with families for a variety of purposes – health care delivery systems, justice systems, welfare systems, educational and occupational support systems. Each of these institutions views and serves families from a somewhat different point of view. Andrews *et al.* argue that an ecological systems approach can help service providers to recognize that what one service does will affect the others. It is hoped that through improved knowledge of interconnected changes, the efficiency and effectiveness of service provision can be improved.

Systems theory also appeals to many professionals and policy-oriented researchers, because of the compatibility between systems concepts and practical interests in the functions that families perform (Walsh, 1982). As Reuben Hill once noted: 'The family is a central systemic concept in theory of high scope while serving as the central target concept for public policy and programmatic services' (1984:10). This dual aspect of the family system concept – as abstract theory and as practical target – makes it a very powerful tool for family science. It was this combination that made general systems theory the most success-ful expression of the standard sociological theory of family life, for the institutionalization of social problem-solving after the Second World War.

The professional benefits to be gained from general systems theory have been well documented in the field of family therapy (Russell *et al*, 1985). Individual symptoms, such as alcoholism, may be best understood not as personal deficiencies but as elements in a pattern of familial interactions, for instance limited emotional warmth that can be expressed only under intoxication. Systems theorizing, then, is a way of reconceptualizing individual problems within a model of relationship dynamics. Furthermore, systems theories are sensitive to the possible existence of multiple symptoms presented by more than one family member. As a result, systems models encourage a holistic approach to the delivery of human services. The significant advantage of systems models here is that they have the potential to reduce administra-tive costs. 'One professional who has a broad understanding of the family's operation may be effective more quickly than several professionals operating with more narrow focuses and less complete information' (Russell *et al.*, 1985:83).

Perhaps the main achievement of family systems theory, however, has been to provide an intellectual framework for beliefs in family strengths (Olson *et al.*, 1983). From a systems perspective, families represent potent therapeutic resources. The potential for positive change is therefore thought to be greatly enhanced when family members are involved in plans for intervention. More generally, systems theories reaffirm the strength of family ties in atomistic modern societies, in which the breakdown of family life is always a possibility. As well, they confirm the resilience of families as groups that are able to gain some control over the conditions of their existence, despite the often disruptive effects of economic, political and military institutions. Pauline Boss has clearly stated the relevance of this point of view for family stress theory:

> We emphasize, therefore, that a crisis does not have to permanently disable a family . . . Human systems, unlike mechanical ones, can learn from their experiences, even painful ones. After a crisis, families can redefine themselves and their

resources . . . or reconstruct their reality by changing the rules by which their system operates . . . Such shifts in the family's perception and organization constitute a turning point, and the recovery process begins. Crisis does not have to break the family structure. It only temporarily immobilizes it and may, in fact, lead to an even higher level of functioning after recovery than before. (Boss, 1987:701).

Implicit in this optimistic judgment are three ideas about families that are basic to all systems theories and related approaches. Those concepts are: family controls, family boundaries and family development. In one version or another these concepts have been very influential. We will therefore examine each of them in turn.

Family controls

Perhaps the most fundamental, and certainly the best known, concept of systems theory is the capacity of a system to control its own behaviour through 'feedback'. The concept of feedback was originally introduced in engineering. It refers to the way in which a system monitors its own behaviour, and feeds this information into a decision-making process. Subsequently the system's behaviour is changed, if the information input attains critical values. This simple idea is the basis for all control systems. According to the family systems theorists, this includes families. Broderick and Smith state directly that 'From a systems perspective the chief function of communication is control' (1979:125).

Broderick and Smith suggest that the interior structure of the family should be understood as a hierarchy of control. At the lowest level of control there are the *family rules* that prescribe particular responses to particular inputs. The second level of control, which Broderick and Smith refer to as *cybernetic control*, occurs when information about the behavioural 'output' of the system is fed back as 'input' to a 'monitoring unit'. This information is then compared to some criterion, such as a goal or a policy, and choices are made between alternative rules that are available for use in the system's repertoire. Finally, the highest level of control occurs when family goals and policies are themselves modified, and a search for new rules is undertaken. This occurs when feedback about the previous range of responses indicates that the system is not working. This highest level of control is referred to as *morphogenesis*, the capacity of a system to change its own structure. However, families are able to do this only for as long as they can retain their integrity as discrete social systems.

Family boundaries

The concept of a social system assumes that a social unit is distinguishable from the objects in its environment. It is therefore thought that families as systems must possess a degree of separation from their surroundings. That separation is conceptualized as a 'boundary' between what is in the system and what is outside the system. At the same time it is emphasized that in order to obtain the resources they need systems must engage in transactions with other systems, and so boundedness is always only a matter of degree – system boundaries are always permeable to some extent. Systems that are highly selective and admit only limited information from the environment are described as *closed*. Systems that are less selective are described as *open*.

Extremely closed and extremely open family systems are both identified with unhealthy forms of family life. The typical family in which children are sexually abused has been described in these terms as 'a closed, undifferentiated and rigid system' (Maddock, 1989:134). It is thought that because there is an overly rigid boundary between the family and the outside world, an implicit rule develops that all important needs are to be met within the family. Furthermore, family members are described as being insulated from the social feedback that might otherwise have exerted a corrective influence upon behaviour.

Open family systems, on the other hand, are believed to have potential problems defining what, or where, their boundaries are. When that occurs they are said to suffer from 'boundary ambiguity' (Boss and Greenberg, 1984). Boundary ambiguity is thought to be associated with disorganized conditions of family living, which give rise to family stress and to a variety of psychological and social pathologies (Boss, 1987; 1988; Ihinger-Tallman, 1988). In recent years difficulties in boundary maintenance, and consequent boundary ambiguity, have been popular issues among some social scientists. That is partly because of new interests in the numbers of 'reconstituted families' or 'step-families' that are now being created as a result of remarriage after divorce (Ihinger-Tallman and Pasley, 1987; Pasley, 1987; Hobart, 1988; Ihinger-Tallman, 1988). It is thought that these families often have difficulties defining who is in the system and who is outside it.

Boundary ambiguity has sometimes been described as a normative feature of the life cycle, since the normal loss of members who leave home or who die entails redefining who is in the family (Boss, 1987; 1988). This focuses explicit attention upon the importance of viewing the family as 'a system moving through time' (Carter and McGoldrick, 1989:4).

Family development

A family that maintains both its boundaries and its control hierarchies is believed to have the capacity for positive adaptation, which enables the family system to grow in complexity and to enhance its functioning. This view of creative morphogenesis in family systems echoes earlier interests in family change, which were expressed in developmental models of the family life cycle.

Concepts of family development were elaborated as a direct application to family life of the idea of progress, in the period of optimistic social reconstruction after the Second World War (Duvall, 1988). This approach rested upon the implicit assumption of a favourable social environment providing abundant opportunities that could be converted into family resources. Families were seen as being in themselves the engines of their own progress. The challenges that families inevitably face came to be defined by many American sociologists as 'developmental tasks' in the normal family life cycle. Duvall has defined a developmental task as 'a thrust from within the individual to narrow the discrepancy between his present behavior and what he might become' (1988:130). The notion of developmental needs and tasks was borrowed from psychology (Hill and Rodgers, 1964). In the work of child psychologists of the time, individuals were seen as facing a predictable series of problems of adjustment due to biological changes as well as changes in social expectations. In the social-psychological models proposed by

Evelyn Duvall (1977) and Joan Aldous (1978), the idea of normal crises was redefined as that of normative transitions between the stages of the family life cycle.

The concept of the family life cycle is rooted in the observation that family life goes through a cycle of birth, growth and decay. This cycle begins with the joining together of two persons of the opposite sex in marriage, and ends with the dissolution of their union when one of them dies. In between, the family expands and contracts as children enter and leave.

Developmental models of the family life cycle conceive of family development as a process of passing through a series of stages. The passage from one stage to another occurs when there is a change in family composition, which brings about a change in family structure. Structural changes in turn have consequences for family functioning. They therefore affect various aspects of family well-being, such as pressure upon economic resources and marital satisfaction. It is claimed that at each stage the family faces distinctive tasks whose completion is essential for successful individual and family development (Duvall and Miller, 1985). For example, the economic burden of establishing a new home at the beginning of the family life cycle may be eased by transfers of resources from families at later stages of the life cycle, when they are under less financial pressure (Hill, 1970).

In the work of Reuben Hill, family development theory was linked with systems theory from an early point in its evolution. As originally proposed, the concept of family development rested upon a view of the family as 'a closed system of interacting personalities [which] is organized in such a way as to meet certain functional prerequisites through the accomplishment of certain individual and developmental tasks' (Hill and Rodgers, 1964:177). Family life cycle stages were therefore defined 'in terms of the dominant developmental tasks being faced by individual members in the family and by the family as a system' (Hill and Rodgers, 1964:178). This systemic approach to family development was continued in Hill's later discussions of family development theory (Hill and Mattessich, 1979; Mattessich and Hill, 1987), and in the work of David Olson and his associates (Olson *et al.*, 1983:70). It has also been found useful by those family therapists who view stress as being greatest at transition points from one stage to another of the family developmental cycle (Carter and McGoldrick, 1989). Whether such a point of view can account adequately for all forms of stress in families is a question that deserves careful consideration. There is evidence to suggest that life-cycle events such as pregnancy or a birth, or moving to a new house or apartment, can precipitate incidents of wife-beating. However, by focusing on such precipitating factors there is a risk that social scientists may overlook larger causes that deserve our attention.

Family conservation and familial conservatism

During the past two decades the established relationships between social knowledge and power have been called into question, in society at large and within institutionalized social science (Witkin, 1989). Dumon notes that in Europe there has been a growing bifurcation in social policy, between traditional family policy and a new 'emancipation policy' that is concerned mainly with women's issues (1988:242–3). A similar division is also to be found in contemporary sociology, between family sociology and feminist sociology, as Gravenhorst reports.

In a feminist look at the sociology of the family, Lerke Gravenhorst (1988) criticizes the emphasis in family development theory upon the family as a system. She argues that since the prime interest is in the development of the system as a whole, the subjective concerns of individual women tend to be overlooked. In her view, family development theory therefore contributes to the repression, distortion and silencing of women's interests. She believes that those interests can be recovered theoretically only when family development concepts are replaced by feminist concepts, such as that of patriarchy. According to Gravenhorst, in a patriarchal society women are assigned the principal tasks in families, and they are therefore committed to financial and social dependence. Gravenhorst claims that in this way structural limits are imposed upon the possibilities for family adaptation that reinforce the position of women as bearers of children for men. The subjective core of female experience in marriage and family, she argues, is not developmental tasks but making a virtue out of necessity (Gravenhorst, 1988:96).

Similar objections have also been made about the limits to theories of family therapy. Theories of family development and those of family therapy have in common a positive evaluation of the continuity of families over time. Feminist critics have claimed that the importance which family therapists attach to maintaining family ties leads to an implicit and inadvertent familial conservatism, which reinforces traditional values that are oppressive for women (Avis, 1985). Boss and Thorne refer to the therapists' approach as a 'conserving micro-functionalism' (1989:80) that emphasizes values of equilibrium and pattern maintenance. In particular, it seems that family systems therapy has often ignored the gendered nature of the cybernetic hierarchy of control (Hare-Mustin, 1988). Rachel Hare-Mustin observes that while generational differences in positions within the family hierarchy are usually recognized in systems approaches, 'Gender, a crucial marker of hierarchy, is disregarded' (1987:21). She therefore claims that:

> Systems approaches, by viewing family members as equal interacting parts in recursive complementarities, tend to ignore differences in power, resources, needs, and interests among family members. Such theories regard the nondifferential treatment of family members as equal treatment, assuming that men and women in the normal family are at the same hierarchical level. (Hare-Mustin, 1987:21)

The reasons for this apparent neglect of power relations within families deserve to be spelled out in some detail, since they raise challenging questions about the prestige of systems theorizing among human service practitioners, and about the influence of practical models upon systems theorizing in family science.

The feminist critique of family therapy begins with an awareness that models of family systems are often blind to gender differences in those relational experiences that lead men and women (usually women) to seek marital therapy (Goldner, 1985; Hare-Mustin, 1987). That blindness is grounded in two features of the therapeutic code, which are in fact pragmatic solutions to practical problems.

First, family therapists have found that in order to reconcile conflicting spouses, it is necessary to get them to break out of the cycle of blaming each other that is found in many troubled marriages (Jacobson, 1985). This is done by focusing on the positive values in the relationship (such as joint accomplishments in the past). As well, the therapist constructs a circular model of relationship causality, in which the partners are encouraged to see how the behaviour of each affects the other. The effect of this strategy is to diffuse attributions of responsibility for problems in the relationship, and to displace attention towards techniques for co-operative problem solving and conflict resolution. Tomm (1980) has recommended a cybernetic systems approach to family therapy for precisely this reason. The key to this approach, he states, is the 'circular pattern diagramming' (CPD) of family interactions, which is used to identify 'stable organizational structure with feedback regulation'. His comments on the therapeutic uses of this method are worth quoting:

> Despite its simplicity, a CPD promotes abstract and integrative conceptualization. It helps the student or clinician focus specifically on a systemic element of the family. Usually when the family initially describes a problem, it is in linear terms with the tendency to blame particular individuals for initiating the problem. If the therapist is drawn into the family's way of perceiving and conceptualizing, he too is liable to end up focusing on and covertly blaming the individual (albeit with somewhat more empathy) and to overlook the interpersonal systemic problem. The use of CPDs concretely facilitates a shift from linear to circular thinking. . . When the therapist can clearly see the full circular patterns(s) he is able to maintain multidirectional partiality and avoid taking sides inappropriately. When a problem is defined as being circular, the issue of initiator or 'first cause' becomes irrelevant. A circle by definition has no beginning or end. It is often very helpful to draw a CPD on a blackboard or piece of paper and explain it to the family. As family members transcend their individual linear conceptualization, a flash of insight may occur with considerable relief of underlying guilt feelings. (Tomm, 1980:14)

This type of approach has often been popular among family therapists, but many feminist therapists have found it hard to accept. The problem here is that 'oppression, from a family systems perspective, is viewed as a mutually regulated dance between oppressor and oppressed, a dance maintained by the cyclical interaction sequences between the participants' (Libow *et al.*, 1982:8). Feminist therapists who want this dance to stop emphasize linear causality rather than circular causality. They do so in order to identify antecedent causes of behavioural problems, such as societal sex-role expectations, male-dominated family structures, and unequal power distribution in the larger society, which women are then encouraged to change through collective action in solidarity with other women.

The second concern about technologies of family therapy is that they have been constrained by a practical need to moderate the behaviour of the therapist, so that she or he will not act in ways that are experienced by clients as threatening. The principal reason for this is that agreement to participate in family therapy is voluntary, and it can always be withdrawn. The 'Utah group' of clinical psychologists notes, in a rejoinder to a feminist critique of their method, that 'No matter how noble our motivation, we cannot afford to prescribe therapist behaviors which alienate one or more family members, who then drop out of treatment' (Alexander *et al.*, 1985:140). In practice it appears that husbands are more likely to drop out of therapeutic treatment than are wives. This is presumably because men have more to lose by any changes in family practices that therapists might wish to recommend, and because maintenance of the existing power structure is often an unstated condition for their involvement in therapy (Goldner, 1985).

As a result of these self-imposed limitations in the scope of therapeutic technology, what tends to be lost in practical models of family systems is knowledge of the socially constructed differences that divide men and women in traditional marriages. This is because the open recognition of those differences is likely to be too threatening to the therapeutic process itself. The role of systems theory here is hardly innocent. It negotiates a construction of reality in which there are no determining causes, but only infinite recursive connections or 'feedback loops' (Goldner, 1985).

Beyond bounded systems

There is another problem with therapeutic family systems theories, to which attention is also drawn by feminism. A major theme in recent criticisms of family therapy's treatment of women is its commitment to the nuclear family system as the unit of diagnosis, as well as the context for intervention (Taggart, 1985; Hare-Mustin, 1987). That commitment is understandable, when we consider the historical situation in which family therapy first became prominent. The formative period of establishment for family therapy was the decade of the 1950s (Goldner, 1985; Hare-Mustin, 1987). That decade was unlike any era before or since in its idealization of the structurally isolated nuclear family as the foundation for socio-emotional normality (see Chapter 1).

Two noteworthy problems have arisen from an undue reliance upon models of nuclear family systems in family therapy, and in family science. One is that individual members' commitments to the existence and continuation of the system tend to be taken for granted (Jacobson, 1985). In actual fact their commitments may be highly variable, ranging from a desire to preserve the system at all costs to a desire to disengage from it. The strength of individual commitments to any system, and the reasons for them, must always be accounted for. That is especially necessary in the case of those members whose continued participation can be expected to bring them few immediate rewards.

The other conspicuous feature of the adherence of family systems theory to a concept of the structurally isolated nuclear family is that it is not grounded in any theory of the larger social system (which Parsonian systems theory did at least provide). The result of this is that analyses of family systems often make little or no reference to important social contexts that shape the forms of family life (James and McIntyre, 1983; Goldner, 1985; Taggart, 1985; Hare-Mustin, 1987; 1988). The moral idealization of structural isolation continues today in the concern expressed by systems theorists about the maintenance of family boundaries. Taggart (1985) has pointed out that the scientific act of locating a system boundary is never simply an ontological issue (i.e. a matter of fact). It is always to some degree a matter of choice, to be decided by the analyst on epistemological grounds (i.e. according to what it is that the analyst wishes to know, and how it is proposed that the data should be collected and interpreted). Viewed in this way, the reliance of family therapists upon family systems concepts is clearly consistent with their tendency to particularize interpersonal problems in ways that do not call into question the larger social structure (James and McIntyre, 1983). From a sociological point of view, the most problematic feature of systems theorizing in this respect is that the concept of a family boundary becomes 'the mere container of the system's substance designed, as it were, to keep context at bay while scientists (or therapists) get on with their work in uncomplicated peace' (Taggart, 1985:120).

The limitations of family systems theorizing are especially visible in relation to the controversial subject of wife-beating (Bograd, 1984). Goldner (1985:33) claims that the assumption of systemic circularity 'looks suspiciously like a hypersophisticated version of blaming the victim'. The difficulties that systems theorists get into here are evident even in a relatively broad account, such as that provided by Jean Giles-Sims (1983). Since this is an important test case for the relative claims of systems theory and feminist theory, it will be discussed in some detail.

Using a systems theory approach, Giles-Sims is most interested in identifying forms of feedback that reinforce violent behaviour. The escalation of interpersonal anger to the level of physical violence is explained systemically by 'deviation-amplifying feedback loops'. Two kinds of feedback loop are identified. There are those within the family system itself, in the ongoing interactions between husbands and wives, and therefore in wives' responses to their husbands' behaviour. Then there are the connections between the family system and its social environment, in particular agents of social control such as neighbours, the police and the courts.

Within the family system, Giles-Sims describes wives as contributing to their husbands' violence towards them in two ways. At the most general level, women's commitment to marriage causes them to sustain their husbands' violence, through their maintenance of the family system within which violent behaviour is established. More specifically, wives are also thought to reinforce violent behaviour when their compliance allows the abusive husband to achieve his goals. Wife-beating, that is to say, is rewarded by the wife's compliant response, or in other words she provides 'positive feedback' for his violent behaviour (Giles-Sims, 1983:127–30). Externally, the major factor in Giles-Sims's systems theoretic account of wife-beating is the lack of significant 'negative feedback' from outsiders. In systems terminology, this is interpreted as the result of difficulties in bridging the boundaries of the family system. Giles-Sims notes that the police and the courts have often provided inadequate protection for battered women seeking refuge, since 'The boundaries of the original family system continue to exist in the view of others in the larger social structure' (1983:138–9). Battered wives, too, are described as actively shaping the impermeable boundaries of their family systems. The stigma associated with family problems in general and family violence in particular leads such women to hide their situation from others. The boundaries of the family's system then become relatively closed (Giles-Sims, 1983:131).

There is no doubt that a systems theoretic account of wife-beating helps to identify some distinctive features of families in which it occurs. However, it must be equally clear that it is insufficient as a general explanation of the phenomenon. Giles-Sims in fact adds other relevant factors, derived from other theoretical approaches. The submission of battered wives to their abusive husbands is thus explained by the partial legitimation of physical coercion towards women in a patriarchal structure. This social structural factor is then glossed in systems terms, as 'acceptable input into the system for some people' (Giles-Sims, 1983:128).

Systems theory accounts of wife-beating, such as that advanced by Giles-Sims, run into four kinds of difficulty. First, the origins of husbands' impulses to act violently against their wives cannot be accounted for in systemic terms. An explanation in terms of feedback loops, like any functional explanation, can only show how an established line of action is maintained, or amplified or dampened: it cannot explain why the behaviour exists in the first place. Second, the commitment of wives to marriage is clearly a critical factor in the apparent self-maintenance of family systems. The work performed by women in the daily reproduction of family life is taken for granted by family systems theory, but in fact women's commitment to doing it is socially constructed. Third, any explanation of wives' submission to violence against them in terms of its cultural legitimacy clearly begs a larger set of questions concerning the nature of culture. And fourth, the respect that the police and the courts have demonstrated for family boundaries needs to be explained in institutional terms. The important theoretical consequence of raising these four issues is that they turn the attention of family sociologists away from family systems theory, and towards other kinds of approach. Those issues have all been hotly debated in the set of theories that are discussed in Chapter 4.

Notes

1. For a description of the role of 'sexual assignments' in the treatment of sexual dysfunction see Jehu (1980b).
2. Sociologists have shown relatively little interest in developing an explicit family policy, but they have nevertheless contributed a great deal to understanding the *implicit* family policies that have shaped government programs in the past (e.g. Eichler, 1983; 1987).
3. The difference between structural-functional models of equilibrium-seeking systems, and models that are premised upon a principle of competitive expansion, can be seen in Oppenheimer's critique of Parsons's theory of gender and family/work roles (1982:259–65). It will be recalled from Chapter 1 that, according to Parsons, wives do not aspire to be economically successful because status competition between spouses might destabilize the marriage. As a matter of fact, increasing numbers of wives have pursued occupational achievement in recent decades, and there is clearly something wrong with Parsons's thesis. Oppenheimer argues that the flaw in Parsons's theory is his failure to analyse the relationships between families, which are engaged in status competition. Viewed in that context, female employment is a strategy that has the competitive advantage of increasing a family's resources for purchasing the symbols of respectable social status. Indeed, the more successful a wife is occupationally, the greater is the status advantage that a dual-earner household will have over a single-earner household. Oppenheimer's conclusion, namely that inter-familial status competition promotes wives' employment, would seem to account for contemporary observations better than does Parsons's focus upon sex roles.

CHAPTER 4

PRIVATE AND PUBLIC: DIALECTICS OF MODERNITY, DIVISION II

Sociological theories about families have benefited greatly from the input of social critics, such as feminists and Marxists. We must consider for a moment why this is so. In everyday life, issues are first experienced as local and particular encounters. It is only with some difficulty that we learn how to thematize those experiences, and to abstract from them, in ways that enable us to generalize the principles involved to other situations. Within the everyday view of the world, we tend to locate the causes of problems in individuals, and in the interactions they initiate. We do not immediately turn to thinking about the larger contexts of action, within which causes that are external to individuals can be specified. Family systems theory is, of course, one framework for contextualizing family interactions. But we have also seen that it does have its self-imposed limits. Social criticism forces us to rethink such limits, and to address larger issues of historic proportions. Feminist thought, for instance, is a form of critical thinking which tends to favour analyses of external constraints, and which attributes world-shaping significance to overarching structures that affect large numbers of women. It is this larger process of determination that we will be concerned with in this chapter, as it has been presented in macro-sociological theories of the modern family.

A number of sociological approaches exist today that supply information about the social contexts within which family relationships are located – information that is missing from family systems models. It is this kind of information that is often most interesting for sociologists. Critics of family systems theory have pointed out, for example, that focusing on interactions within families leaves no way to explain why clients of family therapists present certain kinds of problem more frequently than others. Consider the commonly reported pattern of a mother who is 'over-involved' with her 'symptomatic' child, and who is accompanied to family therapy sessions by her reluctant, 'disengaged' husband (James and McIntyre, 1983). The reasons for this recurring problem require explanation. The first point to note is that this pattern is an extension of a family form in which mother is the central figure because father is absent at work for most of the day. Going a step further, we can say that this pattern is the product of a social structure that separates family and work, and which assigns to women the major responsibility for family, as it assigns to men the major responsibility for work. Here, then, we see that issues in family therapy lead directly into questions of social structure (Bograd, 1988).

Some of the most important contradictions affecting families today arise from this division of social experience into a *private* sphere of interpersonal closeness, and a *public* sphere of employment and state power. It is frequently pointed out that the division between public and private spheres is closely linked to other kinds of dualism, such as those of the political and the personal, the instrumental and the expressive, and male and female (Glennon, 1979; Pateman, 1983; Siltanen and Stanworth, 1984; Yeatman, 1984). Concepts of private and public have therefore been a focal point for much recent discussion on family and gender (K. Hansen, 1987; Storrie, 1987; Coontz, 1988; J. Meyer *et al.*, 1988; Laslett and Brenner, 1989; Osmond, 1989; Richards, 1989).[1] Wife-battering is one issue to which the concept of the private family has been applied.

The invisibility of battered women who experience repeated violence in the home over long periods of time demonstrates how strong the boundaries of family privacy can be (J. Pahl, 1985; Gelles and Straus, 1988). Because the family is an idealized haven from trouble and strife, domestic violence is at odds with the cultural image of the normal family. Battered wives may therefore see themselves as different from other women, because they have failed to manage their husbands' tensions. Loss of self-esteem, and individualization of their problems, can lead them to withdraw from situations that might expose the violence against them to public knowledge. This psychological isolation is not a purely individual phenomenon. It has its roots in the social isolation experienced by many women living in private families. Separation of family life from public life, and the role that women are expected to play as a 'binding agent' in maintaining family integrity (Liljeström, 1982), both reinforce cultural beliefs that family problems are private troubles, and that women have the primary duty of resolving them. The point to be made here is that the structurally isolated nuclear family is both isolated and isolating (Chalmers and Smith, 1987). One aspect of this isolation is public respect for family boundaries.

Feminists have drawn attention to the patterned nature of non-intervention in the private sphere, in contexts such as rape within marriage and wife abuse (Dahl and Snare, 1978). These private problems have been regarded by society as personal tasks that should be solved by individuals rather than by collective agencies. Problems such as wife-battering have been difficult and controversial as public issues, largely because public agencies such as the police and courts are reluctant to breach the privacy of families (J. Pahl, 1985). They have respected the common desire of family members that family life should be an autonomous space, or 'free zone', within which personal affairs can be arranged without interference or official intervention.

The idea that external agencies should have only limited access to things that are considered to be private is one of three general concepts of publicness/privateness (Benn and Gaus, 1983). The other two concepts are agency/accountability, and interest. The first of these concepts draws our attention to whether individuals act as free agents who construct their own lives, or are constrained to perform certain duties for which they can be held publicly accountable. This notion of agency/accountability is closely related to that of interest. Private and public interests are thought to be antithetical. In the one case individuals pursue their own goals, whereas in the other they act with reference to public purposes that are expressed through political institutions and formal organizations.

These three ideas – access; agency/accountability; and interest – together define the cultural ideal of the private family in liberal western democracies. Family members define their projects with reference to personal desires, rather than public goals, and they are free to implement them to the limits of their resources.

Freedom of action is guaranteed by the fact that levels and terms of access by outsiders to the interior of the family are controlled by the members themselves. This ideal of family living has been very attractive to many people living in modern societies, especially in the urban middle class.

The continuing strength of these ideas has recently been confirmed by Lyn Richards, in a study of suburban families in Australia (1989). Ideas about proper family life there are closely linked to images of domestic privacy, and to desires for home ownership. The family home is seen as a source of financial and emotional security, as well as of adult independence and freedom from control by others, and as a place where husbands, wives and children can experience togetherness.

The private family is, of course, only a cultural ideal. It is often modified in practice by other kinds of projects. Official respect for family boundaries may be withdrawn from time to time, for specific purposes. This can happen, for example, when there is great public concern about physical or sexual abuse and child neglect in the home. In general, however, the private family is gratefully regarded as a support network, whose functioning reduces collective burdens of care that would otherwise fall on public agencies (Wenger, 1984; Sauer and Coward, 1985). As Diana Gittins puts it: 'What actually goes on in families is conveniently dismissed as "private" until it becomes "public" by creating a nuisance or a financial responsibility to the State' (1985:154).

The cultural ideal of the private family has had a considerable influence upon family science. Gubrium and Holstein (1987) note that the 'private image' of family has defined an approach to methodology that is exclusively concerned with penetrating the social interiors of households. Similarly, the image of the private family is reflected in theories of families as bounded systems, described in Chapter 3. David Morgan argues that these theories express a cultural preference for a particular kind of family. It is, he says, 'a family centrally concerned with space, with distance, with privacy and invasion' (D.H.J. Morgan, 1985:157). The effect of the terminology of systems theory, Morgan argues, is to hide the historical and cultural particularity of this type of family under universal scientific generalizations.

Systems theories are not the only theories that have the effect of decontextualizing the private family. This effect is also produced by claims for the existence of a unique 'family realm'. Family realm theorists based at Brigham Young University in Utah, and at the University of Utah, believe that 'The irreducible parameter of this realm is the biological, emotional, social, and developmental processes that are inherent in procreation and the nurturing of dependent children' (Beutler *et al.*, 1989). They claim that the realm of human experience created by these processes has seven characteristics that make it fundamentally different from non-family areas of life. Those characteristics are as follows:

(a) the generational nature and permanence of family relationships,
(b) concern with 'total' persons,
(c) the simultaneous process orientation that grows out of familial caregiving,
(d) a unique and intense emotionality,
(e) an emphasis on qualitative purposes and processes,
(f) an altruistic orientation, and
(g) a nurturing form of governance. (Beutler *et al.*, 1989:806)

Critics of this approach have argued that it is not so much a new paradigm as a 'failed nostalgia' for a culturally and historically bound image of the family (Edwards, 1989). As such, it ignores the multiple realities of contemporary families (Jurich, 1989). Even more important, for present purposes, is the point that the family realm perspective gives an isolated description of only one part of human experience (Menaghan, 1989). As a result, this approach does not examine the connections between different realms. It emphasizes (and exaggerates) the differences between the family realm and other realms. Furthermore, it segregates family matters – and family scholars – from other social influences. The most serious consequence of this segregation is that family realm theorists fail to consider how much their own experiences of family uniqueness owe to socially constructed ideological contrasts, rather than fixed biological parameters. In order to understand the historical process by which those contrasts were constructed, we must turn once again to theories of modernity.

One of the most fundamental features of modernization is the segregation of family life from social structures that are far more extensive in space and time. What those structures are, and how they work, is the subject that will occupy us for most of the remainder of this chapter.

The private family

In recent years, the focus of attention in structural theories of family life has shifted away from a concern with contemporary cross-cultural comparisons, to a concern with long-run processes of historical change in the western societies (Kohli, 1986). This is partly because historical demographic studies of our own societies provoked a profound rethinking of structural functional theories of modern families (Anderson, 1979; Elliot, 1986). At one time, comparisons between the western industrial societies and tribal societies in developing nations appeared to suggest that industrialization is the cause of the nuclear family. It was this tradition of work upon which Parsons drew, in formulating his ideas about functional fit between the isolated nuclear family and patterns of industrial employment. Recent historical studies, particularly in England, suggest that in some places nuclear family living in fact preceded industrialization, rather than following from it. Macfarlane (1979), for example, has demonstrated that the nucleation of the English family prior to industrialization produced a 'possessive individualism' that facilitated rational economic calculation and investment.

Social history and social theory of the family are more closely related these days than they used to be (Tilly and Scott, 1978; Liljeström, 1982; 1983; Lamphere, 1987). As a result, sociological interest in family history has considerably broadened, to include many issues besides industrial employment. Today family forms are studied in relation to three great forces of modernization. They are conceptualized in terms of the differentiation of modern society into separate structures of the 'polity', the 'economy', and 'civil society'. Those forces are as follows:

1. The expansion of the state.
2. Industrialization and commodification (i.e. the expanded buying and selling of commodities in markets).
3. Urbanization.

Theories of familial privatization have been developed with respect to each of the three major forces of modernization. In practice, these three types of theory have received unequal amounts of attention in sociological discussions. Later sections of this chapter will therefore focus on aspects of industrialization and commodification, which have been especially prominent concerns for many sociologists. Before moving on to consider those issues in detail, we must first outline briefly each of the three types of family privatization theory, in the order set out above.

The expansion of the public sphere through large construction projects and military campaigns organized by the state is the historical foundation for the private/public division described in liberal political theory. Feminist anthropologists have pointed out that this structural differentiation is also a gendered division. Reiter (1975) believes that a sharp division between a private female world of home and kinship ties, and a public male world of geographically dispersed collegial contacts and hierarchical structures, is characteristic of state-organized societies. In these societies it is the state that holds power, rather than kinship groups. Activities of the state are therefore formalized, legitimated and accorded higher status than domestic activities. The pre-existing division of labour by gender, between female domestic responsibilities and male access to external resources, thus became defined as a separation of spheres. In modern times, it is suggested, this historic separation of spheres was intensified by the growth of public administration, and by related processes of bureaucratic and legal rationalization (M. Stacey and Price, 1981). The legal separation of 'person' from 'office' was also a separation of social spheres. It justified the physical concentration of bureaucratic functionaries, which increased their visibility to and control by centralized authority, in locations that were far removed from their homes. As Max Weber noted: 'In principle, the modern organization of the civil service separates the bureau from the private domicile of the official and, in general, segregates official activity from the sphere of private life' (1968:957).

Other theories of the division between private and public, which are perhaps better known, stress the effects of economic changes. Laslett (1973), for example, has argued that the private family is the consequence of a particular separation between family life and work for financial remuneration. In the West, she says, this separation was historically associated with industrialization. Before that many economic tasks were performed in the household, and family production might have been assisted by

Dialectical relationship

the labour of a variety of non-kin, such as servants and apprentices. The growth of machine production, and the factory system, led to the displacement of this domestic labour force, and to the privatization of family life. We shall have more to say about this line of argument below.

Finally, Sennett (1970) has described the emergence of the private family (or the 'intensive family', as he calls it) in terms of its being a 'bulwark against the industrial city'. This type of family is valued for providing a protective barrier against the risks and instabilities associated with urban heterogeneity and disorder. It defines a sharp separation between internal and external social meanings that relies upon securing the privacy of family life *vis-à-vis* the outside world. The constitution of the family as a private refuge from urban pressures is made possible by its intense emotional intimacy, and by the sanctification of family ties. Fischer (1981) has suggested that intimate ties are a reaction against the anonymity of urban civilization. In modern cities public spaces are peopled by strangers, and these places are experienced as dangerous and alienating environments. Trust is restricted to known others, with whom the individual shares a small, private world (Cheal, 1988a).

The origins of the private family have been of considerable interest to sociologists. However, in practice they have usually been rather more concerned with its consequences, and especially its consequences for women. As noted earlier, those consequences include the invisibility of disadvantages that women may experience in their domestic roles. It has recently been observed, for example, that female poverty due to inequality in marriage has been an invisible problem (Millar and Glendinning, 1987). This is because official studies of poverty have tended to focus on the family as a collective unit in which incomes are presumed to be shared, and upon the male household head as provider. As a result, although the extent and causes of poverty in the market economy are well known, by comparison very little is known about patterns of poverty due to family interactions within the household economy. Recent research has therefore begun to focus on the connections between private and public dimensions of material dependency.

Sociologists have also become interested in the cultural consequences of privatized domesticity. For example, there has been much stress on the ideological exaggeration of the contrast between 'the home' and 'the world' that developed during the nineteenth century. The ideology of separate spheres identified women with homeliness and men with worldliness, and it polarized the ideal personalities of women and men. Cancian (1987) has described one consequence of that ideal as the 'feminization of love'. By this she means that cultural ideals of the feminine qualities of love, such as tenderness and expressiveness, were selectively emphasized as the foundations for family living. Love, Cancian says, 'became a private feeling, disassociated from public life, economic production, and practical action to help others' (1987:24). Feminized love was defined as what women did in the home, and women's privatized labour was defined as a work of love.

The nineteenth century separation of public and private spheres appears to have had a number of consequences for women. Among them, feminist sociologists have been most interested in those aspects that are relatively neglected by the liberal theory of family life. As seen from the point of view of liberal political theory, the private sphere is a protected zone in which individuals can act freely with respect to their personal interests. However, that promise of freedom may prove to be illusory, for two reasons.

First, it may be the case that within the private sphere one category of person is regularly dominant over another. Margrit Eichler (1973) refers to the category of dominant person in domestic relations as the 'personal master', and the category of subordinate person as the 'personal dependent'. She states that all housewives and other attached females who have no independent source of income belong to the category of personal dependent, while their husbands, fathers, lovers, or whoever else it is who supports them, are their personal masters. Typical consequences of personal dependency, she says, include submissiveness and a desire to please.

Second, there is the question of how relations of dependency in domestic life are linked to the social division between private and public spheres. If the dominant category in domestic relations is free to move between the private and public spheres at will, whereas the subordinated category remains within the private sphere, then the members of the former category are agents of their own destinies in a way that the latter can never be. Feminists state that this is in fact the situation in most families, and that the dominators are male while the subordinated are female (Delphy, 1976; 1984; Burton, 1985). In an early statement, Dorothy Smith made this point in the following way:

> The public sphere is that sphere in which 'history' is made. But the public sphere is also the sphere of male activity. Domestic activity becomes relegated to the private sphere, and is mediated to the public sphere by men who move between both. Women have a place only in the private, domestic sphere. . .The division of labour between the sexes does not as such create a relation of oppression of men against women. It is the constitution of public versus private spheres of action, and the relegation of the domestic to that sphere which is outside history – *this* is the contemporarily relevant transformation and the contemporary form of oppression. (D. Smith, 1973:6,7)

Reconsidered from a feminist point of view, the dimensions of publicness/privateness outlined earlier now appear in a different light. The principal point at issue here is inequality of agency. It is held that male agency is sustained by the private labours of females who service the daily needs of their husbands and children (Gamarnikow and Purvis, 1983). Through the domestic labour of women men are freed from many of the practical burdens of housework, and so they can pursue a variety of interests. These may include political pursuits that are inaccessible to women in so far as women are confined to the private sphere. Barrett and McIntosh have argued that in this sense the family must be considered an 'anti-social' institution, in which privacy for women is 'imprisonment' (1982:56). It is further suggested that the social isolation of women through familial commitments is one way in which male domination in the home is sustained. Structurally isolated women are likely to find it more difficult to get together for the purposes of collective efforts to improve their social position. Also, a low level of access to the interior of family life by outsiders renders physical or other abuse against women practically invisible, and thereby insulates oppressive power relations from social pressures and sanctions. In short, it cannot be automatically assumed that men and women are equally autonomous individuals within the private family, or that family privacy has equal effects on women and men (J. Lewis, 1983).

It is possible to argue that there is no necessary causal link between the private family and domestic patriarchy. However, it is also clear that in practice patriarchal relations are facilitated and strengthened by the private family. Some Marxist theorists have gone one step further in asserting a linkage between them. They have claimed that male privilege and the private family are both outcomes of the organization of work in the capitalist mode of production.

Capital, class and labour

The privatized nature of the 'cult of domesticity' in modern family living has been a prominent issue in the Marxist theory of families, and in the considerable amount of neo-Marxist and non-Marxist work that has been stimulated by it (Brenner and Laslett, 1986). Marxism has some distinctive features that require brief explanation, in order to understand the extent of its influence in the social sciences. Marxist social theorists employ a materialist method of analysis that provides them with general principles for the explanation of all social structures. Although the origins of this approach lie in the work of Karl Marx, his writings are of less immediate value for our purposes than those of his collaborator Friedrich Engels. It was in fact Engels who made the clearest linkage between the materialist method and family issues, such as the social value of having children. He stated that:

According to the materialistic conception, the determining factor in history is, in the final instance, the production and reproduction of the immediate essentials of life. This (again) is of a twofold character. On the one side, the production of the means of existence, of articles of food and clothing, dwellings, and of the tools necessary for that production; on the other side, the production of human beings themselves, the propagation of the species (Engels, 1942:5).

Engels established that the organization of social life is determined by the production of two things that are necessary for the continuation of any society – the goods that are necessary for daily living, and the people who renew social life from one generation to the next. In practice, most Marxists emphasize only the necessities of daily living. That narrow approach is often referred to as 'economic determinism', because it stresses the process by which goods are produced, or *mode of production*. According to Seccombe, 'The family is ultimately dependent upon the dominant mode of production for its existence and form' (1974:5).

The essential feature of the capitalist mode of production is its determination by the laws of the investment of capital for profit. Capitalism is driven by the continuous expansion of those processes that contribute to large reductions in manufacturing costs for businesses. Although opinions among Marxists differ on this point, it is thought that in principle this extends to all political and social formations, including families. Marxists therefore believe that the dominant family forms in the western societies are ones that are most useful for owners of industry, or in more abstract terms for 'capital'. Dorothy Smith, for example, believes that the nature of contemporary family life must be understood in terms of its uses for capital. She claims that the middle-class family stands in a 'sub-contractual relation to corporate capitalism' (D. Smith, 1973:14). It produces, supports and moulds the kind of person that corporations need for their survival, and Smith therefore believes that: 'The family is created in the image provided by the corporation' (1973:21).

Materialist studies of families emphasize how necessary the work that is performed in the home is for the maintenance of life (Luxton, 1980). Most of this activity, such as food preparation, is performed by women rather than men, and so it is conventionally considered to be 'women's work' (Charles and Kerr, 1988). Marxist-feminist theorists underscore the way in which this work is unequally distributed according to gender, and the different consequences that it has for men and women (D. Smith, 1981). It is thought that the most important characteristic of domestic labour is that it is performed voluntarily in the home, rather than as paid employment in an organized work setting such as a factory or an office. The consequences that follow from this include the separation of family life from the process of industrial production (Zaretsky, 1986a), and the related division of labour between man as breadwinner and woman as homemaker (McIntosh, 1979). The latter division in turn is described as the cause of women's economic and social dependency, as well as their relative financial deprivation during marriage and, especially, after divorce.

The approach to family life adopted by Marxist theorists is affected by their pursuit of radical change, and it differs significantly from the approach taken by those people who desire to work through conventional social institutions, such as the human service professions. Marxist theorists are typically not very interested in the family as a support system composed of interacting parts. One reason for this is because they stress the vulnerability of working-class families that depend on a 'living wage' or 'family wage' to maintain themselves (Zaretsky, 1982; 1986b). Resource limitations over which working-class people have little control, such as low industrial wages and high unemployment in times of depression, make it difficult for them to keep their families intact. These constraints can also result in delayed childbearing among working-class women, and a permanent reduction in fertility. Marxist life cycle theory differs from the developmental approach described in an earlier chapter, since it does not conceive of financial difficulties as developmental tasks. Instead, financial pressures are treated as budgetary crises that arise from the failure of the capitalist system to provide wages sufficient for human reproduction (Wayne, 1986).

In Marxist family studies, the emphasis is placed upon the underlying economic relations that structure social interactions between men, women and children which are defined ideologically as 'family' (D. Smith, 1985:4–7). Smith states that 'The general emphasis here is on the significance of the economic relations to which the family is articulated as these organize the inner structure of the family' (1981:161). Marxists have theorized that the privatization of social interaction in capitalist societies is an effect of economic relations in three principal ways. The privatization of interaction may be seen as a result of the following:

1. The expanded production of goods.
2. Private property.
3. The reproduction of labour power for industry.

We will consider each of these possibilities in turn.

Capitalist production

In the influential thesis of Eli Zaretsky (1986a), the origin of the dichotomy between private and public is seen to lie in the structure of industrial capitalism, specifically in the dichotomy between 'the family' and 'the economy'. Zaretsky's conceptualization of the capitalist mode of production closely follows that of Marx. Karl Marx described the process of capitalist production as coming into existence

> when each individual capital simultaneously employs a comparatively large number of workers, and when, as a result, the labour-process is carried on on an extensive scale, and yields relatively large quantities of products. A large number of workers working together, at the same time, in one place (or, if you like, in the same field of labour), in order to produce the same sort of commodity under the command of the same capitalist, constitutes the starting-point of capitalist production (Marx, 1977:439)

It is this concept of industrial capitalism that provides the basis for Zaretsky's account of the private family. The overall tendency of capitalist development, he says, has been to remove productive labour from the private efforts of families, and to centralize it in large-scale impersonal units, such as factories. Zaretsky claims that with the rise of capitalist production human activity became divided between the new public forms of work (or 'socialized' forms, as he calls them) and the private labour that continued to be performed predominantly by women within the home.

The structural separation between socialized labour and private labour is experienced subjectively as a division between alienated labour for wages (i.e. 'work') and relations with those people to whom the individual has personal ties (i.e. one's 'personal life'). In Zaretsky's opinion, modern desires for self-fulfilment are stifled by alienated labour. These desires therefore find expression in a search for personal meaning, that can only be realized in personal life. In the personal sphere, he says, we pursue

> our inner lives and social capabilities, our dreams, our desires, our fears, our sense of ourselves as interconnected beings. Reflecting

> the separation of personal life from production, a new idea has emerged on a mass scale: that of human relations, and human beings, as an end in themselves (Zaretsky, 1986a:57)

In actual practice, Zaretsky points out, the separation of work and personal life under capitalism is a common experience only for men. For women who are housewives, personal life and work continue to be fused in the tasks of nurturance and child-rearing that are carried out within the home. Zaretsky notes the social isolation of such women in the family, and he points out that the unpaid housework they perform is devalued by comparison with the paid work in which men are employed. Nevertheless, it also appears to have been the case that the social position of women in early capitalist societies was strengthened in one respect. Women, especially as mothers, were idealized as the core of personal life. Zaretsky claims that the Victorian 'cult of domesticity' assigned a special place to women, as guardians of moral virtue and the higher sentiments, in contrast to the crassness and heartlessness of competitive commerce.

The cult of domesticity, and other forms of private subjectivity that came into prominence later, were brought into popular focus in the imagery of the family. The family need not be the only focus for personal life, of course, but its continuity from former times ensured its prevalence as the main source of personal relations. Zaretsky therefore claims that 'With the rise of corporate capitalism, the family became the major institution in society given over to the personal needs of its members' (1986a:61). As a consequence of this development, the idea grew that family life consists of natural functions, which are performed in a unique realm that has no apparent connection to the rest of society. Zaretsky argues that this idea has shaped the modern view of sexuality, as liberation from traditional sexual repression. He states (1986a:94):

> It is in this context perhaps that we can understand the mysterious significance of sexuality in the lives of modern men and women. It is almost as if sexuality has been invested with all the mystery of society itself. Sex has appeared as the ultimately asocial act, the one in which men and women were the most 'natural', in the dark without clothing . . . sexuality stood for the real life of men and women as opposed to the artificial constraints of society.

Nevertheless, Zaretsky also observes that beneath the modern ideology of sexuality, sexual relations are always social relations, whether they occur inside marriage or outside marriage. As social relations, they consist of exchanges of love and other tokens between partners, as well as the exercise of power. Sexuality, in fact, is sometimes suggested as a principal arena of male domination. Although Zaretsky does acknowledge that sexuality is a medium for the expression of male supremacy, he has been criticized from a feminist point of view for failing to give this point due emphasis (Hartmann, 1981b:6–7). One Marxist who did indeed emphasize this point was Marx's collaborator, Friedrich Engels.

Private property

Engels equated the private family (or the 'individual family' as he called it) with patriarchal monogamy, or in his words 'strictly monogamous marriage under the rule of the man' (1942:62). This type of marriage constitutes families as small groups (i.e. nuclear families), and it separates these groups out from one another into self-contained households. Engels argued that this structural separation had been created by men, for men. They had been able to do this, he thought, because of the greater resources they possessed for the production of food. The purpose of this separation, according to Engels, is to ensure that wives' tasks of childbearing and household management are performed as a 'private service' for their husbands. This privatization of women's services is reinforced by restrictions that are placed upon their participation in 'public production' outside the home. Engels referred to this situation as the 'domestic slavery' of the wife (1942:65).

Engels observed that the strict sexual fidelity of monogamous marriage was in reality 'monogamy for the woman only, but not for the man' (1942:56). He claimed that although the sexual services of most women are privatized, men use prostitutes and other publicly available women too for purposes of sexual gratification. Engels therefore argued that the existence of the private family is not due to desires for emotional closeness, but has to do with control over women's reproductive capacities. With the historic accumulation of private property by men, Engels believed that they wanted to pass on their property to

inheritance

their own children, rather than having it disbursed to the children of other men. Since the biological paternity of children is inevitably uncertain, inheritance from fathers to sons can be assured only if wives are the exclusive sexual property of their husbands. Engels summarized his argument by stating that the monogamous family

> is based on the supremacy of the man, the express purpose being to produce children of undisputed paternity; such paternity is demanded because these children are later to come into their father's property as his natural heirs. (1942:55)

ideas disseminated by ruling class

The principal exception to this state of affairs, Engels thought, was that of love among the propertyless working classes in capitalist societies. Here there is no incentive for monogamy or male supremacy, because there is little or no property to pass on. Engels therefore believed that the liberation of the wife was possible in this class, but only if women were brought into public industry so that they could acquire the means of economic self-sufficiency. Engels realized that this would make marital separation easier, but he did not think that it would result in the complete disappearance of family relations. The most likely consequence of this state of affairs, according to Engels, would be the transformation of monogamous marriage into genuine intimate sexual love. The equality of wage-earning wives with their husbands would ensure that husbands as well as wives were truly sexually monogamous.

The account of family history that Engels advanced has been very influential among feminist social scientists, especially in the last two decades (Sacks, 1974; Vogel, 1983; Sayers *et al.*, 1987). Stolcke (1981), for example, has extended Engels's theory, by arguing that the prevailing arrangements of marriage and family are due to the social structural centrality of hereditary privilege in a class society. At the same time, many feminists have reacted against the work of Marx and Engels, for its tendency to reduce the oppression of women in the family to property relations, and therefore to class oppression (O'Brien, 1979; Barrett, 1980; Hartmann, 1981b; Delphy, 1984; Delphy and Leonard, 1986).

A variety of flaws have been identified in the Marxist account, which are attributed to the over-estimation of the significance of property relations, and of economic transactions more generally.

One objection is that women's participation in the realm of public production does not automatically lead to a more favourable position within the politics of the family (O'Brien, 1979). Here attention is often drawn to the way in which the relative earnings of husbands and wives are affected by the gendered distribution of childcare. It is also pointed out that since Engels attributed great importance to property relations in the monogamous family, his theory does not provide an adequate explanation of why propertyless working-class families do not all disintegrate (Barrett, 1980; Humphries, 1977).

Marxists and feminists have drawn two main kinds of conclusion about family life from the debates around these issues. Both of those conclusions stimulated considerable theoretical development. One conclusion is that the materialism of Marx and Engels is one-sidedly economistic. That is to say, it emphasizes the production of tangible goods such as food and clothing that are necessary for daily living. In doing so it practically ignores the provision of affection, nurturance and sexual satisfaction, which Ferguson and Folbre (1981) refer to as 'sex-affective production'. Furthermore, orthodox Marxism has tended to de-emphasize the reproduction of life itself through procreation. As one influential Marxist theorist has noted, in Marxism

> there has been an unfortunate counterposition of the socio-economic to the demographic, as if these two dimensions of social relations were materially separable under capitalism or elsewhere, and as if the lines of causality ran, undialectically, only one way: from the socio-economic and political to the demographic. (Seccombe, 1986a:23)

Not surprisingly, feminist materialists have often rejected theories of the predominance of relations of production, in order to stress the social importance of women's reproductive work (O'Brien, 1979; Himmelweit, 1983).

The second main conclusion drawn from criticisms of Marx and Engels is that they were wrong in assuming that work for wages is the only significant form of production in which working-class families are engaged in capitalist society. Marx and Engels overlooked the substantial amounts of work performed in the home, such as the preparation of meals and informal health care, that are in fact essential for survival. These forms of domestic production continue to play a major role in individual well-being, even in the most advanced capitalist societies.[2] The main conclusion that is drawn from this point is that materialist theories of working-class families must pay close attention to the study of domestic labour.

Domestic labour

The issue of domestic labour belongs to a definite moment in the history of sociology, in the 1970s. At that time, images of marriage as consisting of male breadwinner/female homemaker roles were still strong, and married women were typically seen as dependent housewives. At the same time, a successful feminist movement had begun to call into question the disadvantages of that status for women (Malos, 1980). Since then, married women have continued to enter paid employment in steadily increasing numbers, and the issues for women have changed. Veronica Beechey has observed that: 'Whereas in the seventies the major debates were about the political economy of domestic labour, about the relationships between production and reproduction, patriarchy and capitalism, today the relationship between gender and work has assumed a greater importance' (1987:13). Selected issues in family, gender and work will be taken up at the end of this chapter. For present purposes it is useful to recall how intense the discussions about domestic labour were during the 1970s, and the reasons for that.

It will be remembered that in the 1950s and the early 1960s family science had been dominated by a convergent style of theorizing that favoured the grand synthesis of Parsonian structural functionalism. We have also seen that this 'orthodox consensus' was subsequently blown apart, and that the process of fragmentation is still going on. The Big Bang of the mid-1970s was due to a combination of several pluralizing forces, among which a resurgent feminism was the most conspicuous. In some countries, such as Italy, the feminist movement raised the question of women's unpaid labour in the home into a major political issue (Dalla Costa, 1988). Similar developments in countries such as Britain and Canada linked feminism to a simultaneous revival of Marxism, with its longstanding interests in labour processes.

The Marxist revival has been very fruitful for family studies, in the form of abundant discussions about the relationship between domestic labour and the capitalist mode of production (B. Fox, 1980; Harris, 1983: 179–200; Close, 1985; Stichter and Parpart, 1988). The 'domestic labour debate', as it came to be known, was premised upon the assumption that there is a fundamental structural separation between public and private spheres that is a result of the capitalist organization of production (Close, 1989:28–9). That structural separation consists of a division between unpaid domestic labour on the one hand, and paid employment (i.e. wage labour) on the other.

The debate began as an attempt to provide Marxist answers to feminist questions about housework as a labour process (Seccombe, 1986b:190). It was an attempt to specify the relationship between women's work in the home and men's wage labour outside the home, as an element in the capitalist mode of production considered as a totality. In fact the issues raised in the debate quickly moved beyond that point to questions that were of greater importance for orthodox Marxism, principally concerning the viability and expansion of capitalism as an economic system (Bennholdt-Thomsen, 1981; Dickinson and Russell, 1986). Here we will be concerned solely with issues raised by the early questions about women's work for their families, since our interest is in family life rather than economic structures.

Marxist analyses of family life in the 1970s and early 1980s focused on the role of the housewife, who purchases and prepares the things that her family members need on a daily basis. The essential feature of the housewife role, in Marxist theory, is that she is seen as mediating between commodity markets (in which goods are bought and sold) and labour markets (in which workers exchange their productive capacity, or labour power, for wages). On one side families consume the goods produced by industry, and on the other they provide the workforce that capitalists employ in industrial production. Both processes are necessary for a capitalist economy to function, but in practice it is the second that has been emphasized by Marxist theorists. Seccombe, for example, announced that his purpose was to 'situate the housewife as a labourer', and that he would therefore 'concentrate almost entirely on the production side of her relation to capital' (1974:7).

From Seccombe's point of view, the productivity of working-class housewives for capital is seen to lie in their contributions to maintaining the labour force that is employed in industry. This economic function is referred to in Marxism as the *reproduction of labour power*. This reproduction is performed in generational cycles through biological reproduction and childcare, and in daily cycles through the physical and psychological sustenance of wage workers. It is the second of these aspects of reproduction that orthodox Marxist theorists consider to be most significant for the economic determination of marriage. Wives, it is thought, are required to perform domestic labour in order to maintain the strength of their husbands, who are engaged in wage labour in factories.

Seccombe stated that the labour process in capitalist societies is split into two separate units (1974:6). On the one hand there is the industrial unit (i.e. the factory), and on the other there is the domestic unit (i.e. the family). The labouring population is therefore described as divided between these two units, with men entering industry and women working in the home. The social experiences of housewives are interpreted as direct consequences of this division of labour. Whereas men earn wages from their employment, women are not paid for their domestic labour. Consequently, married women are materially dependent upon their husbands, who exercise authority over them. Furthermore, if women are to be motivated to work as housewives their housework must be justified in non-economic terms. It is defined ideologically as work performed out of devotion to their families. Finally, domestic labour is privatized in the household, and housewives are therefore socially isolated. In all these ways the determination of the private family by the capitalist mode of production is seen as limiting the possibilities for women's autonomy.

From the perspective of the sociology of the family, what is most important to note here is that Marxist studies of domestic labour brought about a decisive shift away from certain elements of Parsonian structural functionalism. Parsons held that the modern family had evolved from being a unit of production to being a unit of consumption. Marxist domestic labour theorists declared, *contra* Parsons, that productive work *is* carried on in modern households, although their individual interpretations of its significance varied.[3] However, in other respects domestic labour theory involved a return to principles found in structural functionalism. 'Marxist functionalists' explain the form of the working-class family with reference to its functions for capital: the continuation of family life in capitalist societies is thought to result from the advantages that capital gains from women's unpaid domestic labour. The family is believed to benefit capitalist organizations by providing an abundant labour force that can be employed at low wages. It is believed that it does this by making possible a reduction in the wages that capitalists must pay their employees, since it is asserted that personal needs can be met more cheaply by the work of unpaid housewives than by purchasing the same goods and services from commercial suppliers. It is also claimed that full-time housewives constitute a 'reserve army' of labour that is available for wage employment at times of peak economic activity when the number of permanent wage labourers is insufficient to meet the demand for workers (Beechey, 1978; Mackintosh, 1981). The effect of the reserve army is to inhibit wage inflation, and thus once again to enhance the profits earned by capital.

A number of commentators have noted how the line of Marxist reasoning outlined above employs a functionalist logic, and that the difficulties which accompanied the use of that logic in structural functionalism are repeated in Marxism (Kuhn, 1978; Barrett, 1980; Finch, 1983; Creighton, 1985; Cheal, 1988a:65–8). There are two difficulties here that would seem to be particularly serious.

First, there is the problem that Marxist functionalism, like structural functionalism, presupposes an harmonious system of relations, in which every constituent element contributes something to the maintenance of the system. This overlooks the contradictory (and dialectical) nature of modern social life, in which opposed tendencies are set up within a differentiated system. In this respect it is clear that Seccombe is wrong about a very important point. He has claimed that:

> From a Marxist standpoint it is quite incorrect to treat the consumption of the means of subsistence as if it were not, at one and the same time, the production of labour power. From the standpoint of human beings as consumers, their individual

consumption may be the last act in a long labour chain, the satiation of their needs and consequently an end in itself. From the standpoint of analyzing a continuous economic process, however, the failure to turn individual consumption around and see it as the production of labour power vitiates the analysis of a society in full swing. (Seccombe, 1980:34)

In fact it is quite incorrect to treat consumption in late twentieth-century 'consumer societies' as if it were simply the production of labour power. There are forms of consumption which not only do not produce labour power, but which actually destroy it. It is well known that tobacco smoking, and ingesting alcohol and other drugs, have significant effects upon both mortality and morbidity. Those effects are much more important today than they were in the nineteenth century, largely because of the dramatic advances in medical technologies for coping with disease and trauma. Less striking, but perhaps more pervasive, are the ways in which certain leisure life-styles in advanced industrial societies reduce the productivity of labour. Late twentieth-century consumer behaviour includes watching late-night movies, absenteeism from work to attend mid-week sports events, and an increase in sports injuries among middle-class 'fitness' participants. The general point to be made here is that the production of labour power and individual consumption are not identical moments in a cycle of the extended reproduction of capital.

The second major difficulty with Marxist functionalism is that specific family structures cannot be identified with general economic needs, because in practice such needs can be met in a variety of ways. In particular, the material necessity of *some* social division of labour does not account for the patriarchal form of family, nor does it provide a sufficient explanation for the existence of the nuclear family as such (Bruegel, 1978; Miles, 1985). In a modern society the needs of capital could be met through a variety of institutional structures. Patriarchal monogamy is only one of a number of possibilities for the reproduction of labour power, and its social utility appears to be declining at present.

Today, immigration policies are more widely used tools for meeting the labour needs of capital in advanced industrial nations than are family policies. There is now abundant underutilized labour in lesser industrial nations and in the Third World, as a result of their rapid population growth in this century. Furthermore, immigration flows can be turned on and off much more quickly than women's fertility preferences, in response to fluctuations in the business cycle. In addition, feminist resistance to pro-natalism has undoubtedly made the social control of fertility more difficult at the end of the twentieth century than it was in earlier times. In countries such as Canada, immigration policy is currently the favoured instrument for managing the reproduction of labour power for the national labour market. Popenoe has made the same point about Sweden, in the following manner:

> What is actually happening today in advanced societies, most of which have below-replacement birthrates, is that they are replacing their populations with an influx of people from those nations that have excess fertility. Such nations will be in existence for as far into the future as one can reasonably contemplate. Indeed, the growth of many advanced societies in recent years, including Sweden, has depended entirely on the immigration of a foreign population. Thus regardless of what happens to their family systems, population growth (or at least maintenance) through immigration is the probable lot of every advanced society. (Popenoe, 1988:304).

An equally important weakness in early domestic labour theories is that family life in advanced capitalist societies today is clearly not confined to the male breadwinner/female homemaker model that was assumed in the domestic labour debate. It has been necessary to take account of the fact that large numbers of married women are now engaged in both domestic labour and paid employment (Luxton, 1983). Recent European and Scandinavian studies of women and work have introduced new concepts that are intended to describe this pattern. In Norway there is talk about women's 'internal roles' as wives and parents, and their 'external roles' as employees and community volunteers, and about the shifting relations of 'externalization' between them (Jensen, 1989). In Italy there is interest in women's 'double presence', in the family and the market (Bimbi, 1989). The concept of double presence does not only refer to women's double burden of work. It also includes women's double identities, and the contrasting interpretations of the world which they must negotiate. Such concepts are necessary to describe a behavioural variability that is inconsistent with a narrow model of the normal family as a patriarchal, monogamous reproductive unit. Seccombe has acknowledged some of the empirical diversity of contemporary living arrangements in the following manner:

> In all periods of capitalist development, minority subsistence arrangements have been sustained among the proletarian masses: single parent households (mostly female); single persons living alone or in groups with other single people and doing their own housework; unmarried couples; couples who remain childless by choice; couples who share the domestic labour more or less equally; women who own household property and genuinely control their household's income, etc. In all of these cases the people involved are able to fulfill their proletarian duties, and they remain exploitable by capital. It is not easy to live in these ways. For the majority it is preferable to take the path of least societal resistance, to get married and establish nuclear family households. But one can live as a proletarian against the grain of its subsistence norms. Nothing in the capitalist mode of production excludes it. (Seccombe, 1980:60)

A variety of domestic forms exist today, and their diversity has not had any obvious negative effects on the profitability of capital. Indeed, during the 1980s the rate of profit in many industries tended to increase relative to wages. This occurred at the same time as higher divorce rates and other changes were generating multiple living arrangements. Furthermore, family diversity does not appear to have had any adverse effects upon capitalism as a totality, which entered the 1990s in triumph as communism collapsed in Eastern Europe.

In order to overcome these rather substantial difficulties for their approach, Marxist domestic labour theorists must deal with several interconnected issues. To begin with, it is necessary to distinguish between the family as an alliance/kinship group, and the household as an economic unit, in the way that Seccombe has recommended (1986a; 1986b). This reconceptualization has interesting implications for the theoretical presupposition that family life is determined by the mode of production. According to Seccombe's account, while the household is deemed to be 'a necessary part of the capitalist mode of production', the nuclear family is only 'the predominant form for recruitment to and maintenance of private households' (Seccombe, 1980:59). If that is the case, then the existing patterns of family life cannot be determined by the mode of production, but they must be due to the pressure of 'majority family norms' (Seccombe, 1980:60).

Other issues that have not yet been satisfactorily resolved by Marxist domestic labour theorists include problematic methods by which a particular type of living arrangement can be identified as the most profitable for capital (Molyneux, 1979). A further challenge is that, when this problem has been solved, it is still necessary to demonstrate how capitalists are in fact able to shape the forms of everyday life to suit their interests. No sociological explanation is complete until it can be shown why living individuals choose one type of family rather than another, and indeed why they choose family life at all. This weakness in Marxist explanations for the gender distribution of domestic labour has prompted some Marxist-feminists to try to identify social institutions that might link capital and families. The critical question here is what there could be in society that actually has the power to control the internal arrangements of families, but which is itself open to control by a capitalist ruling class. The answer to that question, from the viewpoint of Marxism, is – *The state*.

The family and the state

In Marxist theory, the state is the composite structure of all the levels of government that regulate social life in the name of the general, or public, interest. Despite its claims to generality, the state is not seen as a neutral institution. Rather, it is believed to reflect the relations of power between different social groups, and especially between the classes. The state is therefore held to act in the interests of the dominant, or ruling, class. The interests of the ruling class are expressed in specific state policies, as well as in state maintenance of the social system from which the ruling class derives its privileges.

Marxist feminists have extended the principles of Marxism to the analysis of the family. Accordingly they have defined state regulation of procreation, socialization and domestic caring as related means of ensuring the reproduction of labour power for the capitalist ruling class (McIntosh, 1978; 1979; Ursel, 1984; 1986). In so doing, they have gone beyond the domestic labour debate to examine the contradictory relations between private and public spheres under capitalism.

The important thesis advanced in this work is that an unregulated market economy will tend to undermine the capacity and the desire of working-class women to reproduce, due to low and uncertain 'family wages' earned by male providers, and the pressures upon married women to enter full-time employment. The state intervenes to provide financial supports for maternity and domestic childcare, for example through reduced taxation of men with dependents, and through transfer payments which supplement the earnings of working-class families with children. It is also held that the state regulates women's participation in the labour market, through pro-natalist labour laws.

From the perspective of this approach, the state is seen as a biased arbiter and manager of contradictions between production and reproduction. That conclusion has attracted widespread attention. Here Marxist feminists join with other materialist feminists to analyse the tensions and instabilities arising from the division of social life into separate spheres of work and family. It is therefore necessary to widen our discussion at this point to include broader issues, and broader approaches. The political economy of the relations between private and public spheres, and the managerial role of the state, are of interest to theorists of many persuasions, both Marxist and non-Marxist.

One of the most visible features of modernization in the twentieth century is the expanded role of the state as both a vehicle and an instigator of economic and social progress. The state is expected to maintain a vigilant concern with the pace and direction of change, and to intervene when changes have negative consequences, or when the speed of positive changes is not fast enough. As a result, in this century the state has become heavily involved in providing education, housing, health care and income maintenance for large sections of the population. These state supports – referred to as the *welfare state* – are sometimes consciously linked to policies that are intended to preserve and improve family life. The growth of the welfare state has therefore brought about significant shifts in the relations between private and public spheres.

The changes that have occurred in the balance between private and public spheres in the past century are not the same in all countries. In the Scandinavian countries, for example, ideological oppositions between private and public domains are not as sharp as they often are elsewhere. This has greatly facilitated the expansion of the welfare state. In Scandinavia the focus is on a 'public/private mix' rather than a 'public/ private divide' (Hernes, 1988:202). It follows that there is great concern with ways in which the existing mix can be improved. Typical of this concern is Swedish interest in the 'public child', who spends a considerable part of each day in formal childcare settings (Liljeström, 1983).

Although there are important national differences in the extent of the welfare state, policy processes of opinion formation, programme articulation and institutional transformation have occurred everywhere in this century. These modern social forms have redefined the boundaries between public and private spheres (J. Meyer *et al.*, 1988). They have done so by laying down the conditions which families must satisfy in order to receive support from public agencies, and by setting the standards of conduct towards which families are expected to aspire. The modern state progressively translates selected private problems into public issues, and establishes its jurisdiction over them (P. Morgan, 1985).

In one sense the expanded role of the modern state takes the form of the extension of public regulation over family life (P. Meyer, 1983). State inspectors acquire rights to inform themselves about family affairs, and family privacy is circumscribed. Interestingly, it seems that this change may have occurred at the same time as the growth of a private sphere of personal life and subjective experience. The reason for this conjunction, it is suggested, is that personal relations and the welfare state have both been expanding (from different ends, as it were) while traditional structures of civil society have declined. Personal life and public policy have expanded to fill the gaps created by the weakening of customary social ties, the secularization of beliefs and values, ineffectual community controls, and the lessened capacities of mediating structures to generate comprehensive systems of meaning or power. Zaretsky has therefore concluded that: 'Far from the state "invading" or "replacing" the family, a certain kind of alienated public life and a certain kind of alienated private life have expanded together' (1986b:105).

Zaretsky claims that the rise of economic individualism led to the idea that each nuclear family should be responsible for supporting itself, as a private economic unit. However, the harsh effects of wage labour in early industrialization meant that many nuclear families could not provide for all of their members on a continuous basis. At the same time the weakening of the extended family, which was due to the massive population migration and urbanization that accompanied industrialization, lessened traditional supports during emergencies. Piecemeal efforts by the state to provide for various classes of dependent followed, which in Zaretsky's opinion did not alter the ideal of autonomy for the private family.

Despite the seemingly benevolent role of the welfare state in relation to families, its effects have been treated with suspicion by some feminist theorists, who perceive it as having oppressive consequences for women (Burton, 1985). The critical theoretical questions here have to do with the regulatory role of the state, and its policies toward the family considered as strategies of power (Fahmy-Eid and Laurin-Frenette, 1986). Critics of the existing relations between family and state propose that the family is both the target and the agent of forms of social control. Writing from a Foucauldian point of view, Paterson (1988) makes this argument with respect to education in Scotland. She claims that an official model of appropriate family relations is visible, in the effects of truancy policies on families that do not have a breadwinner in a sedentary job which provides a family wage. With reference to the introduction of this pattern in the nineteenth century, she says:

> State intervention into schooling undermined the legitimacy of the social relations of families who operated as a productive unit. This was because the division of labour involved under these circumstances meant a scheduling of identities such that schooling and work would intersperse with each other. Such families were considered to have faulty mores and these were held to be an indication of problem parents. At the same time, it was in terms of family relations that relations of schooling were legitimated. However, these were family relations of another form, one in

which a man was the primary income earner, through work outside
the home. Within this form a woman was considered as being
primarily concerned with servicing the needs of the man and their
children through unpaid domestic labour which, because it was in
the home, was not defined as work. The children of these families
would be reared under the control of their parents when not
participating in schooling, only doing wage earning work if the
family's low income made this necessary. (Paterson, 1988:65–7)

From the perspective of feminist theory, the principal issue in
relations between family and state is the potential for the use of
state power in confining women to the private sphere. This can
occur because the social policies of modern welfare states have
tended to take for granted the existence of a 'normal' family,
consisting of a male breadwinner and a female housewife (Land,
1979). That presupposition has influenced the levels and conditions of taxation and income supports for husbands and wives,
and the provision of social services to families with special needs.

There are two underlying policy assumptions here that have
been particularly troublesome. One assumption is that a woman
who is married, or who is living in a marriage-like relationship
with a man, should expect to receive financial support from him.
The other is that where there are dependent children, or sick and
infirm relatives, within a household that also contains an able-
bodied woman, then the woman is usually expected to accept the
obligation for providing day-to-day care. That assumption about
the moral order of family life in turn rests upon two fundamental
beliefs: 'firstly, that women in general, and married women in
particular, are the "natural" carers in the domestic setting;
secondly, that married women's earnings, if any, are marginal to
the financial security of the domestic group' (Groves and Finch,
1983:152).

The feature of these policy assumptions that is seen to be
oppressive for women is that they may create financial dependence of wives upon their husbands by cutting them off from
government transfers, and especially earnings, that are otherwise
available to autonomous individuals (Joshi, 1987).[4] Groves and
Finch state that: 'The consequence of the operation of these rules
is that such gender divisions are further reinforced, with the
result that state policies have the effect of *shaping* social life and
social relations, and not merely reflecting them' (1983:149).

As might be expected, there have been disagreements about the precise effects of state policies (Ungerson, 1983), and about their causes. Theories of family and state often differ concerning whose interests state policies really serve. Radical feminists claim that the state is used to oppress women in the interests of men. Marxist feminists, on the other hand, claim that the state serves the interests of capital. Socialist feminists, such as Barrett (1980) and Ferguson (1983), tend to see state policies as outcomes of the intersections of both kinds of interest, in complex historical processes whose variations must be analysed in careful detail. From this point of view, it is important that ambiguities in social life should be recognized in social theory. One such ambiguous pattern is the division between private and public spheres itself, which we have taken for granted up to this point.

Beyond private/public dualism

Dichotomizing social life into private and public domains is not always feasible, and sometimes it works to obscure important connections. Some theorists have therefore criticized concepts of private and public spheres as being oversimplified and deterministic (Eichler, 1980). It is claimed that on close inspection the division between private relations and public institutions dissolves into a multitude of overlapping and interdependent contexts for social interaction. Cheal (1988a) and Oliker (1989), for instance, have pointed out that this conceptual separation ignores women's multiple friendships, which link apparently isolated individuals into a larger network of ties.

Janet Finch has presented a persuasive critique against treating the family and the job as analytically separate spheres. She points out that wives in their domestic roles may work to further their husbands' careers (Finch, 1983), and there are forms of wage work that husbands or wives may perform at home (Finch, 1985). In contrast to Marxist theories of domestic labour, much recent feminist work in the social sciences has been concerned with the interpenetrations of family life and wage employment. Especially, there has been a rediscovery of 'homeworking' – the employment of women to do piecework at home (Boris and

Daniels, 1989). This has been accompanied by an emphasis in social theory upon the disadvantages of a rigid conceptual separation of men's and women's spheres (S. Allen, 1989). In place of the division between private labour in the household and socialized wage labour in the factory, studies conducted in the 1980s were concerned with the social distribution of a number of types of work between the home, the market, the community and the state (Dahlström and Liljeström, 1982; R. Pahl, 1984; Saraceno, 1984; Glazer, 1987). An interesting example of this tendency is Daune-Richard's description of the 'circulation' (or redistribution) of domestic labour in France, from employed women to their non-employed female kin (1988). In this example, and in many others, we see that concepts of separate spheres have been replaced by concepts for describing the effects that wage work and family patterns have upon each other (Pleck, 1977; Mortimer and Sorensen, 1984; Voydanoff, 1988).

From a different perspective – that of critical theory – Jürgen Habermas argued some years ago for an analysis of the interpenetrations of private and public spheres (1989 [1962]). One of the points he sought to make is that family life has lost much of its historical autonomy under contemporary conditions. In his view, the patriarchal conjugal family of early capitalist society claimed for itself an enclosed space of intimacy, set free from the constraints of society. This autonomous domain was held to be constituted by principles of voluntary union between free individuals, a community of love, and cultivation of the non-instrumental faculties of individuals. Habermas argued that in contemporary society these three elements have been 'hollowed out' by public institutions, such as the mass media.

The principal factor in this change is the tendency for market transactions to invade the private sphere, and for personal cultivation to be replaced by consumption. Contemporary consumerism includes not only goods and services, but also meanings produced by 'the culture industry' (e.g. journalism) which are distributed by newspapers, magazines, radio and television. Habermas believes that in late capitalist society the means of communication have 'turned into a conduit for social forces channeled into the conjugal family's inner space by way of a public sphere that the mass media have transmogrified into a sphere of culture consumption' (1989:162). Needs for relaxation and entertainment felt by individuals with disposable leisure time are met in part by movies, dramatized biographies and talk shows that feed upon happenings in private lives. The consequence of this, Habermas claims, is that real processes of familial communication, such as letter writing, decline. We are left with 'the illusion of an untouched private sphere' (Habermas, 1989:171).

In a related argument, Cheal (1987a) has shown that the autonomy of a romantic ideal of love in the private family is limited by meanings derived from the market economy. Market mechanisms, such as the use of money to mediate transactions, are incorporated into the material dimensions of family life. This undercuts the capacities of members to communicate their love for each other. Generalized public media are anonymous, and they are not well adapted to expressing the unique features of personal ties.

Sociological awareness of the unstable boundaries of private and public spheres has increased in recent years. Nevertheless, the different experiences referred to by these concepts still affect the lives of many people in some way. Issues of social division have therefore not been abandoned completely, but they have had to be rethought (Saraceno, 1984; J. Gerson and Peiss, 1985). One response has been to shift the structural properties of conceptual dualism from separate spheres to contrasting principles of social organization. Among several such approaches, Norwegian social scientists have compared 'technically limited rationality' with the 'rationality of responsibility' (Haavind, 1984). The latter concept is described as consisting of the following four elements:

1. Identification with the well-being of others.
2. Attention to the effects of activities upon others.
3. Assuming the responsibility for changing behaviour that affects others.
4. Acceptance of non-reciprocity as the governing principle in transactions (Holter, 1984).

In Canada, Cheal has outlined a similar conceptualization in models of 'moral economy' and 'political economy', considered as parallel systems of social organization, that exist between and within private and public domains (1988a; 1989c).

A related approach to the contrasting principles of social

organization that affect family life has been adopted by Myra Marx Ferree (1985; 1987), from studies in the feminist sociology of work conducted in the former West Germany. Ferree reports that German research on women in the late 1970s and early 1980s moved beyond familiar notions of their 'double burden' of housework and paid employment to consider broader implications of work for women's conceptions of themselves and of social life. The key concept that was introduced here was that of the 'divided life' – divided between two different systems of values. One system, which is associated with the role of wage worker, is oriented toward exchange values. The other system, which is associated with the role of housewife, is oriented toward use values. Taking into account the contradictions between these values, it is not only the demands upon their time that pose problems for employed wives. They also face difficult choices that arise from conflicts between a use-value ethic and an exchange-value ethic, and their commitments to both of them.

This point is nicely illustrated by American research on the care of the children of women who go out to work, undertaken by women who prefer to remain at home (M. Nelson, 1989). Family daycare, as it is sometimes called, is an ambiguous phenomenon of 'waged mothering'. As an employment relationship between two women, it is a market transaction of economic exchange. However, since it is also a partial substitute for the personal relationship between mother and child, it is infused by some of that relationship's emotional and moral characteristics too.

The theoretically interesting point about these work situations that are characterized by overlapping principles of moral economy and political economy is that they reveal in unusually clear terms a general feature of family relationships. Such situations involve relationships that are socially constructed, through negotiations between individuals whose interests are sometimes different and sometimes the same. M. Nelson (1989; 1990) points out that this contradictory situation generates characteristic tensions in the role of family daycare providers. On one side, they are wage workers, and they want to handle their work in a businesslike manner, with respect to terms and conditions of employment. At the same time, their commitments to the children in their care go beyond a merely contractual obligation. Clients' children are assimilated into the mothering which providers give to their own children, and into the systems of reciprocity which link relatives and friends, from among whom most of their clients are drawn. As a result, negotiations over work schedule changes and overtime arrangements are often difficult, and family daycare providers find it hard to say no. Nelson concludes that although providers and parents share some values, 'they must constantly negotiate an emotionally charged territory without established guidelines' (1989:28).

Finch has developed this theme of the negotiated order of relationships in a more theoretical direction. Dealing with practical support between adult kin, she argues that family obligations involve both moral, or normative, rules and negotiated commitments (Finch, 1987). Rules define what is considered to be appropriate behaviour. But because they are general, rules always have to be interpreted in their applications to concrete situations. How rules are interpreted is not a purely psychological process: it is, above all, a social one, since understandings must be negotiated and agreed upon between interested parties. Furthermore, social recognition of who can claim to have a legitimate kinship interest in a particular individual is itself subject to interpretation (Finch, 1989). Viewed in this way, Finch says, 'rules are seen as part of the repertoire of resources which human beings can make use of in constructing social meanings' (1987:160).

Finch makes a general observation about this point which is worth noting, since it is also made in other recent theoretical explorations. We must, she says, develop modes of understanding that recognize the effects that social structures have upon individuals, as well as the ways in which individuals construct their own lives within and through those constraints. How individuals do in fact construct their own lives in relation to structural constraints is known as the problem of 'agency'. Finch points out that the study of family obligations and family negotiations is part of the central sociological task of understanding the puzzle of human agency in contemporary societies. Kathleen Gerson (1985) has argued that the focus of macrostructural theories on the determination of women's lives by capital or patriarchy underestimates women's active role in creating their own lives. And this, she points out, has led to the neglect of the considerable variations among women in their social positions, preferences and interests. Gerson argues that 'The full range of women's behavior cannot be completely understood as the result of external coercion alone. If men make history, but not under conditions of their own choosing, then surely women do also' (1985:29). As Ferree notes about the results from West German studies of women's divided lives, 'The women in these studies emerge as participants who shape their own lives rather than as passive victims of sex and class oppressions' (Ferree, 1985:520).

The final point to be made in this chapter is that the problem of agency has a special place in much recent rethinking of social theories (Giddens, 1979). The reasons for this rethinking include criticisms of the structured differentiation of separate spheres that were noted above. One result of this tendency in current sociological theorizing has been to shift the focus of attention from structures of modernity and the structuring of modernization to destructuring and individualization in post-modernity.

Notes

1. For a bibliography and review of discussions about concepts of public and private see Sharistanian (1987).
2. Interestingly, there have been some signs of convergence between Marxism and theories of families as support systems. From a Marxist perspective, the positive strengths of families are seen as the ways in which they assist poor and powerless individuals in their struggles toward a better life (Humphries, 1982). The family is therefore seen as a 'protective agent in a poor and predatory society' (Humphries, 1987:32). Such endorsements of family life suggest that it is a 'culture of resistance', or 'vanguard', or 'haven', that shelters minority groups, third world peoples and working-class people in capitalist societies from the effects of racist, imperialist and capitalist oppression (e.g. Lasch, 1977:xv). For a critical description of this theoretical tendency see Bishop (1983).
3. The principal issues at stake in the domestic labour debate concerned the precise relationship between labour for the household, which is a non-market activity, and Marx's economic categories, which had been

formulated with reference to market processes of exchange for the purpose of making a profit (Gardiner, 1976; Vogel, 1983). There were several interconnected debates around these issues (Williams, 1988). The central issue concerned how the economic value of domestic labour was to be specified. Briefly, there was a choice to be made – between considering the value of domestic labour to be its contribution to the exchange value of labour power (e.g. the price in wages of the labour power that domestic labour reproduces), and considering the value of domestic labour to be the use value of its products for the household members who consume them. The former approach was tied to a larger set of arguments about the total determination of labour processes by their functions for capital, whereas the latter approach could allow for a range of relationships between capital and different forms of labour.

Totalizing theories of value have generally been most appreciated by Marxists who study advanced capitalist societies as discrete systems. Theories of use values, on the other hand, are more relevant to labour processes, such as peasant householding, that are not organized by capitalists but may nevertheless be partially incorporated into the capitalist world system. Analyses of the articulation of use values to capital tend to be favoured by social scientists interested in the Third World, where capitalist relations are often only weakly developed and subsistence production is still important (Mackintosh, 1979; Bennholdt-Thomsen, 1981; Long, 1984; Stichter and Parpart, 1988). For this reason, and others, the eventual outcome of the domestic labour debate in Britain was a general agreement that was summarized by Harris as follows: 'One of the few consensuses that seem to have emerged from the debate is that domestic labour does not produce labour power. What it produces are use-values which are consumed within the household' (Harris, 1983:187).

At the same time, it must be noted that theories of the household production of labour power continue to be live issues for some Marxists. Paul Close insists that: 'The possibility that domestic labour *does* contribute to the value of labour power has not been finally dismissed, despite the consensuses which have evolved out of the Domestic Labour Debate' (1985:45). In fact the contribution made by domestic labour to the reproduction of labour power in the capitalist mode of production is still of interest to Marxists in North America (Dickinson and Russell, 1986), particularly in relation to issues raised within Canadian socialist feminism (Hamilton and Barrett, 1986).

4. According to Becker's (1981) neoclassical economic theory of the family, the dependence of a non-employed wife on her husband's

income is a rational choice due to the advantage that role specialization has for a higher level of family consumption. There is no doubt some truth to this claim under current labour market conditions, as Ungerson reports in the case of women caring for dependent relatives (1983). Nevertheless, Becker's critics have pointed out that specialization in marriage has some significant limitations (Blau and Ferber, 1986; Owen, 1987). For instance, it seems likely that the gains to be derived from extensive specialization in housework are not great in most cases, because there are narrow limits to both household-specific knowledge and utility which are quickly reached. It is also the case that very few wives can afford to spend their entire married lives within the home, because their husbands' wages are not high enough to sustain an adequate standard of living. The interruptions to employment, and lesser career opportunities, that are experienced by women as childcare specialists result in lower total lifetime incomes and reduced consumption levels for them and their families. Furthermore, specializing in housework is a high-risk strategy for the homemaker to adopt. Divorce, or disability or death of the partner, can result in a substantial drop in income, and as a matter of fact it usually does. This is most likely to occur at a time in life when the job skills of a specialist homemaker have deteriorated, and her opportunities for income replacement are diminished. Finally, there is the problem of selfishness within the family (Folbre, 1988). Even in a life-long marriage, specialization is an efficient strategy only if the breadwinner is in fact prepared to share all earned income without reservation (J. Pahl, 1980; 1983; Brannen and Wilson, 1987; Morris, 1989).

CHAPTER 5

THE ONE AND THE MANY: MODERNITY AND POST-MODERNITY

Changes in family theories often follow changes in family life. As one observer noted about the 1980s: 'studies and research on the family carried out in the last decade may be interpreted as an answer – in the area of knowledge – to the transformations that have occurred in the structure of society' (Sgritta, 1989:90). We saw this in the last chapter, in the way in which the increased tendency for wives to seek employment challenged theories that equated women's roles with domestic labour. Those difficulties prompted social scientists to develop alternative approaches to studying relations between family, work and gender - ones that emphasize historical variation (Jallinoja, 1989). Summarizing the new work, Laslett and Brenner state that 'In the most recent scholarship the accent is on variation and human agency, and particularly on the ways in which women have constructed their own worlds of activity' (1989:384).

Other changes in everyday life have had a related effect upon family theory, which is more profound. In recent years living arrangements have become more diverse (R.N. Rapoport et al., 1982). This new social pluralism was accompanied by the questioning of established images of family life. In particular, the dominant tendency in the sociology of the family - to seek theoretical integration through one coherent model of a specifically modern type of family – has been severely criticized (Denzin, 1987; R. Rapoport, 1989).

Such critiques create a degree of fluidity, and uncertainty, in family theory that is unsettling. The sociology of the family is not alone in this awkward situation. It is part of a much larger problem in social theory, which Alain Touraine (1984) refers to as 'the waning sociological image of social life'. What he means by this is that established theoretical approaches in sociology are less and less able to provide comprehensive, and coherent accounts of how contemporary social forces are connected. More specifically, Touraine explains (1988), it has become increasingly difficult to reconcile the cultural principles of modernity (i.e. reason, progress) with modernization (i.e. ceaseless change, constant revolutionizing of means of production and social forms). Touraine claims that the current state of sociological theory – which he refers to as a crisis – reflects a fundamental dislocation in social life, namely the passage from one culture to another. This *crisis of modernity* appears in sociology as the failure of monolithic theories of history (i.e. of historicism). Touraine comments that 'What is disappearing is social evolutionism, the idea of a natural modernization, commanded by laws of historical development' (1984:38).[1] In this chapter we will explore the thesis of the waning of monolithic theories of social change, with respect to its implications for theories of change in family life.

Family changes revisited: standardization or diversification?

In standard sociological theory a model of family life is held out as a progressive standard, to which everyone is thought to aspire sooner or later. It is believed that all groups converge towards that standard, though they realize it to different degrees according to their unequal capacities to do so. Since the process of modernization brings about a general increase in capacities, this theory of family life assumes that modernization is accompanied by the standardization of family role behaviour.

The theory of modernity has had a deep and lasting effect upon standard sociological theory. In the theory of modernity, powerful institutions that are central to modern society are held to transform everyday life in regular and predictable ways. This process of *institutionalized transformation* shapes and controls social life at the same time as it changes it, so that the result is an increased regularity of social behaviour. As Touraine explains:

The history of modernization is seen as that of the gradual obliteration of cultural and social differences in favour of an increasingly broad participation of everyone in one and the same general model of modernity, defined by applying the general principles of reason to the conduct of human affairs. (1988:443)

An interesting and sophisticated application of modernization theory to the standardization of family life is the argument presented by Michael Young and Peter Willmott (1974) for a trend toward the 'symmetrical family'. They advance a thesis of social change that they refer to as the *principle of stratified diffusion*. This states that, due to the tendency of lower status groups to emulate those above them, important changes always begin high up in the status hierarchy and are gradually diffused downwards. Applying the principle to family history in England, Young and Willmott hypothesize that, as technology replaces the more physically arduous and less interesting jobs, so the greater attachment to work of middle-class people will extend downwards. They believe that this affects the choices between home and employment made by working-class women, who will increasingly choose occupational careers.

According to this thesis, the occupational commitments of husbands and wives will become more similar, or in their terminology 'symmetrical'. At the same time, Young and Willmott expect that the impact of feminism will mean the redistribution of housework, in proportion to occupational demands on time. The result is that the familial division of labour should also become symmetrical. Young and Willmott therefore believe that the segregation of marriage roles will decline.[2]

An earlier thesis of the class-based standardization of family life was Parsons's theory of the modern family. Writing about the United States, Parsons argued that the cultural standard for American family life was that of the urban middle-class family. It defined for practical purposes the 'normal American family' (Parsons, 1971a). The major exceptions to this pattern, Parsons thought, were families in the lower class. Parsons stated that 'family disorganization' was particularly prevalent in this class, as a result of its being rejected by those who were economically more successful. With that important exception, Parsons claimed that the general trend of development in America was 'a massive upgrading of standards in many respects and the inclusion of much higher proportions of the population in the groups enjoying the higher standards' (1971a:63). Parsons believed that as a result of this upgrading, there had been a very substantial homogenization of patterns of life in the population. The consequence of this, he thought, was that there had 'emerged a remarkably uniform, basic type of family' (Parsons, 1971a:53).

Ellen Gee (1986) has presented evidence for women in Canada that broadly supports Parsons's interpretation of family change. She concludes that the principal changes in the occurrence and timing of life course transitions over the last hundred or a hundred and fifty years involve increased standardization. This pattern is due to widespread improvements in the quality of life. The decline in mortality levels has reduced the prevalence of disrupted family relationships, such as early widowhood. As Gee points out, this increases the predictability of family living. Also, greater economic affluence has made it possible for most of those who wish to marry to do so. By comparison with earlier periods of economic difficulty, the result has been an increased standardization of marital status.

The relevance of modernization theory to family studies includes the historical subjection of domestic activities to the rationalization of means and ends. This was done in order to achieve greater efficiencies in the use of time and money, and in order to bring about an upgrading of moral and physical standards of care. Reiger (1985; 1987) has shown how in Australia, between the 1880s and the Second World War, women's traditional chores of cooking, cleaning, sewing, childcare and generally servicing the needs of others became subjected to rational scientific management. Informal practices that were passed on from mothers to daughters were considered to be inadequate. Instead, attempts were made to replace unhealthy and inefficient practices through formal instruction in models produced by the new domestic sciences. Experts from the human service professions played a considerable role in this cultural redefinition, in a self-conscious attempt to improve the quality of family life. This professionally engineered social change extended to redefining the naturalness of mothering, and a major effort was made to teach women how to rear their children more effectively.

The exposure of contemporary populations to family roles and to cultural definitions of levels of family performance has become in certain respects more uniform. But these are not the only changes that have taken place. It also seems to be the case that family interactions have become more diverse. This diversity is not easily described by standard sociological theory, which sees social relationships as governed by a system of roles. In its narrowest form, standard sociological theory conceives of the 'normal family', or 'conventional family', as consisting of the nuclear roles of husband and wife, and their children. In the work of Parsons (1943; 1971a), the norms regulating interactions between family roles require the following:

1. Marriage between adult partners (more specifically, mono-gamy).
2. Superiority of the conjugal bond over other social commit-ments.
3. Fulfilment of the marriage bond through the raising of legitimate children.
4. Co-residence.
5. The employment of one or more adult members outside the home.
6. The unrestricted sharing of incomes between adult members.

The Parsonian model of family life was always an abstraction from reality, like any other ideal type. However, in recent years its links to observed reality have become increasingly tenuous in a number of countries. Furstenberg and Spanier, writing about the United States, conclude:

> In general, the pathways of family formation have become less normatively prescribed insofar as behavioral regularities reveal social rules. Individuals have greater leeway to tailor family arrangements to their personal needs and desires. Hence, the early part of•the life course has become more discretionary in both the timing and the order of family-related transitions, at least compared to a generation ago. (Furstenberg and Spanier, 1984:51–2)

There is evidence (in the United States) of a growing percentage of teenage births occuring to unmarried women (Furstenberg *et al.*, 1987), and more generally of increased cohabitation before or independent of marriage (Trost, 1977; Cotton *et al.*, 1983) and of 'commuter marriages' between partners who live in different cities (Gross, 1980; Gerstel and Gross, 1984). Increased divorce rates and single parenthood by choice indicate that the marriage bond is less binding, and perhaps less important, than it once was (Renvoize, 1985; Ahrons and Rodgers, 1987). This would also seem to be confirmed by the way in which never-married and voluntarily childless life-styles have come to be recognized as viable forms of social life, that are not necessarily devoid of family ties (Veevers, 1980; K. Allen, 1989). It also appears that when husbands and wives both earn large incomes they may decide not to pool them (Hertz, 1986).

Finally, there continue to be significant differences between industrial nations in family patterns, which are not entirely explicable by modernization theories (Boh, 1989). Important cultural differences remain in the modern world. This includes ethnic differences within many industrial societies, especially those which had significant post-Second World War immigration. It has therefore been argued that greater attention should be paid to ethnic variations in family arrangements (Rosenthal, 1983).

The present situation is in many ways ambiguous. It appears to permit interpretations of both familial standardization *and* life-style diversification. Martin Kohli (1986) has described this situation as one of a long-term trend (of approximately three hundred years) towards increased standardization, and a short-term trend (of approximately the last twenty years) towards increased diversification. Until the early 1970s, the secular trend was that of strengthening the normative pattern, of getting married, having children and surviving until at least age 50 in an intact first marriage (Uhlenberg, 1978). However, since the beginning of the 1970s in most western countries, several of the processes that resulted in the standardization of the family life cycle have either stopped or gone into reverse. As a result, there is now an increasing proportion of household configurations and sequences that depart from the normative pattern of family life.

The immediate consequence of the increased prevalence of life-style diversity has been a decline in the utility of sociological approaches that rely upon a concept of the 'normal family' (Bernardes, 1986). Katja Boh emphasizes this point with a play on words. She states that the only common feature in the evolution of family life patterns in Europe is *convergence to diversity* (Boh, 1989:296). She concludes that:

> There is no indication in our analysis that the evolution of family life patterns in European societies would follow a certain pattern to become the model for family modernisation in Europe. Not one but a variety of family patterns have emerged, have become legitimate and practised by people in accordance with their needs and living conditions. And just because the living conditions and the social forces that influence them are so different in the different European countries, we are inclined to believe that the development will not go in one and the same direction, but will lead to a still greater diversification of family patterns in Europe. Nevertheless, there is at least one uniform trend in the overall development of family patterns, and this is the trend towards a recognition of diversity. (Boh, 1989:295-6).

The recognition of diversity, which is so easy as a matter of empirical observation, poses a real challenge for social theory in its positivistic forms. This is because in any scientific field of study there must be some agreement about what the objects of investigation are, so that they can be included in a common theoretical discourse, and so that comparable observations can be generated for the purposes of repeat hypothesis testing. This concern leads to the defining of units of analysis. At present, increased awareness of diversity in family life is leading a number of social scientists into a conscious concern with *redefining* units of analysis, in ways that are appropriate to contemporary conditions. It is this challenge we must take up next.

Rethinking what we study

Defining the object of investigation, or unit of analysis, is an important activity in the social sciences. It is necessary for purposes of clarification, because theorists often have different ideas about what it is that they are studying. The principal unit of analysis is often not the same in different theoretical approaches, even when a common term such as 'family' is employed. The term family is often used to mean different things by different theorists, and in some cases 'the family' has been replaced by other units of analysis in family studies. Current issues include whether 'the family' is a basic unit or a derived unit, or if it is simply one unit of analysis among a number of plausible possibilities (Cheal, 1989b). More fundamentally, the reflexive questions raised by family experts include whether or not we know what 'family' is, and whether or not such a thing as 'the family' even exists at all (Bernardes, 1985b). Trost (1990) has shown that this state of confusion among family experts is a reflection of the enormous variety of family classifications that are employed by lay members of society. He concludes that 'Evidently no one "knows" what a family is: our perspectives vary to such a degree that to claim to know what a family is shows a lack of knowledge' (Trost, 1990:442).

There is much at stake in current debates about definitional problems. Professionally speaking, its consequences include whether or not the scientific study of something called 'the family' is possible. It follows directly from this that the very existence of a specialized discipline of 'the sociology of the family' is called into question. In addition to potential effects upon the organization of academic life, the current debate about definitions also has implications for views on social structure. If there is no concept of 'the family' that can be the subject of general agreement, then how *should* we define the recurring forms of private life? This in turn raises a further question, concerning how to theorize about issues of behavioural uniformity and diversity. Finally, is all the recent concern about theory definitions and models just a temporary phase of intellectual confusion? Or is it symptomatic of larger shifts in the field of social scientific knowledge, and in contemporary culture?

There are four broad approaches to answering these questions which are being actively pursued today. They are: concept specification, concept abandonment, concept displacement, and concept expansion.

Concept specification

Standard sociological theory has regarded the family as a cultural universal. That is to say, it assumes that the culture of any society will contain a general normative expectation that all adults who are mentally and physically capable of doing so should marry and should have children. Clearly, in the contemporary western societies that expectation has been breaking down for some time. But it has not yet disappeared. The 'normal' family continues to be a cultural model for many people, although their precise numbers may be a matter of dispute. Taubin and Mudd (1983) refer to these people as living in 'contemporary traditional families'. For such people, the traditional cultural model of 'the family' continues to be a lived reality, even though it is no longer a cultural universal.

Separation of the concept of 'the family' from any assumption of cultural universality makes possible certain developments in modern social theory that are of some interest. Contemporary traditional families can be seen as shaped not so much by fixed cultural traditions as by the ongoing process of modernization. Ralph Linton's (1936) anthropological theory of cultural change can help to explain why this is so. Linton pointed out that when new cultural elements (such as cohabitation) are introduced into a society, previous cultural universals (such as marriage) become alternatives, about which individuals must now make a conscious choice – to follow the traditional model, or not. Linton thought that in the long run one of two things would happen. One possibility is that if enough people cease to opt for the traditional model, it will drop out of the culture completely. The other possibility is that some people may continue to choose the traditional model, but as a specialized solution to particular requirements. Linton referred to the altered contexts of such cultural elements as 'specialties'.

The fact that 'the family' today may be a 'specialty', in Linton's sense, is one conclusion to be drawn from Nave-Herz's (1989) work on family and marriage in Western Germany. Nave-Herz continues to use the 'normal' definition of 'the family', as a unit made up of an adult couple and their children living together in the same household. The findings from her research lead her to conclude that the social significance of the family has changed, due to the continuing trend toward increased functional specialization in modern societies. Whereas cohabitation is tending to be adopted by young Germans as the social basis for companionship and emotional gratification, the family is adopted as the context in which to bring up children. There is,

Nave-Herz argues, a marked shift in attitudes taking place, towards child-oriented marriage as a rational choice that is based on instrumental reasons.

'The family', considered as a contemporary traditional group, remains the focus of useful sociological investigation, as we have just seen. Nevertheless, many sociologists are not likely to be satisfied with an approach that is limited to studying only one narrowly defined social form. Therefore, other approaches to rethinking what we study have been developed.

Concept abandonment

The most radical solution to difficulties in defining what is meant by 'family' is to abandon the term for all theoretically significant purposes. This is the approach recommended by John Scanzoni (1987). Scanzoni is concerned that emerging forms of everyday living cannot any longer be subsumed under the rubric of 'alternatives' to the normal family. As patterns such as cohabitation and single parenthood become more widespread, so they take on a cultural reality of their own that is no longer definable simply in terms of difference from the benchmark of the conjugal family. Scanzoni therefore argues that a new image or paradigm is needed for the study of structured interpersonal ties. He finds this image in the concept of 'close relationships' (Scanzoni, 1987), and the related concept of 'primary relationships' (Scanzoni *et al.*, 1989).

Scanzoni and his colleagues recommend that the concept of 'the family' should no longer be used by social scientists, because it is too 'concrete', or in other words too historically and culturally specific. Instead they recommend using the 'higher-order' concept of *primary relationships*, under which various kinds of tie that are conventionally defined as family relationships may be subsumed. For example, legal marriages would be included here, along with other kinds of sexual couplings that are not defined in law, under the general heading of 'sexually based primary relationships'.

Scanzoni and his associates state that multifarious and ambiguous meanings of the term 'family' are in fact viable in everyday life, because they help ordinary people to apprehend 'the slippery realities' of families and to communicate lay conceptions of reality effectively (1989:37). However, they insist that a sharp distinction must be drawn between lay and scientific concepts. In particular, they claim that scientific concepts should not be shaped by the 'prevailing symbol-system' (i.e. culture), since the latter is both value-laden and infused with the emotions of ordinary people. Scanzoni *et al.* seek to 'escape' from the distractions and confusions that inevitably accompany lay discourse about families, by using the term 'primary relationships' in its place (1989:44).

The approach taken by Scanzoni and his colleagues is open to some important objections. It is questionable whether it is either possible or desirable to avoid bringing culture into social theory, through the deliberate use of esoteric words and phrases. Indeed, the attempt to do so may simply serve to mask the nature of cultural influences, and thereby make analyses and debates of theoretical issues more difficult.

Clearly, the term 'primary relationship' is not a common phrase in ordinary conversation. Social scientists can therefore realistically expect to control the meanings they give to it, in ways that are not possible with a term such as 'the family'. However, the concept of primary relationships does not stand alone; it is not a pure term. It, too, has a social context, or more precisely a socio-semiotic context. Together with the contrasting term of 'secondary relationships', the use of the term 'primary relationships' reflects an historically specific division between public (i.e. secondary) and private (i.e. primary) spheres of action in industrial societies. The division between private and public powerfully affects family life, as we have seen, and profoundly influences how social scientists think and talk about it. The cultural contradiction between the private world of families and the public world of institutions, such as the state, has a significant but unacknowledged influence upon the theorizing of Scanzoni and his colleagues.

Scanzoni's view of social theory is positivistic in its notions of scientific detachment and conceptual purity. It differs from ideas of the post-positivists in family studies, who seek to uncover the previously unacknowledged influences of everyday common sense upon social science. Post-positivists do not try to escape from lay concepts of reality, but rather attempt to confront them directly, *within* social theory. It is to approaches of this sort that we turn next.

Concept displacement

Post-positivist theorists in family studies recognize that the term 'family' is first of all an element in the everyday stock of knowledge about the social world. They set out to make that knowledge an object of investigation for the social sciences. Here, lay views are not ignored but considered to constitute one part of the subject matter of sociology. There are two broad streams of work in this intellectual tradition, one primarily cognitive, the other primarily discursive.

The cognitive thrust in post-positivist family studies envisages lay ideas about the family as a system of morally charged beliefs, which represent and misrepresent economic and political interests in concrete social relations. 'The family' is described as a mental construct that is the product of a *familial ideology* (Beechey, 1985). This is the approach taken by Jon Bernardes (1985a; 1985b). He argues for a *new* family studies, that will displace 'the family' from its status as a reality that is taken for granted (Bernardes, 1988). This departure from standard sociological theory is important, he claims, because it is necessary for us to recognize how far commonsense knowledge is incorporated into public language, which is in turn taken up by social theory.

A focus on language as the object of social investigation is most characteristic of the second branch of post-positivism that will be considered here. In *discourse theory* the terms with which people describe the world are studied in their practical uses for purposes of communication. Cheal (1988a) states that there is no universal form of 'the family', and that 'family' is a term used by lay actors to label those ties which they believe to involve enduring intimate relations. In a similar manner, Gubrium and Holstein (1990) have drawn attention to the use of language in the social construction of the family. In their words, 'The term "family" is part of a particular discourse for describing human relations in or out of the household' (Gubrium and Holstein, 1990:13). They state that family discourse is a mode of communication, which assigns meanings to actions that are both substantive and active. In its substantive dimensions, family discourse names and makes sense of interpersonal relations. In its active dimensions, it communicates the attitudes which actors intend to adopt towards others, as well as the courses of action which they propose to take.

Post-positivist theorists of all persuasions are very sensitive to the multiple forms and multiple meanings of family life, as these emerge from different social contexts. Bernardes is especially concerned with the way in which talking about *the* family may obscure much real diversity in family situations. He therefore admonishes social theorists that 'This term can and must only have one possible use in future: specifically we must relegate the term "the Family" to denoting only the usage of everyday actors' (Bernardes, 1985b:210). Notwithstanding Bernardes's position, other social theorists who do use the term 'the family' have attempted to make use of some of the multiple meanings of everyday life, in complex sociological models of family structures (Wilson and Pahl, 1988). The basic question to ask about their line of work is how many such models we will need in order to understand contemporary societies.

Concept expansion

Structural sociologists have worked for some time to produce family concepts which would enable them to apply established theories to emerging phenomena. One solution has been to extend the definition of 'the family' into a normal form and at least one secondary form that is a transformation of it. The work of Harris (1983) is a good example of this approach. In a manner that is influenced by social anthropology, Harris speaks of 'the family' as a *class* of groups. It is all those groups which are formed by extension from the elementary relations of the nuclear family; namely relations between spouses, between parents and children and between siblings.

A related, but simpler, approach was deployed by Ahrons (1979) and later taken up by Ahrons and Rodgers (1987). Ahrons was concerned with the reorganization of the nuclear family after divorce, which frequently results in the formation of two households. Because of the connections between these households, through their shared rights over children in common,

Ahrons argued that they form one family system – a 'binuclear family system'. Ahrons therefore defines family life as consisting of the pre-divorce structure of the nuclear family, and the post-divorce structure of the binuclear family.

Jan Trost, too, is concerned with definitional problems that arise in part from the increased prevalence of divorce. In an elegant theoretical model, he has demonstrated in principle how a wide variety of living arrangements can be generated from a limited number of fundamental social properties (Trost, 1980). Trost is particularly interested in two types of group which he defines as families. They are the parent–child unit, consisting of one parent and one child related to each other, and the spousal unit, consisting of two cohabiting adults, either married or unmarried (Trost, 1988). Both these types are in effect theoretical reductions of the nuclear family that reflect contemporary conditions of social fragmentation.

Rather than proliferate types which are transformations of the normal family, Rhona Rapoport has recommended that we adopt a generalized 'diversity model'. She describes this approach as follows: 'With the diversity model, each particular family form – conventional, dual-worker, single-parent, reconstituted, etc. – is seen as providing the structure for a lifestyle' (R. Rapoport, 1989:60). Rapoport justifies this position on two grounds: first, because there are so many unknowns today that a new intellectual flexibility is required; and second, because past ideologies about family forms have proved inadequate for understanding contemporary changes. She does, however, note one potential problem with the diversity model. This is the tendency to reduce analysis to a micro-sociological level. In this approach large-scale social structural factors may be ignored, in favour of individual and small-scale interpersonal analyses.

Individualization

In so far as the sociology of the family has been moving in the direction of more individual-focused analyses, it may be because structural changes in society have made relations between autonomous individuals the principal basis for everyday social life. Observations of increased cultural diversity and heightened individuality are closely related in contemporary family theory, because the loosening of social controls that accompanies diversification allows individuals to choose between alternative life-styles. This *destandardization* of the family increases the freedoms that are open to individuals, and expands their sense of individuality and personal autonomy (Buchmann, 1989). Boh expresses this point as follows:

> Whatever the existing patterns are, they are characterised by the acceptance of diversity that has given men and women the possibility to choose inside the boundaries of the system of available options the life pattern that is best adapted to their own needs and aspirations. (1989:296)

Modernist social theorists are inclined to believe that increased individualism is a logical extension of the long-term trend of structural differentiation. This is the *individualization* thesis of modernity, which has been especially popular in recent German social theory (Kohli, 1986; Buchmann, 1989). It is thought that in the process of modernization, individuals become differentiated from each other as autonomous social units. This point was made by Parsons in one of his later works, although it is little known. Parsons noted that 'a strong case can be made that the trend of *modern* society, because it has become so highly differentiated and pluralistic, is positively to favor individuality' (1977:198). More recent theories have also pointed to the important role of the state in the public institutionalization of individual rights, and in undermining the powers of traditional groups such as families, which are consequently less able to act as corporate units (J. Meyer, 1986; Mayer and Schoepflin, 1989).

Cheal (1988a) has argued that contemporary family relations take the principal form of a *moral individualism*, due to the increased indeterminacy of cultural codes under conditions of social pluralism. Acquired rights to individual autonomy are aligned with commitments to others mainly through interpersonal bonding that is socially constructed. Characteristic consequences of this situation for family interactions include the search for inter-subjective agreement about members' biographies (P. Berger and Kellner, 1970), and increased sentimentality and increased ritualization of family ties (Cheal, 1988a; 1988b). The combination of the last two features produces an expanded significance of symbolic media for communicating to significant others the message that they are loved (Cheal, 1987a).

Luhmann (1986) claims that love should be understood not as a natural feeling, but as a generalized medium of communication. He argues that this code of communication, with its rules for expressing, forming and stimulating feelings, has become an increasingly important means for the management of intimate relationships. Luhmann attributes the origin of this state of affairs to functional differentiation in social systems. Progressive system differentiation has produced a great variety of specialized structures. Since individuals participate in a number of these they are no longer firmly located in any one of them. As a result, individuals now believe themselves to possess unique combinations of experiences, which they attribute to their unique personal qualities. Stable interaction between individuals requires that they confirm each other's personal, inner experiences. The code of love has evolved, Luhmann argues, as a mode of *interpersonal interpenetration*, which relies upon the internalization of another person's view of the world.

Interest in inner, subjective views of the objects that individuals perceive as relevant to them is an important theme in the theoretical approach known as *phenomenology*. This approach has its origins in the philosophy of human experience, and it is intensely individualistic. For example, in the sociology of the family McLain and Weigert have objected to any assumption that 'some construct called family actually behaves' (1979:187). Instead, they claim that only individuals behave.

The theme of individualization which runs through much modern social theory revolves around issues of autonomy, personhood, choice and identity. Those themes have sometimes been set out as formal assumptions of sociological theories, particularly in the United States.

Exchange

One well-known approach to theorizing about individuals in families is *exchange theory* (Nye, 1979; 1980; 1982). With its origins in behavioural psychology and in micro-economics, exchange theory has often been a preferred basis for deductive theorizing about patterns of interaction in families (Aldous, 1977; Tallman, 1988). The heart of exchange theory is a model of rational choice. It is assumed that individuals choose between lines of action in such a way as to minimize their costs and maximize their rewards. Exchange theorists believe that individuals engage in interaction only if it is profitable for them to do so. It is therefore thought that family life takes the general form of an exchange of goods and services.

Most exchange analyses of family life have been concerned with relations between husbands and wives. Topics include the choice of marriage partner (Murstein, 1973), the quality of the marriage relationship (R. Lewis and Spanier, 1982), marital separation (Levinger, 1979) and remarriage (Giles-Sims, 1987). One of the best-known applications of this approach is Scanzoni's work on marital interaction as a bargaining process, in which failure to agree on the rules of exchange may result in open conflict (Scanzoni, 1972; 1978; 1979; Scanzoni and Szinovacz, 1980).

Exchange theory is the most single-mindedly individualistic of the recent approaches in sociology that emphasize human agency. As a result, it has a simplicity and clarity that is admired by positivist theorists. At the same time, exchange theory has been criticized for oversimplification.[3] Other approaches often seek to combine notions of individual agency with notions of collective agency. This combination opens up wider possibilities for sociological explanation, but it also leads to conflicting interpretations and the possibility of theoretical confusion. Examples of this can be found in discussions of the concept of 'strategy'.

Strategy

It has been noted that the boundaries between sociology and social history are no longer as strong as they once were. There is today greatly increased traffic of people and ideas between these two fields. For the most part, this traffic has taken the form of theories and concepts moving from sociology to history, and data and interpretations moving from history to sociology. Occasionally the process of cross-fertilization works the other way, when concepts developed by historians are introduced into sociological discussions. The emergence of the concept of strategy is an example of this (Modell, 1978; Moch *et al.*, 1987; D.H.J. Morgan, 1989).

Many social historians and other social scientists have increasingly argued for a view of human beings as active strategists (Hareven, 1987; Lamphere, 1987). People are not seen as passively determined by their economic situations, but as actively adapting to them (Cheal, 1987b). They do this by setting long-term goals, and by weighing alternative means to achieve their ends within the possibilities existing in particular environments. The concept of strategy also conveys the idea that in evaluating alternatives open to them people adopt a comprehensive view of their situations, including taking account of the actions of others with whom they interact. If it is assumed that all the members of a group adopt an identical view of their situation, then there may exist not only individual strategies but also collective strategies, such as *family strategies* (Brenner and Laslett, 1986).

The concept of family strategy is thought to be particularly useful for analysing decisions about the allocation of persons to family positions – such as the timing of marriage, the number of children to have, co-residence with extended kin, and which family members should work outside the home and which should work within it (Hareven, 1987; Laslett and Brenner, 1989). However, the relationships between family interests and individual interests are often ambiguous, and sometimes conflicting (Crow, 1989). This can create some uncertainty as to which explanatory models are most appropriate for which kinds of data (Moch *et al.*, 1987).

Interaction

The moral ideal that all members of a family should adopt an identical view of their collective situation has been explicitly incorporated into sociology, in the theoretical approach known as *symbolic interactionism*. The usual definition of the family employed here is that given by Burgess (1926), namely that the family is a unity of interacting personalities. By this Burgess meant, in the first instance, that family life is constituted by interactions, which maintain the relationships of husband and wife and parents and children. In addition, he believed that 'the family develops a conception of itself' (Burgess, 1926:5). This conception includes a sense of the responsibilities that each member has to the others, as defined in family roles, and notions of what family life is or ought to be.

Burgess's emphasis on family unity was reflected in his concept of 'marital adjustment', which he saw as a precondition for a stable marriage.[4] He defined marital adjustment as involving processes of accommodation and assimilation, as follows:

> In certain of its phases, marital adjustment may be measured by accommodation, the mode of living that minimizes conflict and promotes harmony. Many, perhaps the majority of, marriages remain on the level of accommodation.
>
> From the standpoint of assimilation, adjustment is to be defined as the integration of the couple in a union in which the two personalities are not merely merged, or submerged, but interact to complement each other for mutual satisfaction and the achievement of common objectives. The emphasis is upon intercommunication, interstimulation, and participation in common activities.
>
> A well-adjusted marriage from the point of view of this study may then be defined as a marriage in which the attitudes and acts of each of the partners produce an environment which is favorable to the functioning of the personality of each, particularly in the sphere of primary relationships. (Burgess and Cottrell, 1939)

Burgess and his associates and followers were very interested in the relations between personality and marital interaction. It has been characteristic of the symbolic interactionist approach since then that attention is paid to the ways in which individuals' images of themselves are shaped by their interactions with others. Each person's sense of his or her identity is assumed to be derived from the communications that take place in everyday life, including family life. Stryker (1968) described this in terms of the 'familial identities' to which individuals are committed. These identities, he says, 'exist insofar as persons are participants in structured social relationships' (Stryker, 1968:559).

Symbolic interactionism has been a diverse, complex and influential approach to the sociology of the family over many years (R. Turner, 1970; Hutter, 1985). Much of this symbolic interactionist work has been absorbed into the standard sociological theory of the family, in the form of social psychological *role theory* (Burr, Leigh *et al.*, 1979). Here the focus is typically upon how individuals 'take' family roles, in processes of socialization and identity formation (Mackie, 1987). Interactionists also study how individuals 'make' and sometimes break roles as they try to shape family life to fit their emerging definitions of themselves. Interactionist work on shifting patterns of family life thus includes studying ways in which behaviour is negotiated, and renegotiated, among family members (Backett, 1987; Finch, 1987).

From a feminist standpoint, the interactionist perspective has been criticized for obscuring asymmetry in relations between women and men, and for encouraging a benign view of family life that ignores the capacity of men to impose their definitions of reality upon women (Glenn, 1987). Prompted by emergent gender issues, symbolic interactionists have had to recognize that families are not always united. They have therefore extended their investigations to include conflict situations. This involves them in studying the interactive dynamics of control and domestic violence (Stets, 1988).

One sign of increased interest in gender issues by interactionists is the *micro-structural theory* of gender (Risman and Schwartz, 1989). From this perspective, gendered behaviour is held to be the result of ways in which meanings are constructed within social relationships. Gender stereotypes are thought to be mapped onto the sexes from the typical activities in which men and women engage, as a result of their roles in the sexual division of labour. In turn, stereotypical behaviour is reproduced in cycles of interaction rituals (Cheal, 1989d). The consequences of this pattern include female dependence. Women's greater reliance on marriage gives them a stronger interest in respectability, which enables men to exercise greater control in premarital interactions (DiIorio, 1989).

A shift in emphasis has occurred within interactionist family studies, from an assumption of unity to looser models of individuals and their relationships. This shift has become more marked in recent years. Focusing on individuals rather than families has in turn meant an increased awareness of the fact that not all intimate interactions occur in family settings. Sociologists influenced by this emphasis upon methodological individualism stress the extent to which sexual encounters occur in non-family contexts. They have demonstrated how role commitments may be redefined, new relationships entered into and plural involvements sustained (Atwater, 1979; 1982; Richardson, 1988). All of this leads to increased questioning of developmental models of the changes that occur in individuals' family roles over time.

Life course

Interactionists' openness to the prevalence of social instability in modern societies was an important factor in the emergence of the interdisciplinary field known as 'life course dynamics' (Elder, 1984; 1985). The concept of the *life course* refers to the changes that occur in an individual's relationship to his or her environment over time. Like the concept of strategy, conceptualizations of the life course received much of their impetus from sociologically informed historical investigations (Elder, 1977; Hareven, 1978; 1982; 1987). However, it is the particular relevance of the life course concept to the analysis of present conditions that attracts the attention of many sociologists, who have become increasingly dissatisfied with notions of the family life cycle (Cheal, 1987b).

Family life cycle theory defines the existence of a universal set of family stages (marriage, birth, etc.), in terms of the evolution of the role system of the normal family. The underlying difficulty with family life cycle theory is the impossibility of fitting all the different sequences of domestic arrangements that exist today into any one set of stages (Trost, 1977; M. Murphy, 1987; Eichler, 1988).[5] Glen Elder (1984) has suggested that the notion of a normative sequence of family stages did in fact make some sense in the 1950s, which was an historically unusual era of marital stability and high fertility. But he believes that family life cycle models are no longer useful in the context of current behavioural diversity. He therefore recommends that we adopt the individual rather than the family as the basic unit of analysis for the purpose of studying changes in family relationships. Individuals' lives are followed across time, as they engage in family building and dissolving.

The focus in life course analysis is on the individual's passage through a sequence of social situations, and on how each individual is affected by the passages of others. The total sequence of an individual's situations is referred to as a life course 'trajectory' or 'pathway'. The passage from one situation to another is referred to as a 'transition'. Life course studies in the sociology of the family have dealt mainly with transitions, such as passages into and out of the married status (Wallace, 1987; Cheal, 1988c).

Life course studies exploded in the 1980s, when they had a considerable impact on the sociology of the family (Bernardes, 1986). From the life course perspective, a family is considered to be a set of 'interlocking trajectories'. Glen Elder (1985) points out that failed marriages and careers frequently lead adult sons and daughters to return to their parental household, and economic setbacks and divorce among parents of adolescents can impede their transition to adulthood. Each generation in the family is therefore seen as affected by decisions and events in the life courses of others. Among sociologists there has been particular interest in the extent to which 'problem behaviours' may result from the disadvantages caused by early experiences of other family members, especially parents, as in the case of adolescent childbearing (Elder, 1974; Elder *et al.*, 1986; Furstenberg *et al.*, 1987).

A major emphasis of life course research is the search for social patterns in the timing, duration, spacing and order of transitions. As studies on these issues have accumulated, it has become increasingly apparent that there is a great deal of variability and fluidity in life course trajectories. One advantage of the life course concept here is that it permits drawing comparisons between individuals and classes of individual in the degree of life course predictability and order (Rindfuss *et al.*, 1987). An important conclusion to emerge from such studies is that women's lives are less predictable and less standardized than those of men. Two issues appear to be particularly important here.

First, it has been noted that the social dimensions of women's lives are more plural, and more finely balanced, than those of men. Glen Elder (1977) has stated as a matter of paradigmatic principle that any individual's life course is multidimensional. Individuals engage in multiple roles, such as work, marriage and parenthood, whose trajectories are affected by different events. The multidimensionality of the life course is especially important in accounts of women's lives. Men's life course trajectories are tied to and controlled by the institutions in which they are employed, and by related public regulatory bodies. Women's life course trajectories, on the other hand, are more influenced by their family roles, and so they are more affected by the transitions of other family members (Lopata, 1987). This is most obvious in the effects of having children upon women's employment patterns. However, it is also visible in patterns of caring for elderly dependents. Whereas caring by men usually takes the form of looking after their wives during the retirement phase of the life course, women occupy a wide variety of life course positions at the time when they begin caring (Ungerson, 1987).

The second point about female life course diversity stressed in recent sociological studies is that the normative identification of women with the private sphere, which was so important in the recent past, has become less strong. Women have increasingly taken up occupational careers, in combination with or as alternatives to domestic responsibilities. As they have done so, they have made different choices that reflect their particular circumstances and values. Gerson, for example, has described the different ways in which women resolve the 'hard choices' between employment and family commitments (K. Gerson, 1985; 1987). Women today make many different kinds of choice, ranging from the traditional model of domesticity, through rising employment aspirations and ambivalence about motherhood, to rejection of motherhood and homemaking in favour of a non-traditional career. This new diversification of women's roles, it is argued, reflects a trend toward increased individualization of the female life course (Buchmann, 1989). This trend is sometimes described as a long-term feature of modernity, and sometimes seen as inaugurating a new epoch of post-modernity.

Something is happening

We have noted at several points, and most recently in the discussion of the life course approach, that changes in family theories often follow changes in family life. We have also seen that in the search for new understandings sociologists have explored a number of new approaches, including a variety of redefinitions of 'family'. In all this blooming, buzzing confusion there is no clear line of theoretical development, nor should we expect to find one. Nevertheless, there is a tendency in some of the most recent writings for discussions of theoretical possibilities to crystallize into two contrasting views of the state of theory (Buchmann, 1989:70–5). These come together in the modernism/ post-modernism debate over the future of social life and the future of the social sciences. In the remainder of this chapter we will be concerned with the future of family life. The future of the social sciences will be taken up in the concluding chapter.

The theoretical framework of modernism has provided the guiding thread for our discussions up to this point. It includes the theory of modernity, and related concepts of processes of modernization and anti-modernist reactions. The unifying theme here is that of the *rationalization* of social life. The progressive rational organization of human affairs is thought to be due to the emancipation of human beings from arbitrary limits of poverty and ignorance. As a result, people become free to order their activities guided by the powers of reason. Accounts of the standardization of the life course illustrate this idea very well. It is held that the timing and spacing of family transitions in the western societies has become more orderly. It is also thought that this has occurred not so much because of intensified normative controls of the traditional sort, but because individuals have chosen common patterns of life course management under conditions of material improvement and institutional bureau-cratization.

But we have noted too that this grand vision of human progress has been disturbed in recent years. There is a bewildering variety of alternative life-styles. Also, disorderly sequences of transitions have become more prevalent. Parenthood may come before marriage, and individuals may cycle into and out of marriage and family formation many times, without ever completing the task of raising their children into independent adults.

In addition to the practical difficulty of providing explanatory models for these more complex patterns, there is a deeper problem for social theory. Are these recent changes simply a short-term interruption to the secular trend of western modernization? Or are they the beginning of a cultural transformation, to which the classical sociological theories of social order will no longer apply?

Post-modernist theorists agree with the second of these statements. Höhn and Lüscher (1988), for example, consider the ambivalent situation of the family in Germany today to be indicative of a societal transition that they think should be characterized by the term 'post-modernity'. Whatever social forms eventually emerge from this transition, Höhn and Lüscher seem to think that they will involve a break with core ideas of modernity.

Modernist theorists generally disagree with claims of such a break. They do so by arguing for either a dualistic or a cyclical model of modernization. On the one hand, it is thought that there are secular tendencies toward greater collective control and social order, achieved through the expansion of powerful institutions such as the state. On the other hand, it is thought that the changes required by a modern society engaged in the progressive transformation of itself entail the frequent destruction of existing social forms, which have become outmoded. Too much destruction would, of course, render social life impossible. Tendencies towards disorganization are therefore held to be counteracted by creative forces of reorganization, which recombine the fragments of the old order in new and more advantageous ways.

Marshall Berman is a persuasive exponent of the idea that modernity is unstable. He states that in its destructive aspect, modern society 'pours us all into a maelstrom of perpetual disintegration and renewal, of struggle and contradiction, of ambiguity and anguish' (Berman, 1982:15). The causes of these great upheavals include industrialization, urbanization, international migration, and violent swings in access to economic resources and in levels of economic security. These themes were in fact very prominent in American studies in the sociology of the family during the first half of the twentieth century (Elder, 1984). Although not presented in the terms that we today would want to call the theory of modernity, the work of Burgess and his colleagues none the less illustrates the nature of this approach very well.

In their justifiably famous book which summarized the best of American family sociology between the two world wars, Burgess and Locke (1945) argued that the American family was in a state of transition – from *institution* to *companionship*. In the past, they thought, a stable and secure family life was guaranteed by external pressures of law, custom and public opinion. Those controls were reinforced inside the family by the authority of the male family head, the rigid discipline exercised by parents over their children, and elaborate private and public rituals. That system of control, they argued, had broken down in America in the twentieth century. This was due to a complex combination of causes – economic deprivation among the lower classes, particularly during the Great Depression; individualism that permitted greater autonomy within and from families; a democratic ethos that loosened public controls over morality as well as internal authority relationships; the decline of domestic production and thus of an economic focus to family life; and migration and the growth of cities, with consequent exposure to new and shifting patterns of behaviour (Burgess and Locke, 1945; Burgess, 1973).

Burgess claimed that the result of all these changes was family disorganization; that is, a situation characterized by normative uncertainty, behavioural fluidity and relationship disintegration. But he was not pessimistic. Burgess believed that *disorganization* was always followed eventually by *reorganization*. Since he thought that the external, institutional supports for family life had declined, Burgess located the potential for reorganization in the desires and capacities of individuals to construct meaningful lives for themselves. Family life, he thought, was being reconstituted on the basis of interpersonal relationships of mutual affection and understanding. The result of that process would be the companionship family.

Significantly, Burgess seems to have believed it was unlikely that individuals could reconstitute family life on their own. He thought that individuals' limited resources of self-understanding and social skills would have to be supplemented and upgraded by the knowledge generated from social scientific research. Translated by family experts into practical techniques, this knowledge was to be communicated and implemented by a variety of social agencies that we have noted in our earlier discussions of modernity. Burgess was deeply concerned with advancing the programmes of child guidance clinics, marriage counselling centres, psychiatrists and clinical psychologists in their efforts to treat the behaviour problems of children and adults. He also stressed the preventative value of family studies courses for college students.

Today it is the existence of the companionship family that is in question. Perhaps Burgess and Locke would not have been too surprised at this. They pointed out that ties of affection are not as strong as ties of duty, when the latter are publicly enforced. They also noted the greater vulnerability of the socially isolated companionship family, especially to the effects of economic insecurity (Burgess and Locke, 1945:719).

All this is well known. What is new today – and what may justify applying the term 'post-modern' to our present condition – is that the human service programmes that Burgess recommended no longer work in precisely the way he envisaged. He seems to have simply assumed that therapeutic agencies would inevitably be committed to the values of familism, and in particular to the preservation of the family as a unity of interacting personalities. But today it is the values of individualism and emancipation from social limitations that are increasingly evident in the work of human service practitioners. We have noted in an earlier chapter how this is related to critical rethinking of social scientific theory and practice, especially in relation to abuse of women within their families. That rethinking is part of a trend which is not likely to reconstitute family life. Today, feminist therapists and workers in women's shelters often see it as their responsibility to provide women with personal resources with which to *leave* their families.

The post-modern family?

Post-modernist theorists have begun to grapple with the possibility that many of the features of social life that were taken for granted for a long time will have to be rethought. This is not simply a question of rethinking specific social arrangements, such as family life, or even the sex/gender role system. Rather, post-modernism poses the question of a general rethinking of 'the social' and of 'theory'. Post-modernism is an elusive approach to the study of human existence, which has only recently begun to be incorporated into the sociology of social life (Denzin, 1986; Bauman, 1988a; 1988b; Featherstone, 1988; Kellner, 1988; J. Murphy, 1988; 1989). The remarks that follow are therefore intended to be merely suggestive of current lines of development.

Post-modernist thought begins with experiences of pluralism, disorder and fragmentation in contemporary culture that are not predicted by the modern paradigm of universal reason. Post-modernists go on to argue that if modernity, and hence our concepts of reason and progress, have in some sense failed, then presumably a very different set of principles must be at work in the world. Unlike the modernist theorists, however, the post-modernists do not think these alternative principles will eventually produce a total reorganization of social life.[6] Rather, they are inclined to believe that what is most characteristic of the post-modern era is its continuous production of instability. This production of instability – in science, art and literature as well as in life-styles and family relationships – is described by a set of ideas that are unlike the standard theories of social evolution (such as that of Talcott Parsons), which presupposed convergence to equilibrium. The following points deal with some current questions about the future of family life in post-modern society.

The end of progress

Faith in modernity has included the belief in a continuous upward path of improvement for all that leads to an ever more glorious future of popular well-being and social harmony. This romantic view of modernity has been severely eroded by recent events in the western societies. There is a growing realization that economic growth and the expansion of the welfare state since the end of the Second World War did not solve all social ills. Many individuals remain trapped in poverty and ignorance, and for some social groups – such as American blacks – conditions have got measurably worse. Stories about increasing numbers of children growing up in poverty reach us from many different directions, like a bad echo from the nineteenth century.

Social change continues, of course – at an ever more rapid pace – but it is thought that it does so in ways that bring only dubious benefits, or benefits for some but not others, or benefits that have side-effects whose accumulation will eventually cost us dearly. It therefore appears to some observers that, in the western societies at least, progress has come to an end and with it modernity (Vattimo, 1988). If that is the case, then what does the post-modern family look like?

Norman Denzin argues that the traditional concept of a family can no longer be applied to the post-modern situation. The modern nuclear family, in which children were cared for by two parents within a protective and emotionally secure environment, is no longer the norm in America, he believes. He therefore proposes a definition of a new type of family for the post-modern period. His bleak assessment is that 'It is a single-parent family, headed by a teenage mother, who may be drawn to drug abuse and alcoholism. She and her children live in a household that is prone to be violent' (Denzin, 1987:33).[7]

In addition to these structural and interactional features, Denzin refers to two other aspects of post-modern family life. They have to do with the connections that family members have with the social environment. First, Denzin suggests that increasing numbers of children are now cared for by someone other than a parent. The daycare setting is therefore an important factor in contemporary child development. Second, there is the presence of the television set in the home, which is left on for up to seven hours a day. It is from television that children learn cultural myths today, Denzin insists. He concludes that the post-modern child 'is cared for by the television set, in conjunction with the day-care center' (Denzin, 1987:33). The mass media and daycare providers also figure prominently in other accounts of post-modernization.

Simulations and the death of the subject

Post-modernist theories of popular culture attach considerable importance to the ways in which mass-mediated meanings penetrate all corners of contemporary social life. Jean Baudrillard, especially, argues that the media's insatiable urge to

communicate creates an excess of cultural products. This excess
of meanings erases all boundaries, and it produces a de-
differentiated mass society (Baudrillard, 1983a).[8] One aspect of
this situation, in Baudrillard's view (1983b), is the disappearance
of any separation between public and private spheres. This is
because intimate details of private lives are picked up by
journalists and talk-show hosts, processed through electronic
networks, and relayed into millions of homes through television
and newspapers.

Denzin (1987) is concerned that 'television set family myths',
which are portrayed in soap operas and situation comedies, are
out of touch with the realities of family life for most people. They
are 'cultural fantasies', which do not provide practical guidelines
for how to live today. The television 'families' that fascinate mass
audiences are, in Baudrillard's terminology, *simulations* (1988).
These images are not real families, nor are they signs that refer to
real families. Nevertheless, these imaginary families are 'real' to
millions of viewers, who discuss the events of their lives at work
the next day just as they discuss the details of their own lives.
This is, Baudrillard says, 'the generation by models of a real
without origin or reality: a hyperreal' (1988:166).

Hyperreal mediated fantasies are of particular interest to
feminist theorists, who detect in them sites for the ideological
construction of male-dominated heterosexual couples. Popular
romance narratives, such as the Harlequin Romance paperbacks,
have drawn especial attention (Ebert, 1988; Finn, 1988). The
precise subjective effects produced by reading these texts are
important issues in contemporary social theory. Post-modernist
interpretations of romance narratives see them as constituting the
'subjectivity' of the individual, or in other words as creating the
individual's sense of self. Of course, romance stories are only one
source of subjectivity. They are therefore described as existing in
(partially) contradictory relations to other constitutive sources,
such as everyday family life. These other sources are also thought
to contain contradictory experiences, such as love and fear,
submission and autonomy, sexual desire and asexual care-giving.
The self, or 'subject', produced by this complex of experiences is
seen not as a coherent, stable essence, but as a fragmented
participant in various discourses. Ebert, for instance, holds that
today,

gender instability and identity confusion threaten to undermine the individual's imaginary sense of a whole self. As a result, individuals readily seek out and embrace those ideological representations that symbolically resolve these contradictions and produce the illusion of a unified, stable subjectivity. (Ebert, 1988:38)

The claim that individuals do not now (and perhaps never did) possess a stable inner identity is sometimes expressed in the phrase 'the death of the subject'. Behind this phrase lies the argument that individuals who do not possess a coherent sense of their own identity will not be able to act consistently upon, or especially against, their environment. It is at this point that the sociology of the family comes back in. The shifting contexts of childhood socialization in post-modern society are sometimes thought to contribute to subjective instability. It is here that current research into the experiences of children in daycare acquires its theoretical relevance.

Chaos

Leavitt and Power (1989) question whether children can develop authentic understandings of their emotions in daycare interactions, if the care-givers' own lack of emotional investment in them results in a failure to legitimize childrens' emotional expressions. Dencik (1989) considers such anxieties to be themselves indicative of the post-modern condition of a quickening 'social acceleration'. Old patterns have been abandoned, but the new ones are not stable. Dencik argues that in Denmark, parents and other care-givers distance themselves from their own experiences as children, which they consider to be invalidated as models for childhood today. But at the same time they lack confidence in the alternative models proposed by experts, since their effects are unknown and they are subject to endless revision. In Dencik's words:

Modern parents know a lot about children and child development as compared with previous generations. Still, many of them simply feel at a loss at what to do. They listen eagerly to the advice of experts, but soon discover they often change their minds and prove themselves to be unreliable. One year we hear the children absolutely must eat at regular times, next year they must be allowed to eat whenever they feel hungry. One year the children must have as much freedom as possible, the next year strict rules of behavior must be enforced. Nobody can give hard and fast advice, the know-how changes just as quickly as the development itself. Uncertainty is chronic. (Dencik, 1989:174)

Forced to make decisions in a much shorter time than that needed to assemble the requisite information, people may panic and abandon reason in favour of simplified codes. The resulting social structure is not a product of social reorganization, but a temporary order within a constant instability. It is this instability of knowledge, uncertainty of judgment and lack of confidence in experts that make the present era merit the description 'post-modern' (Bauman, 1987). Lack of confidence pervades all expert systems now, since they are continuously being outmoded, scrapped, broken down and reassembled. This is notoriously the case with computer technology, as Dencik notes. It is also the situation in social theory.

Notes

1. Touraine has criticized as outmoded the dominant sociological view of the relationship between social life and social history, which he says was 'based on the unity between the stage of evolution of a society and its form of social and cultural organization; this is an idea that S.M. Lipset has defended with great talent through a series of influential books beginning with *Political Man*' (Touraine, 1984:41). For an empirical critique of Lipset's hypotheses along these lines see Cheal (1978).
2. Young and Willmott's hypothesis of a trend toward the symmetrical family has been subjected to close scrutiny, from which mostly negative conclusions have been drawn. See Hunt and Hunt (1982), Lupri and Symons (1982) and Finch (1983; 1985).
3. Critics include Cheal (1984) and Glenn (1987). Hartsock (1985) argues that exchange theory is incompatible with a feminist standpoint. First, she says that the prevalence of empathy in women's self-definition contradicts the key assumption in exchange theory, that individuals are fundamentally separate and concerned only with their own interests. Second, women's experiences do not support the

view that all social relations are voluntaristic. Women who are responsible for small children typically have little choice over whether or not to accept them. And third, unlike the opposition of interests in competitive market relations, conflict is not at the core of the relationships between most mothers and their children.

A relevant example of the issues here can be seen in Ivan Nye's (1982) discussion of transactions between parents and their children. Nye points out that in an industrial society children provide few material benefits which would compensate their parents for the enormous costs of their upbringing. This leads him to question why parents continue to shoulder heavy costs on behalf of their children, when they can expect to get few rewards in return. In searching for ways to deal with this problem in exchange theoretic terms, Nye suggests that parental support might be induced by non-material rewards from children, and by social rewards from the larger community. The possibility that family life might be a complex relational nexus constituted by mixed motives is not even considered.

4. Marital adjustment has been a topic of enduring interest among American family scientists, particularly in relation to the concept of 'marital quality' (Spanier, 1976; R. Lewis and Spanier, 1979; Vannoy-Hiller and Philliber, 1989).

5. One option for family life cycle theory in the 1980s was to follow the route of concept expansion, outlined above. This involved identifying a normal model of the family life cycle, and one or more secondary models. Expanded family life cycle models have sometimes been proposed as a means of adapting family life cycle theory to contemporary conditions of social diversification (Stapleton, 1980; Mattessich and Hill, 1987). Reuben Hill (1986), for example, took this approach towards the end of his career, when he outlined a complex model of the paths of development of three types of single-parent family. The principal disadvantage of this approach is the proliferation of typologies and models. Eventually this reaches the point at which the originally simple and powerful idea of the family life cycle becomes too unwieldy to be of practical value for social scientific explanation. At that point more or less arbitrary typological reductions must be carried out (Höhn, 1987).

6. Reorganization is a possibility in post-modern society, but it is likely to appear only in patches, in unique configurations that emerge under particular, local conditions.

7. There are some striking similarities between the post-modernist critique of the failure of modern institutions and the anti-modernist critique of modernity as cultural decline. For example, anti-modernists and post-modernists are generally highly critical of welfare

bureaucracies, which they believe provide only partial solutions to some problems, while creating new problems which they cannot solve. This similarity is one of the most controversial aspects of post-modernism. Some observers claim that post-modernism is simply a new form of conservatism in disguise (Habermas, 1981; Sangren, 1988). Denzin's post-modernism does not identify with anti-modernist calls for a return to tradition. He insists that 'We must stop defining problems in terms of a middle-class morality', and we must avoid 'proposals that take freedom away from those they are intended to serve' (1987:35).

8. The process of cultural de-differentiation in post-modernization is the opposite of the process of structural differentiation in modernization (e.g. as described by Parsons).

CHAPTER 6

CONCLUSION:
THE INSTABILITIES OF POST-MODERN
SOCIAL THEORY

At the beginning of this book we noted how in the 1970s a Big Bang occurred in family theory that brought the post-Second World War move towards theoretical convergence to an end. That rupture initiated a dramatic period of diversification in family studies. We have seen in subsequent chapters that the breaches made in the walls of the 'orthodox consensus' allowed a flood of new ideas to sweep over the field. Old ideas were revised, or overthrown. Throughout the period there was often an exciting sense of remaking the sociology of the family, which continues today. The outcome of all this is that the field of family theory is now a tremendously diverse terrain. As a result, the current challenges facing family theorists are not the same as they once were. Talcott Parsons no longer dominates the field intellectually, and 'Parsons bashing' is an increasingly irrelevant exercise.[1]

Since the mid-1970s, a great deal of energy has been expended on the task of tearing down the orthodox consensus about the normal family. That task is now complete. The challenge for us is to renew family theory, in the aftermath of the Big Bang. Whatever conclusions are drawn about the state of family theory today, they must be made in full knowledge of the situation as it exists now. That situation is complex, and unstable, but it is not random.

The present-day divisions between theoretical approaches to the family have some noteworthy resemblances to those that existed in the 1930s. However, the present situation is different from the pre-war context in one very important respect. The magnitude of diversity is much greater now than it was then, due to the enormous expansion of professional social science in the post-Second World War period. Large numbers of social scientists are currently working on related issues, but in different ways, in many countries. In this book I have tried to document the main directions taken by this international diversification. The picture presented here is no doubt incomplete, but it does permit some general conclusions.

One distinctive aspect of the present situation is the way in which the diversification of ideas about families coincided with the high point of the institutionalization of sociology as a positivist social science. Current divisions can no longer be understood, as they once were understood (and sometimes still are), in terms of comparisons between science and myth, or fact and value, or theory and ideology. Today we are forced to acknowledge that what we are dealing with are the ideological processes of science itself (Harding, 1986a; Harding and O'Barr, 1987). It appears now that formulations of *the* structure and of 'social reality' can only be constituted from a single universalizing perspective. Any such perspective is constituted by, and thereby privileges, one particular kind of socially constructed world – or its negative reflection in a particular social imaginary.

Accepting this conclusion is hard for positivist social scientists. This is not surprising. It threatens to destabilize the entire edifice of modern social science, which they created. Once it is assumed that no scientific position is epistemologically privileged, then presumably any given position can be called into question from some point of view other than that in which it is grounded. And *this*, of course, is precisely what *has* happened in the last two decades (Sprey, 1990).

This does not mean that family social science is any less important than it once was. Indeed, it can be stated that the opposite is the case. The issues debated by most sociologists of the family are not the artificial inventions of a priesthood of scholars, remote from the daily concerns of ordinary people and of policy makers. The issues, and the divisions, arise from important social processes that sociologists try to understand, at the same time as they are themselves influenced by those processes. If today we must pay much more attention than we once did to the way in which sociology is shaped by social influences, it is also the case that we are in a much stronger position to describe what those influences are and how they work. The contributions that sociologists have made to social theory provide us with a range of tools, with which to understand the intellectual contexts in which sociologists operate. It is important that these tools should be used to improve professional self-understanding, and that this reflexive knowledge should be linked to our understanding of social life. Only in this way can we hope to produce a social science that is grounded in the world in which we live, rather than being imposed upon it.

In this book I have shown how family theorists responded to, and how they were also influenced by, a set of contradictions arising from the twentieth-century experience with modernity. I began by contrasting the modernist faith in reason and progress with the anti-modernist fear of cultural disintegration and moral decline. I then moved on to consider two divisions within modernity itself, whose frictions generated much of the heat in recent years, in the sociology of the family and in family relationships. They are: first, the division between systematizing models of developmental change, and radical models of rupture and liberation; and second, the division between a private sphere of idealized domesticity, and a public sphere within which power and prestige are concentrated. Finally, I showed how the modern vision of reason, as revealing one path of progress which is true for everyone, has been contradicted by unexpected forms of pluralism. These latter patterns were described in the last chapter as potentially inaugurating a new era of post-modernity.

It remains to consider what the distinctive characteristics of social theory in a post-modern era might be. Any suggestions with respect to this issue are necessarily highly speculative. Nevertheless, there may be something of value in such an exercise, if it can be shown that the lines of development proposed already exist in current tendencies. That task will be taken up in the rest of this, our concluding, chapter.

From polarization to pluralization

A principal characteristic of family theory today is its instability. This instability is most evident in the way in which new ideas emerge, and sometimes become popular with extraordinary rapidity, only to disappear almost as quickly. Marxist theorizing about female domestic labour in the household, as being explicable in terms of the reproduction of male wage labour for industry, is a conspicuous illustration. It is well known that extreme swings in theoretical orthodoxy are not uncommon in Marxism, since Marxists frequently trim their sails to catch shifting political winds. It must be emphasized, therefore, that the instability of social theory is not a characteristic only of the more overtly politicized approaches. It is also to be found in areas where there is less at stake (at least in terms of political positions), such as the disjunction between models of standardization and models of individualization that we observed in life course analyses.

The expert's models of standardization and individualization in life course studies are profoundly contradictory. It is of course possible to think of ways in which they could be reconciled, as I attempted to do in part by drawing attention to the distinction between short-term and long-term trends. The important point to note here is that any attempt to theorize along these lines begins with an explicit recognition of the existence of contradictory models. That recognition marks an important moment in the history of family theory. It is the moment of a self-consciously critical, and reflexively self-limiting, mode of theorizing. The principal characteristic of this type of theorizing is the absence of any claim to a singular truth. Accounts are localized – in time, and in space, and with respect to institutional structures (language, the mode of production, etc.).[2]

The localization of theory, and the instability of theory, are related phenomena within post-modern knowledge. In the first place, this is so because localized theories develop along many different lines, in relation to different patterns of events. When such theories are brought together the ensuing contradictions and indeterminacies – or worse, incomprehensions and misunderstandings – create tensions that are not easily resolved. In so far as the protagonists do not retreat into closed worlds, which are carefully fortified against alternative ideas, the inevitable result is the destabilization of *all* theoretical discourses.[3] There is an important conclusion which follows from this point: appeals for more science, and more social scientists, are not likely to resolve our present difficulties in reaching agreement on important questions.

Theory localization and theory instability are related in another way, in so far as unstable theoretical frameworks have a tendency to break down into alternative models that are applied in particular contexts. With respect to issues in the sociology of the family, this is most obvious at present in feminist theory. A particularly well known example of this (because it has been controversial) is Heidi Hartmann's 'dual systems theory' (1981b). She argued that there is no necessary connection between the capitalist economic system that produces goods and the patriarchal sex/gender system that produces people. From Hartmann's point of view, understanding women's experiences requires concrete analyses of the contingent relations between patriarchy and capitalism, considered as autonomous systems.

Jean-François Lyotard (1984) has labelled the distinctive combination of localization and instability in post-modern knowledge as *paralogy*. In his view, the status of science today does not rest upon the expert's command over a universal body of knowledge, but upon the inventor's capacity to create new ideas and to produce new kinds of data. Unlike modernist theorists of knowledge, he does not view this situation negatively, as a 'paradigm crisis'. Rather, as a post-modernist, he positively embraces paralogy in a celebration of pluralism, and as a way of avoiding all forms of totalitarianism.

If there is any one theme which links the various interests in post-modernism, it is pluralism (McKinney, 1986; Hassan, 1987). It is thought that there are multiple meanings in social life, and in social theory, that define multiple realities. As this idea has gradually taken hold, in different forms and to different degrees, it has reshaped how social theorists think about the relationships between new theories and established theories. It no longer appears to be the case that established ideas, such as standard sociological theory, represent a core of accumulated knowledge which we must either build upon, or destroy. Standard sociological theory is no longer taken for granted, but it has not disappeared. Many people continue to work effectively within its traditions, producing work that is both interesting and useful. This is not the end of the matter, however. There are other sociologists whose aim is to test where the limits of existing approaches lie, and who seek to find out what lies beyond those limits. Such work brings into sociology the neglected knowledges of the many 'others' who stand outside the dominant expert discourses – such as the parents of disabled children (Voysey, 1975). The effect of the latter kind of work is to produce a plurality of concepts and models. In so doing, it opens up spaces within sociology for a plurality of points of view.

The shift that is underway in social theory today is best described as that *from polarization to pluralization*. In the era of polarization that began in the 1960s, and which continued in some places right through to the beginning of the 1990s, contradictions between opposing principles of social organization were the most dynamic factors in sociological change. That is no longer the case. In sociology today, change has ceased to be dialectical. Instead, change is created by instabilities in the constitutive procedures that make *any* kind of organization possible. From the point of view of modern sociology, this must appear to be a deepening of the perceived crisis in the project of an integrated and coherent theoretical framework. I want to argue that it need not be, and should not (yet) be seen to be, a crisis. Rather, it is the price we pay for an accelerated pace of change in the activity of theorizing.

A discipline that is engaged in constantly recasting its foundations, as well as its theoretical structures, is capable of more flexible responses to changing conditions than a discipline whose only choices are between the contradictory poles of fixed divisions. In that sense, post-modern social theory can be understood as an advance over modern social theory. This does not mean that doing post-modern sociology is simply science-as-usual. It has its own peculiar characteristics, which we would do well to understand.

Since the 1960s, sociology has moved further and further into an epistemological practice of *self-conscious pluralization*. The scientific status of knowledge was profoundly altered by this post-modern condition. The impact of an item of knowledge today does not arise from its having a clearly definable place within a cumulative body of work, whether that corpus is understood in terms of the discipline as a whole or in terms of specific programmes within it. Instead, the significance of an item is derived from its role as an element in the continuous production of conceptual pluralism.

There is a noteworthy consequence which follows from this. The most important ideas in social theory today are not those which make the greatest 'contribution' to science, in terms of an increase in the power of a theory. Rather, the most important ideas are those which are most 'productive', in terms of their capacity to generate new ideas and hence more scientific activity. The latter direction is strongly recommended by the feminist philosopher, Sandra Harding. She insists that destabilization of thought has often advanced understanding more effectively than its restabilization. Harding therefore claims that we should see theoretical disputes 'not as a process of naming issues to be resolved but instead as opportunities to come up with better problems than those with which we started' (1986b:19).

In Harding's philosophy of science, solving problems is projected into the indefinite future. This is a distinctly post-modern move. A potential end to a process is conceptualized, only to be followed by the announcement of an infinite set of future possibilities. Here, philosophy mirrors post-modern family science.

In search of the future

One of the most visibly striking features of family studies in recent years has been the pursuit of new and emerging patterns of behaviour. Sociologists have been eager to describe these patterns while they were still forming. They have also been keen to theorize about them in terms of concepts of the new, such as 'new families', 'the new man', 'the new grandparent', and so forth. The list of 'new' issues that have been subjected to the sociological gaze since the 1960s is long indeed – dual career families, swinging couples (i.e. mate swapping), lesbian mother-hood, the feminization of poverty, etc. The introduction of many of these issues is clearly related to feminist concerns about understanding how women live today, and how their lives are changing. However, a fascination with the new in family studies has not been confined only to feminists, or only to women. Men as well as women have been interested in such issues as changing male attitudes towards masculinity and fatherhood. D.H.J. Morgan (1990), for example, emphasizes the plurality of masculinities which is possibly emerging among men in contemporary western societies.

The intense interest of many family scientists in patterns that are new and emerging is striking, particularly since it is contrary to a fundamental rule of positivist sociology, set down by Emile Durkheim (1964). Durkheim argued that the goal of sociology as a science should be to uncover general laws about the operation of social facts. He concluded that in order to achieve this goal, certain definite procedures would be necessary. One of the procedures he recommended was that sociologists should avoid studying 'changeable and unstable' patterns of behaviour. That is because such phenomena cannot provide the kinds of observational data that scientists require if they are to uncover objective social facts. Durkheim held that in order to arrive at correct sociological laws, it would be necessary progressively to eliminate subjective influences upon researchers' judgments, through repeated testing of their hypotheses. Repeat testing requires repeat observations of the same objects. It is essential for this procedure that the objects under investigation should be stable, so that the same measurements will produce the same results in successive experiments. Durkheim therefore urged sociologists to study only phenomena which 'constitute a fixed object', and not the 'free currents' that are 'perpetually in the process of transformation and incapable of being mentally fixed by the observer' (1964:45). Durkheim summarized his argument in the following aphorism: 'In order to follow a methodical course, we must establish the foundations of science on solid ground and not on shifting sand' (1964:46).

Durkheim's recommended procedure is not followed by most sociologists of the family today. This includes many sociologists who profess to be very concerned about the scientific basis of family theory. Indeed, they often seem to prefer 'shifting sand' to 'solid ground'. Why is this?

Durkheim was prepared to disregard shifting social practices in order to focus upon more slowly changing social structures, for two reasons. These reasons are closely related to the modernist foundations of his sociology. First, Durkheim clearly believed that the knowledge produced by scientific sociology would be cumulative. He thought that sociologists would eventually arrive at a comprehensive body of knowledge, by means of 'successive approximations'. His confidence in the long-term potential of sociology enabled him to set aside the 'fleeting reality' of short-term changes. Short-term interests and possibilities could be sacrificed in favour of greater long-term gains. Second, Durkheim (like his successor Parsons) thought that it was possible to distinguish between social forms that are 'normal' (i.e. progressive) and those that are 'pathological' (i.e. retrogressive). He believed that through deduction the sociologist could distinguish between healthy and unhealthy conditions of the social organism. On this basis Durkheim proceeded to identify the normal conditions that are most important for the sociologist to study, in order to describe the path of social evolution.

We have seen during the course of this book that both of the presuppositions upon which Durkheim relied are no longer taken for granted. Ideas of the 'inventorying of propositions', 'theory building' and theory convergence are heard less often in the sociology of the family these days than ideas of 'beginning from ourselves', 'theory critique' and dissonance. Concepts of the normal family are now suspect, and they are either relativized as ideology or deconstructed in order to reveal more basic social processes. On both counts, the unquestioned faith in progress and in reason that once inspired Durkheim's neglect of the new has gone.

Knowledge of the new has a greater value today than it did in Durkheim's day. That is because the focus of attention in much of the sociology of the family has moved from the present to the future. Since the future itself is not observable, the practical interest of many sociologists now is in the forward horizon of the present, which it is hoped will yield valuable clues about what is going to happen next.

Viewed from the perspective of modernism, the future is the outcome of a developmental process of overcoming the limitations of the present. Since the future is thought to be immanent in the present, it is believed that its outlines can be deduced from a careful analysis of current contradictions. These contradictions define the points of strain and struggle in the system, from which progressive solutions can be expected to emerge.

Recent surprises, and reversals of long-term trends, have dealt this point of view some rather severe blows. The pursuit of new and emerging phenomena has suddenly acquired a new significance. We know that family life is changing, but we do not know which of the emergent social forms will set the pattern for the future. We still assume that *some* pattern must emerge sooner or later, and that it is therefore the business of the sociologist to keep in touch with all possible changes, in order not to miss significant developments when they occur. The leading sociologists of the family today are engaged in a search for the future, in order to discover who will occupy it, and which claims made in the present will prevail. One of the consequences of this situation, as Durkheim anticipated, is the instability of analytical categories.

The instability of analytical categories

In an earlier chapter we noted that sociologists are divided – and often confused – about how 'family' should be defined. This confusion has not arisen because sociologists failed to think deeply enough about the matter. It exists largely because they have tried to modify certain conventional meanings of the term 'family', in ways that it was hoped would facilitate the sociological description of new and emerging social practices.

It might be thought that this instability, in what is surely *the* major concept in the field, must have a devastating effect upon the work of family theorists. But that is not the case. Most social scientists have learned to work with that instability, through migrating between different uses of concepts in different language games. In fact, the instability of analytical categories is sometimes positively recommended as a basis for theorizing at this time. Sandra Harding has stated that: 'Feminist analytical categories *should* be unstable – consistent and coherent theories in an unstable and incoherent world are obstacles to both our understanding and our social practices' (Harding, 1986b:19). From this point of view, social theory is ideally positioned in a space between all positions, so that it is able to take advantage of every possibility, and so that it avoids all forms of closure. This 'position', which is more common than we might think, has some interesting implications for analyses of current trends in social theory.

The fuzziness of 'schools of thought'

One of the most common methods of analysing major patterns within social theory is to describe the emergence and growth of 'schools of thought' (Mullins, 1973; 1983; Tiryakian, 1979; Boss *et al.*, forthcoming). The underlying rationale for this method is derived from familiar sociological concepts of social structure and social process.

The structural dimension of this approach is provided by concepts of academic social networks, within which significant clusters, or 'theory groups', may form. Groups of scholars are shown to share certain assumptions, perhaps due to a common education in certain universities, or as a result of common exposure to ideas conveyed through specialized journals and conferences. As a form of theory description, a social network analysis identifies concepts which have circulated widely through influential channels of communication. As a form of theory explanation, it stresses how knowledge production and diffusion rely upon social interaction, which is shaped by channels of network expansion.

The social process dimension of the schools-of-thought approach is provided by accounts of intellectually significant historical events. Well-known examples include the radicalizing effect of the Vietnam War upon the growth of academic Marxism in North America, and the emergence of 'second wave' feminism as a major social movement. Structure and process models of theory formation can be usefully combined. It may be important to know how the bearers of certain ideas became established in, or were excluded from, the academy during periods of institutional growth or retrenchment.

Several schools of thought were mentioned in earlier chapters of this book, including most notably discussions of the impact of feminism. Other schools of thought too were described, such as

Marxism, exchange theory and symbolic interactionism. However, the schools-of-thought approach has not been heavily stressed in this book. The most conspicuous limitation of that approach is the weak explanations that it provides for the contents of theoretical arguments. Particularly problematic are those explanations that take a narrative form, consisting of stories about the exceptional influences exerted by particular individuals, alone or in conjunction with others (for instance in certain university departments). Some of these descriptions of schools of thought have a tendency to degenerate into biographies of the 'great-men-and-women-of-science' type (e.g. Ritzer, 1988). Such accounts under-emphasize the contextual effects of larger societal processes of culture formation. As a result, the contents of sociological theories are under-determined. In any situation other than their own intellectual history, sociologists would surely be quick to criticize such accounts as poor sociology.

The overarching conceptual framework in this book is not provided by a typology of academic schools of thought, but by a cultural theory of knowledge. This theory emphasizes the great importance for sociology of the relationship between disciplinary knowledge and modernity. Some of the reasons for preferring an account of sociological theorizing from the perspective of a cultural theory of modernity should be evident from earlier discussions. The ideas that are communicated in social networks are located within a larger cultural idiom, over which theory groups typically have little control. Their cultural matrix provides the set of discourses within which theorists find a place to talk, and the words to talk with.

The range of possibilities for discourse that can be generated from within an unstable culture far exceeds the number of patterns that can be rendered socially effective as traditions. Under the post-modern conditions that were described above – i.e. pluralization, the pursuit of the new, and the instability of analytical categories – there are few constraints upon breaking with tradition. Social theorists constantly seek out new sources of ideas, and they seek to combine existing ideas in new ways. Today there are so many scholars working as theorists, and the influences upon and between them are so multifarious, that the division of a field into a finite number of schools is much too simple to be used as anything other than a provisional orientation. Problematic simplifying procedures include the drawing of boundaries between unique schools of thought, as well as the assumption that all significant scholarship can only be produced by theorists working from inside one school or another.

The socially constructed reality of a set of unique schools of thought is an especially prominent feature of American family studies. Yet even here it can no longer be taken for granted. The problem of boundary specification for schools of thought is illustrated by the career of John Scanzoni. At one time Scanzoni could be described as an exemplar of exchange theory in the sociology of the family. However, that is no longer the case. Although he still has a micro-sociological focus, exchange principles are now combined in his work with issues drawn from the social psychology of personal relationships. The result is a line of theorizing that is both richer and more complex than before. These days it is not at all uncommon for active social scientists, such as Scanzoni, to stray across intellectual borders. In so doing, these theorists lessen the value of the schools-of-thought approach for comparative theoretical analysis.

There is a point of some general significance here, with which this discussion concludes. During the 1980s certain theoretical boundaries, such as those surrounding the various micro-sociologies, became increasingly open. Symbolic interactionism, in particular, became a looser approach which absorbed a variety of influences. Norman Denzin's career, and his recent writing on the family, illustrate this point. Today the boundaries between a number of 'schools of thought' are fuzzy. They will be even more difficult to define by the end of the twentieth century. The globalization of social theory is following the globalization of economic and political institutions. The state of social theory today is driven by an increased velocity in the circulation of social ideas, and of social theorists.

Notes

1. For an argument that the time is now ripe for a partial rehabilitation of Parsons within feminist theory, by discarding some ideas and

developing others, see Johnson (1989). Johnson argues in favour of the general dimensions of Parsons's evolutionary model of progress, by claiming that women's perspectives are now being integrated into a more widely shared definition of morality. She describes this process in Parsonian terms as 'value generalization'.

2. One sign of the localization of sociological explanation is a greater interest in 'locality research', in studies that focus on particular regions as units within which proximity effects can be observed. Savage *et al.* state that the emergent focus on the concept of locality is due to 'a movement away from theoreticism (where empirical investigation was disparaged), over-generalization (in which specific variations between places or countries were ignored), and against structural determinacy (in which human agency was dispelled from social scientific explanation)' (1987:28).

3. For a discussion of closure in sociology see R. Murphy (1983).

REFERENCES

Adams, B. (1988), 'Fifty years of family research', *Journal of Marriage and the Family*, **50**.

Ahrons, C. (1979), 'The binuclear family', *Alternative Lifestyles*, **2**.

Ahrons, C. and R. Rodgers (1987), *Divorced Families* (W.W. Norton: New York and London).

Aldous, J. (1977), 'Family interaction patterns', in *Annual Review of Sociology, vol. 3*, ed. A. Inkeles (Annual Reviews Inc.: Palo Alto).

Aldous, J. (1978), *Family Careers* (Wiley: New York).

Alexander, J., J. Warburton, H. Waldron and C.H. Mas (1985), 'The misuse of functional family therapy: a non-sexist rejoinder', *Journal of Marital and Family Therapy*, **11**.

Allen, K. (1989), *Single Women/Family Ties* (Sage: Newbury Park).

Allen, S. (1989), 'Locating homework in an analysis of the ideological and material constraints on women's paid work', in *Homework*, eds. E. Boris and C. Daniels, (University of Illinois Press: Urbana and Chicago).

Anderson, M. (1979), 'The relevance of family history', in *The Sociology of the Family*, ed. C. Harris (University of Keele: Keele).

Andrews, M., M. Bubolz and B. Paolucci (1980), 'An ecological approach to study of the family', *Marriage and Family Review*, **3**.

Askham, J. (1984), *Identity and Stability in Marriage* (Cambridge University Press: Cambridge).

Atwater, L. (1979), 'Getting involved', *Alternative Lifestyles*, **2**.

Atwater, L. (1982), *The Extramarital Connection* (Irvington: New York).

Avis, J.M. (1985), 'The politics of functional family therapy', *Journal of Marital and Family Therapy*, **11**.

Backett, K. (1987), 'The negotiation of fatherhood', in *Reassessing Fatherhood*, eds. C. Lewis and M. O'Brien (Sage: London).

Badham, R. (1986), *Theories of Industrial Society* (Croom Helm: London).

Bane, M.J., and P. Jargowsky (1988), 'The links between government policy and family structure', in *The Changing American Family and Public Policy*, ed. A. Cherlin (Urban Institute Press: Washington, DC).

Barrett, M. (1980), *Women's Oppression Today* (Verso: London).

Barrett, M., and M. McIntosh (1982), *The Anti-social Family* (Verso: London).

Baudrillard, J. (1983a), *In the Shadow of the Silent Majorities* (Semiotext(e): New York).

Baudrillard, J. (1983b), 'The ecstasy of communication', in *The Anti-Aesthetic*, ed. H. Foster (Bay Press: Port Townsend).

Baudrillard, J. (1988), *Selected Writings* (Stanford University Press: Stanford).

Bauman, Z. (1987), *Legislators and Interpreters* (Cornell University Press: Ithaca, NY).

Bauman, Z. (1988a), 'Is there a postmodern sociology?', *Theory Culture and Society*, **5**.

Bauman, Z. (1988b), 'Sociology and postmodernity', *Sociological Review*, **36**.

Beaujot, R. (1988), 'The family in crisis', *Canadian Journal of Sociology*, **13**.

Beavers, W.R. (1982), 'Healthy, midrange, and severely dysfunctional families', in *Normal Family Processes*, ed. F. Walsh (Guilford Press: New York and London).

Becker, G. (1981), *A Treatise on the Family* (Harvard University Press: Cambridge, MA).

Beechey, V. (1978), 'Women and production', in *Feminism and Materialism*, eds. A. Kuhn and A. Wolpe (Routledge and Kegan Paul: London).

Beechey, V. (1985), 'Familial ideology', in *Subjectivity and Social Relations*, eds. V. Beechey and J. Donald (Open University Press: Milton Keynes).

Beechey, V. (1987), *Unequal Work* (Verso: London).

Bellah, R., R. Madsen, W. Sullivan, A. Swidler and S. Tipton (1985), *Habits of the Heart* (University of California Press: Berkeley, CA).

Benn, S., and G. Gaus (1983), 'The public and the private', in *Public and Private in Social Life*, eds. S. Benn and G. Gaus (Croom Helm: London and Canberra).

Bennholdt-Thomsen, V. (1981), 'Subsistence production and extended reproduction', in *Of Marriage and the Market*, eds. K. Young, C. Wolkowitz and R. McCullagh, (CSE Books: London).

Berardo, F., and C. Shehan (1984), 'Family scholarship', *Journal of Family Issues*, **5**.

Berger, B., and P. Berger (1983), *The War Over the Family* (Doubleday: Garden City).

Berger, P., and H. Kellner (1970), 'Marriage and the construction of reality', in *Recent Sociology No.2*, ed. H. Dreitzel (Macmillan: New York).

Berman, M. (1982), *All That Is Solid Melts Into Air* (Simon and Schuster: New York).

Bernard, J. (1972) *The Future of Marriage*, (World Publishing: New York).

Bernardes, J. (1985a), '"Family ideology": identification and exploration', *Sociological Review*, **33**

Bernardes, J. (1985b), 'Do we really know what "the family" is?', in *Family and Economy in Modern Society*, ed. P. Close and R. Collins (Macmillan: Basingstoke).

Bernardes, J. (1986), 'Multidimensional developmental pathways: a proposal to facilitate the conceptualisation of "family diversity"', *Sociological Review*, **34**.

Bernardes, J. (1987), '"Doing things with words": sociology and "family policy" debates', *Sociological Review*, **35**.

Bernardes, J. (1988), 'Founding the *new* "family studies"', *Sociological Review*, **36**.

Beutler, I., W. Burr, K. Bahr and D. Herrin (1989), 'The family realm', *Journal of Marriage and the Family*, **51**.

Bimbi, F. (1989), '"The double presence": a complex model of Italian women's labor', *Marriage and Family Review*, **14**.

Bishop, L. (1983), 'The family: prison, haven or vanguard?', *Berkeley Journal of Sociology*, **28**.

Blau, F., and M. Ferber (1986), *The Economics of Women, Men, and Work* (Prentice-Hall: Englewood Cliffs, NJ).

Bograd, M. (1984), 'Family systems approaches to wife battering: a feminist critique', *American Journal of Orthopsychiatry*, **54**.

Bograd, M. (1988), 'Power, gender, and the family', in *Feminist Psychotherapies*, eds. M. Dutton-Douglas and L. Walker (Ablex: Norwood).

Boh, K. (1989), 'European family life patterns – a reappraisal', in *Changing Patterns of European Family Life*, eds. K. Boh, M. Bak, C. Clason, M. Pankratova, J. Qvortrup, G. Sgritta and K. Waerness (Routledge: London and New York).

Boh, K., M. Bak, C. Clason, M. Pankratova, J. Qvortrup, G. Sgritta and K. Waerness, eds. (1989), *Changing Patterns of European Family Life* (Routledge: London and New York).

Boris, E., and C. Daniels, eds. (1989), *Homework* (University of Illinois Press: Urbana and Chicago).

Boss, P. (1987), 'Family stress', in *Handbook of Marriage and the Family*, eds. M. Sussman and S. Steinmetz (Plenum: New York).

Boss, P. (1988), *Family Stress Management* (Sage: Newbury Park).

Boss, P., W. Doherty, R. LaRossa, W. Schumm and S. Steinmetz, eds. (forthcoming), *Sourcebook of Family Theories* (Plenum: New York).

Boss, P., and J. Greenberg (1984), 'Family boundary ambiguity', *Family Process*, 23.

Boss, P., and B. Thorne (1989), 'Family sociology and family therapy: a feminist linkage', in *Women in Families*, eds. M. McGoldrick, C. Anderson and F. Walsh (W.W. Norton: New York).

Brannen, J., and G. Wilson, eds. (1987), *Give and Take in Families* (Allen and Unwin: London).

Brenner, J., and B. Laslett (1986), 'Social reproduction and the family', in *Sociology: From Crisis to Science?*, vol. 2, ed. U. Himmelstrand (Sage: London).

Broderick, C. (1971), 'Beyond the five conceptual frameworks', *Journal of Marriage and the Family*, 33.

Broderick, C. (1988), 'To arrive where we started: the field of family studies in the 1930s', *Journal of Marriage and the Family*, 50.

Broderick, C., and J. Smith (1979), 'The general systems approach to the family', in *Contemporary Theories About the Family*, vol. 2, eds. W. Burr, R. Hill, F.I. Nye and I. Reiss (Free Press: New York).

Bruegel, I. (1978), 'What keeps the family going?', *International Socialism*, 2.

Brym, R., with B. Fox (1989), *From Culture to Power* (Oxford University Press: Toronto).

Buchmann, M. (1989), *The Script of Life in Modern Society* (University of Chicago Press: Chicago and London).

Burch, T. (1987), 'Age-sex roles and demographic change', *Canadian Studies in Population*, 14.

Burgess, E. (1926), 'The family as a unity of interacting personalities', *The Family*, 7.

Burgess, E. (1973), *On Community, Family, and Delinquency* (University of Chicago Press: Chicago and London).

Burgess, E., and L. Cottrell (1939), *Predicting Success or Failure in Marriage* (Prentice-Hall: New York).

Burgess, E., and H. Locke (1945), *The Family* (American Book Company: New York).

Burr, W. (1973), *Theory Construction and the Sociology of the Family* (Wiley: New York).

Burr, W. (1989), 'Levels of analysis in family systems theory', presented to the Theory and Methods Workshop, *National Council on Family Relations*, New Orleans.

Burr, W., D. Herrin, R. Day, I. Beutler and G. Leigh (1988), 'Epistemologies that lead to primary explanations in family science', *Family Science Review*, **1**.

Burr, W., R. Hill, F.I. Nye and I. Reiss (1979), 'Introduction', in *Contemporary Theories About the Family, vol. 1*, eds. W. Burr, R. Hill, F.I. Nye and I. Reiss (Free Press: New York).

Burr, W., and G. Leigh (1983), 'Famology: a new discipline', *Journal of Marriage and the Family*, **45**.

Burr, W., G. Leigh, R. Day and J. Constantine (1979), 'Symbolic interaction and the family', in *Contemporary Theories About the Family, vol. 2*, eds. W. Burr, R. Hill, F.I. Nye and I. Reiss (Free Press: New York).

Burton, C. (1985), *Subordination* (Allen and Unwin: Sydney).

Cancian, F. (1987), *Love in America* (Cambridge University Press: Cambridge).

Carlson, A. (1988), *Family Questions* (Transaction Books: New Brunswick, NJ, and Oxford).

Carter, B., and M. McGoldrick (1989), 'Overview: the changing family life cycle – a framework for family therapy', in *The Changing Family Life Cycle*, second edn, eds. B. Carter and M. McGoldrick (Allyn and Bacon: Boston).

Chalmers, L., and P. Smith (1987), 'Wife battering: psychological, social and physical isolation and counteracting strategies', in *Women: Isolation and Bonding*, ed. K. Storrie (Methuen: Toronto).

Chappell, N. (1989), 'Aging and the family', in *Marriage and the Family in Canada Today*, ed. G.N. Ramu (Prentice-Hall: Scarborough, Ont.).

Charles, N., and M. Kerr (1988), *Women, Food and Families* (Manchester University Press: Manchester and New York).

Cheal, D. (1978), 'Models of mass politics in Canada', *Canadian Review of Sociology and Anthropology*, **15**.

Cheal, D. (1984), 'Transactions and transformational models', in *Studies in Symbolic Interaction, vol. 5*, ed. N. Denzin (JAI Press: Greenwich CT).

Cheal, D. (1987a), '"Showing them you love them": gift giving and the dialectic of intimacy', *Sociological Review*, **35**.

Cheal, D. (1987b), 'Intergenerational transfers and life course management', in *Rethinking the Life Cycle*, eds. A. Bryman, B. Bytheway, P. Allatt and T. Keil (Macmillan: Basingstoke).

172   *Family and the state of theory*

Cheal, D. (1988a), *The Gift Economy*, (Routledge: London and New York).

Cheal, D. (1988b), 'The ritualization of family ties', *American Behavioral Scientist*, **31**.

Cheal, D. (1988c), 'Relationships in time: ritual, social structure and the life course', in *Studies in Symbolic Interaction, vol. 9*, ed. N. Denzin (JAI Press: Greenwich, CT).

Cheal, D. (1989a), 'Theoretical frameworks', in *Marriage and the Family in Canada Today*, ed. G.N. Ramu (Prentice-Hall: Scarborough, Ont.).

Cheal, D. (1989b), 'The meanings of family life', in *Family and Marriage*, ed. K. Ishwaran (Wall and Thompson: Toronto).

Cheal, D. (1989c), 'Strategies of resource management in household economies: moral economy or political economy?', in *The Household Economy*, ed. R. Wilk (Westview Press: Boulder, CT).

Cheal, D. (1989d), 'Women together: bridal showers and gender membership', in *Gender in Intimate Relationships*, eds. B. Risman and P. Schwartz (Wadsworth: Belmont).

Chilman, C. (1983), 'Prologue: the 1970s and American families (a comitragedy)', in *Contemporary Families and Alternative Lifestyles*, eds. E. Macklin and R. Rubin (Sage: Beverly Hills).

Christensen, H., ed. (1964), *Handbook of Marriage and the Family* (Rand McNally: Chicago).

Close, P. (1985), 'Family form and economic production', in *Family and Economy in Modern Society*, eds. P. Close and R. Collins (Macmillan: Basingstoke).

Close, P. (1989), 'Toward a framework for the analysis of family divisions and inequalities in modern society', in *Family Divisions and Inequalities in Modern Society*, ed. P. Close (Macmillan: Basingstoke).

Cohen, S., and M.F. Katzenstein (1988), 'The war over the family is not over the family', in *Feminism, Children, and the New Families*, eds. S. Dornbusch and M. Strober (Guilford Press: New York and London).

Collier, J., M. Rosaldo and S. Yanagisako (1982), 'Is there a family? New anthropological views', in *Rethinking the Family*, eds. B. Thorne and M. Yalom (Longman: New York and London).

Collins, R. (1985), *Sociology of Marriage and the Family* (Nelson-Hall: Chicago).

Constantine, L. (1983), 'Dysfunction and failure in open family systems', *Journal of Marriage and the Family*, **45**.

Coontz, S. (1988), *The Social Origins of Private Life* (Verso: London and New York).

Cotton, S., J. Antill and J. Cunningham (1983), 'Living together', in *The*

Family in the Modern World, eds. A. Burns, G. Bottomley and P. Jools (Allen and Unwin: Sydney).

Coward, R. (1983), *Patriarchal Precedents* (Routledge and Kegan Paul: London).

Creighton, C. (1985), 'The family and capitalism in Marxist theory', in *Marxist Sociology Revisited*, ed. M. Shaw (Macmillan: Basingstoke).

Crow, G. (1989), 'The use of the concept of "strategy" in recent sociological literature', *Sociology*, **23**.

Currie, D. (1988), 'Re-thinking what we do and how we do it', *Canadian Review of Sociology and Anthropology*, **25**.

Dahl, T.S., and A. Snare (1978), 'The coercion of privacy', in *Women, Sexuality and Social Control*, eds. C. Smart and B. Smart (Routledge and Kegan Paul: London).

Dahlström, E, (1989), 'Theories and ideologies of family functions, gender relations and human reproduction', in *Changing Patterns of European Family Life*, eds. K. Boh, M. Bak, C. Clason, M. Pankratova, J. Qvortrup, G. Sgritta and K. Waerness (Routledge: London and New York).

Dahlström, E., and R. Liljeström (1982), 'Gender and human reproduction', *Polish Sociological Bulletin*, **57–60**.

Dalla Costa, M. (1988), 'Domestic labour and the feminist movement in Italy since the 1970s', *International Sociology*, **3**.

Darling, C. (1987), 'Family life education', in *Handbook of Marriage and the Family*, eds. M. Sussman and S. Steinmetz (Plenum: New York).

Daune-Richard, A.-M. (1988), 'Gender relations and female labor', in *Feminization of the Labor Force*, eds. J. Jenson, E. Hagen and C. Reddy (Oxford University Press: New York).

Davids, L. (1980), 'Family change in Canada', *Journal of Marriage and the Family*, **42**.

Davis, K. (1948), *Human Society* (Macmillan: New York).

Davis, K., ed. (1985), *Contemporary Marriage* (Russell Sage Foundation: New York).

Davis, K. (1988), 'Wives and work: a theory of the sex-role revolution and its consequences', in *Feminism, Children, and the New Families*, eds. S. Dornbusch and M. Strober (Guilford: New York and London).

Delphy, C. (1976), 'Continuities and discontinuities in marriage and divorce', in *Sexual Divisions and Society*, eds. D. Barker and S. Allen (Tavistock: London).

Delphy, C. (1979), 'Sharing the same table', in *The Sociology of the Family*, ed. C. Harris (University of Keele: Keele).

Delphy, C. (1984), *Close to Home* (University of Massachusetts Press: Amherst).

Delphy, C., and D. Leonard (1986), 'Class analysis, gender analysis and the family', in *Gender and Stratification*, eds. R. Crompton and M. Mann (Polity Press: Cambridge).

Dencik, L. (1989), 'Growing up in the post-modern age', *Acta Sociologica*, **32**.

Denzin, N. (1986), 'Postmodern social theory', *Sociological Theory*, **4**.

Denzin, N. (1987), 'Postmodern children', *Society*, **24**.

Dhruvarajan, V. (1988), 'Religious ideology and interpersonal relationships within the family', *Journal of Comparative Family Studies*, **19**.

Dickinson, J., and B. Russell (1986), 'Introduction: the structure of reproduction in capitalist society', in *Family, Economy and State*, eds. J. Dickinson and B. Russell (St Martin's Press: New York).

DiIorio, J. (1989), 'Being and becoming coupled', in *Gender in Intimate Relationships*, eds. B. Risman and P. Schwartz (Wadsworth: Belmont).

Donzelot, J. (1979), *The Policing of Families* (Pantheon: New York).

Dornbusch, S., and M. Strober, eds. (1988), *Feminism, Children, and the New Families* (Guilford Press: New York and London).

Dumon, W. (1988), 'The meaning of family policy in western Europe and the United States', in *Social Stress and Family Development*, eds. D. Klein and J. Aldous (Guilford Press: New York).

Durkheim, E. (1964), *The Rules of Sociological Method* (Free Press: New York).

Duvall, E. (1977), *Marriage and Family Development*, fifth edn. (J.B. Lippincott: Philadelphia).

Duvall, E. (1988), 'Family development's first forty years', *Family Relations*, **37**.

Duvall, E., and B. Miller (1985), *Marriage and Family Development* (Harper and Row: New York).

Ebert, T. (1988), 'The romance of patriarchy', *Cultural Critique*, **10**.

Edelman, M. (1987), *Families in Peril* (Harvard University Press: Cambridge, MA).

Edgell, S. (1980), *Middle-Class Couples* (Allen and Unwin: London).

Edwards, J. (1989), 'The family realm: a future paradigm or failed nostalgia?', *Journal of Marriage and the Family*, **51**.

Ehrlich, C. (1971), 'The male sociologist's burden: the place of women in marriage and family texts', *Journal of Marriage and the Family*, **33**.

Eichler, M. (1973), 'Women as personal dependents', in *Women in Canada*, ed. M. Stephenson (New Press: Toronto).

Eichler, M. (1980), *The Double Standard* (St Martin's Press: New York).

Eichler, M. (1981a), 'Power, dependency, love and the sexual division of labour', *Women's Studies International Quarterly*, **4**.

Eichler, M. (1981b), 'The inadequacy of the monolithic model of the family', *Canadian Journal of Sociology*, **6**.

Eichler, M. (1983), 'Women, families and the state', in *Perspectives on Women in the 1980s*, eds. J. Turner and L. Emery (University of Manitoba Press: Winnipeg).

Eichler, M. (1985), 'The connection between paid and unpaid labour', in *Women's Paid and Unpaid Work*, ed. P. Bourne (New Hogtown Press: Toronto).

Eichler, M. (1987), 'Family change and social policies', in *Family Matters*, eds. K. Anderson, H. Armstrong, P. Armstrong, J. Drakich, M. Eichler, C. Guberman, A. Hayford, M. Luxton, J. Peters, E. Porter, C.J. Richardson and G. Tesson (Methuen: Toronto).

Eichler, M. (1988), *Families in Canada Today* (Gage: Toronto).

Eichler, M., and J. Lapointe (1985), *On the Treatment of the Sexes in Research*, (Social Sciences and Humanities Research Council of Canada: Ottawa).

Eisenstein, Z. (1982), 'The sexual politics of the New Right', in *Feminist Theory*, eds. N. Keohane, M. Rosaldo and B. Gelpi (University of Chicago Press: Chicago).

Elder, G. (1974), *Children of the Great Depression* (University of Chicago Press: Chicago and London).

Elder, G. (1977), 'Family history and the life course', *Journal of Family History*, **2**.

Elder, G. (1984), 'Families, kin, and the life course', in *Review of Child Development Research*, *vol. 7*, ed. R. Parke (University of Chicago Press: Chicago).

Elder, G. (1985), 'Perspectives on the life course', in *Life Course Dynamics*, ed. G. Elder (Cornell University Press: Ithaca, NY, and London).

Elder, G., A. Caspi and G. Downey, (1986), 'Problem behavior and family relationships', in *Human Development and the Life Course*, eds. A. Sørensen, F. Weinert and L. Sherrod (Lawrence Erlbaum: Hillsdale, NJ).

Elliot, F.R. (1986), *The Family: Change or Continuity?* (Humanities Press: Atlantic Highlands).

Engels, F. (1942), *The Origin of the Family, Private Property and the State* (International Publishers: New York).

Fahmy-Eid, N., and N. Laurin-Frenette (1986), 'Theories of the family and family/authority relationships in the educational sector in Québec and France, 1850–1960', in *The Politics of Diversity*, eds. R. Hamilton and M. Barrett (Verso: London).

Fararo, T. (1989), 'The spirit of unification in sociological theory', *Sociological Theory*, **7**.

Featherstone, M. (1988), 'In pursuit of the postmodern', *Theory Culture and Society*, **5**.

Ferguson, A. (1983), 'On conceiving motherhood and sexuality', in *Mothering*, ed. J. Trebilcot (Rowman and Allanheld: Totowa).

Ferguson, A. (1989), *Blood at the Root: Motherhood, sexuality and male dominance* (Pandora: London).

Ferguson, A., and N. Folbre (1981), 'The unhappy marriage of patriarchy and capitalism', in *Women and Revolution*, ed. L. Sargent (South End Press: Boston).

Ferree, M. (1985), 'Between two worlds: German feminist approaches to working-class women and work', *Signs*, **10**.

Ferree, M. (1987), 'Family and job for working-class women', in *Families and Work*, eds. N. Gerstel and H. Gross (Temple University Press: Philadelphia).

Finch, J. (1983), *Married to the Job* (Allen and Unwin: London).

Finch, J. (1985), 'Work, the family and the home', *International Journal of Social Economics*, **12**.

Finch, J. (1987), 'Family obligations and the life course', in *Rethinking the Life Cycle*, eds. A. Bryman, B. Bytheway, P. Allatt and T. Keil (Macmillan: Basingstoke).

Finch, J. (1989), *Family Obligations and Social Change* (Polity Press: Cambridge).

Finn, G. (1988), 'Women, fantasy and popular culture', in *Popular Cultures and Political Practices*, ed. R. Gruneau (Garamond: Toronto).

Fischer, C. (1981), 'The public and private worlds of city life', *American Sociological Review*, **46**.

Fletcher, R. (1988), *The Shaking of the Foundations* (Routledge: London and New York).

Fogarty, M., and B. Rodgers (1982), 'Family policy – international perspectives', in *Families in Britain*, eds. R.N. Rapoport, M. Fogarty and R. Rapoport (Routledge and Kegan Paul: London).

Folbre, N. (1988), 'The black four of hearts: toward a new paradigm of household economics', in *A Home Divided*, eds. D. Dwyer and J. Bruce (Stanford University Press: Stanford).

Foucault, M. (1978), *The History of Sexuality, vol. 1*, (Pantheon: New York).

Fox, B., ed. (1980), *Hidden in the Household* (The Women's Press: Toronto).

Fox, B. (1988), 'Conceptualizing "patriarchy"', *Canadian Review of Sociology and Anthropology*, **25**.

Fox, G.L. (1981), 'Family research, theory, and politics', *Journal of Marriage and the Family*, **43**.

Franklin, A. (1983), 'The family as the patient', in *Family Matters*, ed. A. Franklin (Pergamon: Oxford).

Furstenberg, F., J. Brooks-Gunn and S.P. Morgan (1987), *Adolescent Mothers in Later Life* (Cambridge University Press: Cambridge).

Furstenberg, F., and G. Spanier (1984), *Recycling the Family* (Sage: Beverly Hills).

Gagnon, A.-G. (1989), 'Social sciences and public policies', *International Social Science Journal*, **41**.

Gamarnikow, E., and J. Purvis (1983), 'Introduction', in *The Public and the Private*, eds. E. Gamarnikow, D.H.J. Morgan, J. Purvis and D. Taylorson (Heinemann: London).

Garbarino, J. (1982), *Children and Families in the Social Environment* (Aldine: New York).

Gardiner, J. (1976), 'Political economy of domestic labour in capitalist society', in *Dependence and Exploitation in Work and Marriage*, eds. D. Leonard Barker and S. Allen (Longman: London and New York).

Gee, E. (1986), 'The life course of Canadian women', *Social Indicators Research*, **18**.

Gelles, R., and M. Straus (1988), *Intimate Violence* (Simon and Schuster: New York).

Genov, N. (1989), 'National sociological traditions and the internationalization of sociology', in *National Traditions in Sociology*, ed. N. Genov (Sage: London).

Gerson, J., and K. Peiss (1985), 'Boundaries, negotiation, consciousness: reconceptualizing gender relations', *Social Problems*, **32**.

Gerson, K. (1985), *Hard Choices* (University of California Press: Berkeley, CA).

Gerson, K. (1987), 'How women choose between employment and family', in *Families and Work*, eds. N. Gerstel and H. Gross (Temple University Press: Philadelphia).

Gerstel, N., and H. Gross (1984), *Commuter Marriage* (Guilford Press: New York and London).

Giddens, A. (1979), *Central Problems in Social Theory* (Macmillan: London).

Giddens, A. (1987a), *Sociology: A brief but critical introduction*, second edn. (Harcourt Brace Jovanovich: San Diego).

Giddens, A. (1987b) *Social Theory and Modern Sociology* (Stanford University Press: Stanford).

Giles-Sims, J. (1983), *Wife Battering* (Guilford Press: New York).

Giles-Sims, J. (1987), 'Social exchange in remarried families', in *Remarriage and Stepparenting*, eds. K. Pasley and M. Ihinger-Tallman, (Guilford Press: New York and London).

Gittins, D. (1985), *The Family in Question* (Macmillan: Basingstoke).

Glazer, N. (1987), 'Servants to capital: unpaid domestic labor and paid work', in *Families and Work*, eds. N. Gerstel and H. Gross (Temple University Press: Philadelphia).

Glendinning, C., and J. Millar, eds. (1987), *Women and Poverty in Britain* (Harvester Wheatsheaf: Hemel Hempstead).

Glenn, E.N. (1987), 'Gender and the family', in *Analyzing Gender*, eds. B. Hess and M. Ferree (Sage: Newbury Park).

Glennon, L. (1979), *Women and Dualism* (Longman: New York and London).

Glick, P. (1984), 'American household structure in transition', *Family Planning Perspectives*, **16**.

Goldner, V. (1985), 'Feminism and family therapy', *Family Process*, **24**.

Goldthorpe, J.E. (1987), *Family Life in Western Societies* (Cambridge University Press: Cambridge).

Goode, W. (1963), *World Revolution and Family Patterns* (Free Press: New York).

Goode, W. (1964), *The Family* (Prentice-Hall: Englewood Cliffs, NJ).

Goode, W., E. Hopkins and H. McClure (1971), *Social Systems and Family Patterns* (Bobbs-Merrill: Indianapolis).

Graham, H. (1984), *Women, Health and the Family* (Harvester Wheatsheaf: Hemel Hempstead).

Gravenhorst, L. (1988), 'A feminist look at family development theory', in *Social Stress and Family Development*, eds. D. Klein and J. Aldous (Guilford Press: New York and London).

Gross, H. (1980), 'Dual-career couples who live apart', *Journal of Marriage and the Family*, **42**.

Groves, D., and J. Finch (1983), 'Natural selection: perspectives on entitlement to the invalid care allowance', in *A Labour of Love*, eds. J. Finch and D. Groves (Routledge and Kegan Paul: London).

Gubrium, J. (1987), 'Organizational embeddedness and family life', in *Aging, Health and Family*, ed. T. Brubaker (Sage: Newbury Park).

Gubrium, J, (1988), 'The family as project', *Sociological Review*, **36**.

Gubrium, J., and J. Holstein (1987), 'The private image: experiential location and method in family studies', *Journal of Marriage and the Family*, **49**.

Gubrium, J., and J. Holstein (1990), *What Is Family?* (Mayfield: Mountain View, CA).

Gubrium, J., and R. Lynott (1985), 'Family rhetoric as social order', *Journal of Family Issues*, **6**.

Haavind, H. (1984), 'Love and power in marriage', in *Patriarchy in a Welfare Society*, ed. H. Holter (Oslo: Universitetsforlaget).

Habermas, J. (1981), 'Modernity versus postmodernity', New German *Critique*, **22**.

Habermas, J. (1989), *The Structural Transformation of the Public Sphere* (MIT Press: Cambridge, MA).

Hadden, J. (1983), 'Televangelism and the mobilization of a New Christian Right family policy', in *Families and Religions*, eds. W. D'Antonio and J. Aldous (Sage: Beverly Hills).

Hall, C. (1979), 'The early formation of Victorian domestic ideology', in *Fit Work for Women*, ed. S. Burman, (Croom Helm: London).

Hamilton, R. (1978), *The Liberation of Women* (Allen and Unwin: London).

Hamilton, R., and M. Barrett, eds. (1986), *The Politics of Diversity* (Verso: London).

Hansen, D., and R. Hill (1964), 'Families under stress', in *Handbook of Marriage and the Family*, ed. H. Christensen (Rand McNally: Chicago).

Hansen, D., and V. Johnson (1979), 'Rethinking family stress theory', in *Contemporary Theories About the Family*, vol. *1*, eds. W. Burr, R. Hill, F.I. Nye and I. Reiss (Free Press: New York).

Hansen, K. (1987), 'Feminist conceptions of public and private', *Berkeley Journal of Sociology*, **32**.

Harding, S. (1986a), *The Science Question in Feminism* (Cornell University Press: Ithaca, NY, and London).

Harding, S. (1986b), 'The instability of the analytical categories of feminist theory', *Signs*, **11**.

Harding, S., and J. O'Barr, eds. (1987), *Sex and Scientific Inquiry* (University of Chicago Press: Chicago and London).

Hare-Mustin, R. (1987), 'The problem of gender in family therapy theory', *Family Process*, **26**.

Hare-Mustin, R. (1988), 'Family change and gender differences', *Family Relations*, **37**.

Hareven, T., ed. (1978), *Transitions* (Academic Press: New York).

Hareven, T. (1982), 'The life course and aging in historical perspective', in *Aging and Life Course Transitions*, eds. T. Hareven and K. Adams (Guilford Press: New York and London).

Hareven, T. (1987), 'Historical analysis of the family', in *Handbook of Marriage and the Family*, eds. M. Sussman and S. Steinmetz (Plenum Press: New York and London).

Hargrove, B. (1983), 'The church, the family, and the modernization process', in *Families and Religions*, eds. W. D'Antonio and J. Aldous (Sage: Beverly Hills).

Harris, C., ed. (1979), *The Sociology of the Family* (University of Keele: Keele).

Harris, C. (1983), *The Family and Industrial Society* (Allen and Unwin: London).

Hartmann, H. (1981a), 'The family as the locus of gender, class, and political struggle', *Signs*, **6**.

Hartmann, H. (1981b), 'The unhappy marriage of marxism and feminism', in *Women and Revolution*, ed. L. Sargent (South End Press: Boston).

Hartsock, N. (1983), 'The feminist standpoint', in *Discovering Reality*, eds. S. Harding and M. Hintikka (Reidel: Dordrecht).

Hartsock, N. (1985), 'Exchange theory', in *Current Perspectives in Social Theory*, vol. *6*, ed. S. McNall (JAI Press: Greenwich, CT).

Hassan, I. (1987), *The Postmodern Turn* (Ohio State University Press: Columbus).

Hernes, H. (1988), 'The welfare state citizenship of Scandinavian women', in *The Political Interests of Gender*, eds. K. Jones and A. Jónasdóttir (Sage: London).

Hertz, R. (1986), *More Equal than Others* (University of California Press: Berkeley, CA).

Hill, R. (1949), *Families Under Stress* (Harper: New York).

Hill, R. (1966), 'Contemporary developments in family theory', *Journal of Marriage and the Family*, **28**.

Hill, R. (1970), *Family Development in Three Generations* (Schenkman: Cambridge, MA).

Hill, R. (1971), 'Modern systems theory and the family', *Social Science Information*, **10**.

Hill, R. (1977), 'Social theory and family development', in *The Family Life Cycle in European Societies*, ed. J. Cuisenier (Mouton: The Hague).

Hill, R. (1984), 'Family studies and home economics: towards a theoretical orientation', *Canadian Home Economics Journal*, **34**.

Hill, R. (1986), 'Life cycle stages for types of single parent families', *Family Relations*, **35**.

Hill, R., and D. Hansen (1960), 'The identification of conceptual frameworks utilized in family study', *Marriage and Family Living*, **22**.

Hill, R., and P. Mattessich (1979), 'Family development theory and life-span development', in *Life-Span Development and Behavior*, vol. *2*, eds. P. Baltes and O. Brim (Academic Press: New York).

Hill, R., and R. Rodgers (1964), 'The developmental approach', in *Handbook of Marriage and the Family*, ed. H. Christensen (Rand McNally: Chicago).

Himmelstrand, U. (1986), 'Introduction', in *Sociology: From crisis to science?*, vol, *1*, ed. U. Himmelstrand (Sage: London).

Himmelweit, S. (1983), 'Production rules OK? Waged work and the family', in *What Is To Be Done About the Family?*, ed. L. Segal (Penguin: Harmondsworth).

Hobart, C. (1988), 'The family system in remarriage', *Journal of Marriage and the Family*, **50**.

Hobsbawm, E. (1983), 'Introduction: inventing traditions', in *The Invention of Tradition*, eds. E. Hobsbawm and T. Ranger (Cambridge University Press: Cambridge).

Höhn, C. (1987), 'The family life cycle: needed extensions of the concept', in *Family Demography*, eds. J. Bongaarts, T. Burch and K. Wachter (Clarendon Press: Oxford).

Höhn, C., and K. Lüscher (1988), 'The changing family in the Federal Republic of Germany', *Journal of Family Issues*, **9**.

Holman, T., and W. Burr (1980), 'Beyond the beyond: the growth of family theories in the 1970s', *Journal of Marriage and the Family*, **42**.

Holstein, J. (1988), 'Studying "family usage"', *Journal of Contemporary Ethnography*, **17**.

Holter, H. (1984), 'Women's research and social theory', in *Patriarchy in a Welfare Society*, ed. H. Holter (Oslo: Universitetsforlaget).

Humphries, J. (1977), 'Class struggle and the persistence of the working-class family', *Cambridge Journal of Economics*, **1**.

Humphries, J. (1982), 'The working-class family: a marxist perspective', in *The Family in Political Thought*, ed. J. Elshtain (University of Massachusetts Press: Amherst).

Humphries, J. (1987), 'The origin of the family', in *Engels Revisited*, eds. J. Sayers, M. Evans and N. Redclift (Tavistock: London and New York).

Hunt, J., and L. Hunt (1982), 'The dualities of careers and families', *Social Problems*, **29**.

Hutter, M. (1985), 'Symbolic interaction and the study of the family', in *Studies in Symbolic Interaction, Supplement 1*, ed. R.S. Perinbanayagam (JAI Press: Greenwich, CT).

Ihinger-Tallman, M. (1988), 'Research on stepfamilies', in *Annual Review of Sociology, vol. 14*, ed. W.R. Scott (Annual Reviews Inc.: Palo Alto).

Ihinger-Tallman, M. and K. Pasley (1987), *Remarriage* (Sage: Newbury Park).

Jacobson, N. (1985), 'Beyond empiricism: the politics of marital therapy', in *Family Studies Review Yearbook, vol. 3*, eds. B. Miller and D. Olson, (Sage: Beverly Hills).

Jallinoja, R. (1989), 'Women between the family and employment', in *Changing Patterns of European Family Life*, eds. K. Boh, M. Bak, C. Clason, M. Pankratova, J. Qvortrup, G. Sgritta and K. Waerness (Routledge: London and New York).

James, K., and D. McIntyre (1983), 'The reproduction of families: the social role of family therapy?', *Journal of Marital and Family Therapy*, **9**.

Jehu, D. (1980a), 'Assessment of sexual dysfunction', in *Perspectives on Family Therapy*, ed. D. Freeman (Butterworth: Vancouver).

Jehu, D. (1980b), 'Treatment of sexual dysfunction', in *Perspectives on Family Therapy*, ed. D. Freeman, (Butterworth: Vancouver).

Jensen, A.-M. (1989), 'Care giving and socialization in the view of declining fertility and increasing female employment', *Marriage and Family Review*, **14**.

Johnson, M. (1989), 'Feminism and the theories of Talcott Parsons', in *Feminism and Sociological Theory*, ed. R. Wallace (Sage: Newbury Park).

Joshi, H. (1987), 'The cost of caring', in *Women and Poverty in Britain*, eds. C. Glendinning and J. Millar (Harvester Wheatsheaf: Hemel Hempstead).

Joshi, H., ed. (1989), *The Changing Population of Britain* (Blackwell: Oxford).

Jurich, J. (1989), 'The family realm: expanding its parameters', *Journal of Marriage and the Family*, **51**.

Kantor, D., and W. Lehr (1975), *Inside the Family* (Jossey-Bass: San Francisco).

Kaslow, F. (1987), 'Marital and family therapy', in *Handbook of Marriage and the Family*, eds. M. Sussman and S. Steinmetz, (Plenum: New York and London).

Katz, R., and R. Briger (1988), 'Modernity and the quality of marriage in Israel', *Journal of Comparative Family Studies*, **19**.

Kellner, D. (1988), 'Postmodernism as social theory', *Theory Culture and Society*, **5**.

Kelly, R. (1988), 'Poverty, the family, and public policy', in *Families and Economic Distress*, eds. P. Voydanoff and L. Majka (Sage: Newbury Park).

Kerber, U. (1987), 'German social report: marriage and family', *Social Indicators Research*, **19**.

Kiernan, K. (1988), 'The British family', *Journal of Family Issues*, **9**.

Kitzinger, S. (1978), *Women as Mothers* (Random House: New York).

Kobrin, F. (1976), 'The primary individual and the family', *Journal of Marriage and the Family*, **38**.

Kohli, M. (1986), 'The world we forgot: a historical review of the life course', in *Later Life*, ed. V. Marshall (Sage: Beverly Hills).

Komarovsky, M. (1988), 'The new feminist scholarship', *Journal of Marriage and the Family*, **50**.

Kooistra, P. (1989), 'Misconstruction of the American family', presented to the American Sociological Association, San Francisco.

Kuhn, A. (1978), 'Structures of patriarchy and capital in the family', in *Feminism and Materialism*, eds. A. Kuhn and A. Wolpe (Routledge and Kegan Paul: London).

Lamphere, L. (1987), *From Working Daughters to Working Mothers* (Cornell University Press: Ithaca NY, and London).

Land, H. (1979), 'The boundaries between the state and the family', in *The Sociology of the Family*, ed. C.C. Harris (University of Keele: Keele).

Land, H. (1983), 'Poverty and gender', in *The Structure of Disadvantage*, ed. M. Brown (Heinemann: London).

Land, H., and H. Rose (1985), 'Compulsory altruism for some or an altruistic society for all', in *In Defence of Welfare*, eds. P. Bean, J. Ferris and D. Whynes (Tavistock: London).

Lasch, C, (1977), *Haven in a Heartless World* (Basic: New York).

Laslett, B. (1973), 'The family as a public and private institution', *Journal of Marriage and the Family*, **35**.

Laslett, B., and J. Brenner (1989), 'Gender and social reproduction', in *Annual Review of Sociology, vol. 15*, ed. W.R. Scott (Annual Reviews Inc.: Palo Alto).

Laws, J.L. (1971), 'A feminist review of the marital adjustment literature', *Journal of Marriage and the Family*, **33**.

Lawson, A. (1988), *Adultery* (Basic: New York).

Leavitt, R., and M. Power (1989), 'Emotional socialization in the postmodern era', *Social Psychology Quarterly*, **52**.

Lee, G. (1980), 'Kinship in the seventies', *Journal of Marriage and the Family*, **42**.

Lenero-Otero, L., ed. (1977), *Beyond the Nuclear Family Model*, (Sage: London).

Levinger, G. (1979), 'A social exchange view on the dissolution of pair relationships', in *Social Exchange in Developing Relationships*, eds. R. Burgess and T. Huston (Academic Press: New York).

Lewis, J. (1980), *The Politics of Motherhood* (Croom Helm: London).

Lewis, J. (1983), 'Introduction', in *Women's Welfare/Women's Rights*, ed. J. Lewis (Croom Helm: London).

Lewis, R., and G. Spanier (1979), 'Theorizing about the quality and stability of marriage', in *Contemporary Theories About the Family, vol. 1*, eds. W. Burr, R. Hill, F.I. Nye and I. Reiss (Free Press: New York).

Lewis, R., and G. Spanier (1982), 'Marital quality, marital stability, and social exchange', in *Family Relationships*, ed. F.I. Nye (Sage: Beverly Hills).

Libby, R., and R. Whitehurst, eds. (1973), *Renovating Marriage*, (Consensus Publishers: Danville).

Libby, R., and R. Whitehurst, eds. (1977), *Marriage and Alternatives* (Scott, Foresman and Company: Glenview).

Libow, J., P. Raskin and B. Caust (1982), 'Feminist and family systems therapy', *American Journal of Family Therapy*, **10**.

Liljeström, R. (1982), 'Planning and organizing alternatives stemming from the sphere of reproduction', *Acta Sociologica*, **25**.

Liljeström, R. (1983), 'The public child, the commercial child, and our child', in *The Child and Other Cultural Inventions*, eds. F. Kessel and A. Siegel (Praeger: New York).

Liljeström, R. (1986), 'Gender systems and the family', in *Sociology: From Crisis to Science?*, vol. 2, ed. U. Himmelstrand (Sage: London).

Linton, R. (1936), *The Study of Man* (Appleton-Century: New York).

Long, N. (1984), 'Introduction', in *Family and Work in Rural Societies*, ed. N. Long (Tavistock: London and New York).

Lopata, H. (1987), 'Women's family roles in life course perspective', in *Analyzing Gender*, eds. B. Hess and M. Ferree (Sage: Newbury Park).

Luhmann, N. (1986), *Love as Passion* (Polity Press: Cambridge).

Lupri, E., and G. Symons (1982), 'The emerging symmetrical family: fact or fiction?', *International Journal of Comparative Sociology*, **23**.

Luxton, M. (1980), *More Than a Labour of Love* (The Women's Press: Toronto).

Luxton, M. (1983), 'Two hands for the clock: changing patterns in the gendered division of labour in the home', *Studies in Political Economy*, **12**.

Lyotard, J.-F. (1984), *The Postmodern Condition* (University of Minnesota Press: Minneapolis).

Mace, D. (1986), 'Marriage and family enrichment', in *Family Therapy Sourcebook*, eds. F. Piercy and D. Sprenkle (Guilford Press: New York and London).

Macfarlane, A. (1979), *The Origins of English Individualism* (Cambridge University Press: New York).

Mackie, M. (1987), *Constructing Women and Men* (Holt, Rinehart and Winston: Toronto).

Mackintosh, M. (1979), 'Domestic labour and the household', in *Fit Work for Women*, ed. S. Burman (Croom Helm: London).

Mackintosh, M. (1981), 'Gender and economics', in *Of Marriage and the Market*, eds. K. Young, C. Wolkowitz and R. McCullagh (CSE Books: London).

Maddock, J. (1989), 'Healthy family sexuality', *Family Relations*, **38**.

Malos, E., ed. (1980), *The Politics of Housework* (Allison and Busby: London).

Marshall, B. (1988), 'Feminist theory and critical theory', *Canadian Review of Sociology and Anthropology*, **25**.

Marx, K. (1977), *Capital, vol. 1* (Vintage Books: New York).

Mattessich, P., and R. Hill (1987), 'Life cycle and family development', in *Handbook of Marriage and the Family*, eds. M. Sussman and S. Steinmetz (Plenum: New York and London).

Mayer, K., and U. Schoepflin (1989), 'The state and the life course', in *Annual Review of Sociology, vol. 15*, ed. W.R. Scott (Annual Reviews Inc.: Palo Alto).

McBride, B. (1989), 'Stress and fathers' parental competence', *Family Relations*, **38**.

McDaniel, S. (1988), 'The changing Canadian family', in *Changing Patterns: Women in Canada*, eds. S. Burt, L. Code and L. Dorney (McClelland and Stewart: Toronto).

McIntosh, M. (1978), 'The state and the oppression of women', in *Feminism and Materialism*, eds. A. Kuhn and A. Wolpe (Routledge and Kegan Paul: London).

McIntosh, M. (1979), 'The welfare state and the needs of the dependent family', in *Fit Work for Women*, ed. S. Burman (Croom Helm: London).

McKinney, R. (1986), 'Toward a resolution of the modernist/postmodernist debate', *Philosophy Today*, **30**.

McLain, R., and A. Weigert (1979), 'Toward a phenomenological sociology of family', in *Contemporary Theories About the Family, vol. 2*, eds. W. Burr, R. Hill, F.I. Nye and I. Reiss (Free Press: New York).

Menaghan, E. (1989), 'Escaping from the family realm', *Journal of Marriage and the Family*, **51**.

Merton, R. (1957), *Social Theory and Social Structure* (Free Press: New York).

Meyer, J, (1986), 'The self and the life course', in *Human Development and the Life Course*, eds. A. Sørensen, F. Weinert and L. Sherrod (Lawrence Erlbaum: Hillsdale, NJ).

Meyer, J., F. Ramirez, H. Walker, N. Langton and S. O'Connor (1988), 'The state and the institutionalization of the relations between women and children', in *Feminism, Children, and the New Families*, eds. S. Dornbusch and M. Strober (Guilford Press: New York and London).

Meyer, P. (1983), *The Child and the State* (Cambridge University Press: Cambridge).

Miles, A. (1985), 'Economism and feminism', in *Feminist Marxism or Marxist Feminism*, eds. P. Armstrong, H. Armstrong, P. Connelly and A. Miles (Garamond: Toronto).

Millar, J., and C. Glendinning (1987), 'Invisible women, invisible poverty', in *Women and Poverty in Britain*, eds. C. Glendinning and J. Millar (Harvester Wheatsheaf: Hemel Hempstead).

Mitterauer, M., and R. Sieder (1982), *The European Family*, (Blackwell: Oxford).

Moch, L., N. Folbre, D. Smith, L. Cornell and L. Tilly (1987), 'Family strategy: a dialogue', *Historical Methods*, **20**.

Modell, J. (1978), 'Patterns of consumption, acculturation, and family income strategies in late nineteenth-century America', in *Family and Population in Nineteenth-Century America*, eds. T. Hareven and M. Vinovskis, (Princeton University Press: Princeton, NJ).

Moen, P., and A. Schorr (1987), 'Families and social policy', in *Handbook of Marriage and the Family*, eds. M. Sussman and S. Steinmetz (Plenum Press: New York and London).

Molyneux, M. (1979), 'Beyond the domestic labour debate', *New Left Review*, **116**.

Montgomery, J., and W. Fewer (1988), *Family Systems and Beyond* (Human Sciences Press: New York).

Morgan, D.H.J. (1975), *Social Theory and the Family* (Routledge and Kegan Paul: London and Boston).

Morgan, D.H.J. (1979), 'New directions in family research and theory', in *The Sociology of the Family*, ed. C.C. Harris (University of Keele: Keele).

Morgan, D.H.J. (1985), *The Family, Politics and Social Theory* (Routledge and Kegan Paul: London and Boston).

Morgan, D.H.J. (1989), 'Strategies and sociologists', *Sociology*, **23**.

Morgan, D.H.J. (1990), 'Issues of critical sociological theory: men in families', in *Fashioning Family Theory*, ed. J. Sprey (Sage: Newbury Park).

Morgan, P. (1985), 'Constructing images of deviance: a look at state intervention into the problem of wife-battery', in *Marital Violence*, ed. N. Johnson (Routledge and Kegan Paul: London).

Morris, L. (1989), 'Household strategies: the individual, the collectivity, and the labour market – the case of married couples', *Work, Employment and Society*, **3**.

Mortimer, J., and G. Sorensen (1984), 'Men, women, work, and family', in *Women in the Workplace*, eds. K. Borman, D. Quarm and S. Gideonse (Ablex: Norwood).

Mowrer, E. (1932), *The Family*, (University of Chicago Press: Chicago).

Mullins, N. (1973), *Theories and Theory Groups in Contemporary American Sociology* (Harper and Row: New York).

Mullins, N. (1983), 'Theories and theory groups revisited', in *Sociological Theory 1983*, ed. R. Collins (Jossey-Bass: San Francisco).

Münch, R. (1989), 'Structures, cultures, and knowledge', in *Social Structure and Culture*, ed. H. Haferkamp (De Gruyter: Berlin and New York).

Murphy, J. (1988), 'Making sense of postmodern sociology', *British Journal of Sociology*, **39**.

Murphy, J. (1989), *Postmodern Social Analysis and Criticism* (Greenwood: New York).

Murphy, M. (1987), 'Measuring the family life cycle', in *Rethinking the Life Cycle*, eds. A. Bryman, B. Bytheway, P. Allatt and T. Keil (Macmillan: Basingstoke).

Murphy, R. (1983), 'The struggle for scholarly recognition', *Theory and Society*, **12**.

Murphy-Lawless, J. (1988), 'The obstetric view of feminine identity', in *Gender and Discourse*, eds. A. Todd and S. Fisher (Ablex: Norwood).

Murphy-Lawless, J. (1989), 'Male texts and female bodies', in *Text and Talk as Social Practice*, ed. B. Torode (Foris: Dordrecht).

Murstein, B. (1973), 'A theory of marital choice applied to interracial marriage', in *Interracial Marriage*, eds. I. Stuart and L. Abt (Grossman: New York).

Nave-Herz, R. (1989), 'The significance of the family and marriage in the Federal Republic of Germany', in *Family Divisions and Inequalities in Modern Society*, ed. P. Close (Macmillan: Basingstoke).

Nelson, M. (1989), 'Negotiating care: relationships between family daycare providers and mothers', *Feminist Studies*, **15**.

Nelson, M. (1990), 'Mothering others' children', *Signs*, **15**.

Nelson, R., and F. Skidmore, eds. (1983), *American Families and the Economy* (National Academy Press: Washington, DC).

Nicholson, L. (1986), *Gender and History* (Columbia University Press: New York).

Nissel, M. (1982), 'Families and social change since the Second World War', in *Families in Britain*, eds. R.N. Rapoport, M. Fogarty and R. Rapoport (Routledge and Kegan Paul: London).

Nock, S. (1979), 'The family life cycle: empirical or conceptual tool?', *Journal of Marriage and the Family*, **41**.

Nye, F.I. (1979), 'Choice, exchange, and the family', in *Contemporary Theories About the Family*, vol. 2, eds. W. Burr, R. Hill, F.I. Nye and I. Reiss (Free Press: New York).

Nye, F.I. (1980), 'Family mini theories as special instances of choice and exchange theory', *Journal of Marriage and the Family*, **42**.

Nye, F.I. (1982), 'The basic theory', in *Family Relationships*, ed. F.I. Nye (Sage: Beverly Hills).

Nye, F.I. (1988), 'Fifty years of family research, 1937–1987', *Journal of Marriage and the Family*, **50**.

Nye, F.I. and F. Berardo, eds. (1966), *Emerging Conceptual Frameworks in Family Analysis* (Macmillan: New York).

Oakley, A. (1974), *The Sociology of Housework* (Martin Robertson: London).

Oakley, A. (1976), 'Wisewoman and medicine man: changes in the management of childbirth', in *The Rights and Wrongs of Women*, eds. J. Mitchell and A. Oakley (Penguin: Harmondsworth).

Oakley, A. (1979), *Becoming a Mother* (Martin Robertson: Oxford).

Oakley, A. (1980), *Women Confined* (Schocken: New York).

Oakley, A. (1984), *The Captured Womb* (Blackwell: Oxford).

Oakley, A. (1987), 'From walking wombs to test-tube babies', in *Reproductive Technologies*, ed. M. Stanworth (Polity Press: Cambridge).

O'Brien, M. (1979), 'Reproducing marxist man', in *The Sexism of Social and Political Theory*, eds. L. Clark and L. Lange (University of Toronto Press: Toronto).

O'Brien, M. (1981), *The Politics of Reproduction* (Routledge and Kegan Paul: London and Boston).

Oliker, S. (1989), *Best Friends and Marriage* (University of California Press: Berkeley, CA).

Olson, D., H. McCubbin, H. Barnes, A. Larsen, M. Muxen and M. Wilson (1983), *Families: What Makes Them Work* (Sage: Beverly Hills).

O'Neill, J. (1986), 'The medicalization of social control', *Canadian Review of Sociology and Anthropology*, **23**.

Oppenheimer, V. (1982), *Work and the Family* (Academic Press: New York).

Ory, M., and R. Leik (1983), 'A general framework for family impact analysis', in *Family Studies Review Yearbook*, vol. 1, eds. D. Olson and B. Miller (Sage: Beverly Hills).

Osmond, M. (1987), 'Radical-critical theories', in *Handbook of Marriage and the Family*, eds. M. Sussman and S. Steinmetz (Plenum: New York).

Osmond, M. (1989), 'Demystifying the public–private dichotomy', presented to the Theory and Methodology Workshop, National Council on Family Relations (New Orleans).

Owen, S. (1987), 'Household production and economic efficiency', *Work, Employment and Society*, **1**.

Pahl, J. (1980), 'Patterns of money management within marriage', *Journal of Social Policy*, **9**.

Pahl, J. (1983), 'The allocation of money and the structuring of inequality within marriage', *Sociological Review*, **31**.

Pahl, J. (1985), 'Introduction', in *Private Violence and Public Policy*, ed. J. Pahl (Routledge and Kegan Paul: London).

Pahl, R. (1984), *Divisions of Labour* (Blackwell: Oxford).

Paolucci, B., O. Hall and N. Axinn (1977), *Family Decision Making: An Ecosystem Approach* (Wiley: New York).

Parsons, T. (1943), 'The kinship system of the contemporary United States', *American Anthropologist*, **45**.

Parsons, T. (1949), 'The social structure of the family', in *The Family: Its function and destiny*, ed. R. Anshen (Harper: New York).

Parsons, T. (1955), 'The American family', in *Family, Socialization and Interaction Process*, T. Parsons and R. Bales (Free Press: Glencoe, IL).

Parsons, T. (1964), *The Social System* (Free Press: New York).

Parsons, T. (1966), *Societies: Evolutionary and Comparative Perspectives* (Prentice-Hall: Englewood Cliffs).

Parsons, T. (1971a), 'The normal American family', in *Readings on the Sociology of the Family*, eds. B. Adams and T. Weirath (Markham: Chicago).

Parsons, T. (1971b), *The System of Modern Societies* (Prentice-Hall: Englewood Cliffs, NJ).

Parsons, T. (1977), *Social Systems and the Evolution of Action Theory* (Free Press: New York).

Pasley, K. (1987), 'Family boundary ambiguity', in *Remarriage and Stepparenting*, eds. K. Pasley and M. Ihinger-Tallman (Guilford Press: New York and London).

Pateman, C. (1983), 'Feminist critiques of the public/private dichotomy', in *Public and Private in Social Life*, eds. S. Benn and G. Gaus (Croom Helm: London and Canberra).

Paterson, F. (1988), 'Schooling the family', *Sociology*, **22**.

Perlman, D., and K. Rook (1987), 'Social support, social deficits, and the family', in *Applied Social Psychology Annual, vol. 7: Family processes and problems*, ed. S. Oskamp (Sage: Newbury Park).

Piotrkowski, C. (1979), *Work and the Family System* (Free Press: New York).

Pleck, J. (1977), 'The work-family role system', *Social Problems*, **24**.

Popenoe, D. (1988), *Disturbing the Nest* (Aldine de Gruyter: New York).

Rapoport, R. (1989), 'Ideologies about family forms: towards diversity', in *Changing Patterns of European Family Life*, eds. K. Boh, M. Bak, C. Clason, M. Pankratova, J. Qvortrup, G. Sgritta and K. Waerness (Routledge: London and New York).

Rapoport, R.N., M. Fogarty and R. Rapoport, eds. (1982), *Families in Britain* (Routledge and Kegan Paul: London).

Rapp, R. (1978), 'Family and class in contemporary America', *Science and Society*, **42**.

Reiger, K. (1985), *The Disenchantment of the Home* (Oxford University Press: Melbourne).

Reiger, K. (1987), 'All but the kitchen sink: on the significance of domestic science and the silence of social theory', *Theory and Society*, **16**.

Reiss, I. (1965), 'The universality of the family', *Journal of Marriage and the Family*, **27**.

Reiss, I. (1981), 'Some observations on ideology and sexuality in America', *Journal of Marriage and the Family*, **43**.

Reiss, I. (1986), *Journey Into Sexuality* (Prentice-Hall: Englewood Cliffs, NJ).

Reiss, I., and B. Miller (1979), 'Heterosexual permissiveness', in *Contemporary Theories About the Family*, vol. *1*, eds. W. Burr, R. Hill, F.I. Nye and I. Reiss (Free Press: New York).

Reiter, R. (1975), 'Men and women in the South of France: public and private domains', in *Toward an Anthropology of Women*, ed. R. Reiter (Monthly Review Press: New York).

Renvoize, J. (1985), *Going Solo* (Routledge and Kegan Paul: London).

Richards, L. (1989), 'Family and home ownership in Australia – the nexus of ideologies', *Marriage and Family Review*, **14**.

Richardson, L. (1985), *The New Other Woman* (Free Press: New York).

Richardson, L. (1988), 'Secrecy and status: the social construction of forbidden relationships', *American Sociological Review*, **53**.

Riley, D. (1983), *War in the Nursery* (Virago: London).

Rindfuss, R., C.G. Swicegood and R. Rosenfeld (1987), 'Disorder in the life course', *American Sociological Review*, **52**.

Risman, B., and P. Schwartz (1989), 'Being gendered: a microstructural view of intimate relationships', in *Gender in Intimate Relationships*, eds. B. Risman and P. Schwartz (Wadsworth: Belmont).

Ritzer, G. (1988), *Sociological Theory*, second edn. (Knopf: New York).

Rosenthal, C. (1983), 'Aging, ethnicity and the family: beyond the modernization thesis', *Canadian Ethnic Studies*, **15**.

Roussel, L., and I. Théry (1988), 'France: demographic change and family policy since World War II', *Journal of Family Issues*, **9**.

Rueschemeyer, M. (1988), 'New family forms in a state socialist society', *Journal of Family Issues*, **9**.

Russell, C., D. Olson, D. Sprenkle and R. Atilano (1985), 'From family symptom to family system', in *Family Studies Review Yearbook*, vol. *3*, eds. B. Miller and D. Olson (Sage: Beverly Hills).

Ryant, J. (1989), 'The family, law, and social policy', in *Marriage and the Family in Canada Today*, ed. G.N. Ramu (Prentice-Hall: Scarborough, Ont.).

Sacks, K. (1974), 'Engels revisited: women, the organization of production, and private property', in *Woman, Culture, and Society*, eds. M.Z. Rosaldo and L. Lamphere (Stanford University Press: Stanford).

Sangren, S. (1988), 'Rhetoric and the authority of ethnography: "postmodernism" and the social reproduction of texts', *Current Anthropology*, **29**.

Saraceno, C. (1984), 'Shifts in public and private boundaries: women as mothers and service workers in Italian daycare', *Feminist Studies*, **10**.

Sauer, W., and R. Coward (1985), 'The role of social support networks in the care of the elderly', in *Social Support Networks and the Care of the Elderly*, eds. W. Sauer and R. Coward, (Springer: New York).

Savage, M., J. Barlow, S. Duncan and P. Saunders (1987), 'Locality research', *Quarterly Journal of Social Affairs*, **3**.

Sayers, J., M. Evans and N. Redclift, eds. (1987), *Engels Revisited* (Tavistock: London and New York).

Scanzoni, J. (1972), *Sexual Bargaining* (Prentice-Hall: Englewood Cliffs, NJ).

Scanzoni, J. (1978), *Sex Roles, Women's Work, and Marital Conflict* (D.C. Heath: Lexington).

Scanzoni, J. (1979), 'Social processes and power in families', in *Contemporary Theories About the Family, vol. 1*, eds. W. Burr, R. Hill, F.I. Nye and I. Reiss (Free Press: New York).

Scanzoni, J. (1987), 'Families in the 1980s: time to refocus our thinking', *Journal of Family Issues*, **8**.

Scanzoni, J., K. Polonko, J. Teachman and L. Thompson (1989), *The Sexual Bond* (Sage: Newbury Park).

Scanzoni, J., and M. Szinovacz (1980), *Family Decision-Making* (Sage: Beverly Hills).

Seccombe, W. (1974), 'The housewife and her labour under capitalism', *New Left Review*, **83**.

Seccombe, W. (1980), 'Domestic labour and the working-class household', in *Hidden in the Household*, ed. B. Fox (The Women's Press: Toronto).

Seccombe, W. (1986a), 'Marxism and demography', in *Family, Economy and State*, eds. J. Dickinson and B. Russell (St Martin's Press: New York).

Seccombe, W. (1986b), 'Reflections on the domestic labour debate and prospects for marxist-feminist synthesis', in *The Politics of Diversity*, eds. R. Hamilton and M. Barrett (Verso: London).

Sennett, R. (1970), *Families against the City* (Harvard University Press: Cambridge, MA).

Sgritta, G. (1989), 'Towards a new paradigm', in *Changing Patterns of*

European Family Life, eds. K. Boh, M. Bak, C. Clason, M. Pankratova, J. Qvortrup, G. Sgritta and K. Waerness (Routledge: London and New York).

Shanas, E. (1979), 'The family as a social support system in old age', *The Gerontologist*, **19**.

Sharistanian, J. (1987), 'Bibliographical essay', in *Beyond the Public/ Domestic Dichotomy*, ed. J. Sharistanian (Greenwood Press: New York).

Shera, W., and S. Willms (1980), 'Family impact statements', in *Perspectives on Family Therapy*, ed. D. Freeman (Butterworth: Vancouver).

Shkilnyk, A. (1984), *A Poison Stronger than Love* (Yale University Press: New Haven).

Siltanen, J., and M. Stanworth (1984), 'The politics of private woman and public man', in *Women and the Public Sphere*, eds. J. Siltanen and M. Stanworth (St Martin's Press: New York).

Skolnick, A. (1983), *The Intimate Environment* (Little, Brown: Boston).

Slater, P. (1984), 'Sexual adequacy in America', in *Framing the Family*, eds. B. Adams and J. Campbell (Waveland Press: Prospect Heights).

Sluzki, C. (1985), 'Process, structure and world views: toward an integrated view of systemic models in family therapy', in *Family Studies Review Yearbook, vol. 3*, eds. B. Miller and D. Olson (Sage: Beverly Hills).

Smart, C., and B. Smart, eds. (1978), *Women, Sexuality and Social Control* (Routledge and Kegan Paul: London).

Smith, D. (1973), 'Women, the family and corporate capitalism', in *Women in Canada*, ed. M. Stephenson (New Press: Toronto).

Smith, D. (1974), 'Women's perspective as a radical critique of sociology', *Sociological Inquiry*, **44**.

Smith, D. (1975), 'An analysis of ideological structures and how women are excluded', *Canadian Review of Sociology and Anthropology*, **12**.

Smith, D. (1981), 'Women's inequality and the family', in *Inequality*, eds. A. Moscovitch and G. Drover (University of Toronto Press: Toronto).

Smith, D. (1985), 'Women, class and family', in *Women, Class, Family and the State*, eds. V. Burstyn and D. Smith, (Garamond: Toronto).

Smith, D. (1987), *The Everyday World as Problematic* (Northeastern University Press: Boston).

Smith, J. (1985), 'A familistic religion in a modern society', in *Contemporary Marriage*, ed. K. Davis (Russell Sage Foundation: New York).

Spanier, G. (1976), 'Measuring dyadic adjustment', *Journal of Marriage and the Family*, **38**.

Sprey, J. (1990), 'Theoretical practice in family studies', in *Fashioning Family Theory*, ed. J. Sprey (Sage: Newbury Park).

Stacey, J., and B. Thorne (1985), 'The missing feminist revolution in sociology', *Social Problems*, **32**.

Stacey, M. (1981), 'The division of labour revisited or overcoming the two Adams', in *Practice and Progress*, eds. P. Abrams, R. Deem, J. Finch and P. Rock (Allen and Unwin: London).

Stacey, M., and M. Price (1981), *Women, Power, and Politics* (Tavistock: London and New York).

Stapleton, C. (1980), 'Reformulation of the family life-cycle concept', *Environment and Planning A*, **12**.

Stark, E., and A. Flitcraft (1983), 'Social knowledge, social policy, and the abuse of women', in *The Dark Side of Families*, eds. D. Finkelhor, R. Gelles, G. Hotaling and M. Straus (Sage: Beverly Hills).

Stets, J. (1988), *Domestic Violence and Control* (Springer-Verlag: New York).

Stichter, S., and J. Parpart (1988), 'Introduction: towards a materialist perspective on African women', in *Patriarchy and Class*, eds. S. Stichter and J. Parpart (Westview Press, Boulder: CT, and London).

Stolcke, V. (1981), 'Women's labours: the naturalisation of social inequality and women's subordination', in *Of Marriage and the Market*, eds. K. Young, C. Wolkowitz and R. McCullagh (CSE Books: London).

Storrie, K. (1987), 'Introduction: the ecology of gender', in *Women: Isolation and bonding*, ed. K. Storrie (Methuen: Toronto).

Stryker, S. (1968), 'Identity salience and role performance', *Journal of Marriage and the Family*, **30**.

Sussman, M. (1976), 'The family life of old people', in *Handbook of Aging and the Social Sciences*, eds. R. Binstock and E. Shanas (Van Nostrand Reinhold: New York).

Sydie, R.A. (1987), *Natural Women, Cultured Men* (Methuen: Toronto).

Taggart, M. (1985), 'The feminist critique in epistemological perspective', *Journal of Marital and Family Therapy*, **11**.

Tallman, I. (1988), 'Problem solving in families', in *Social Stress and Family Development*, eds. D. Klein and J. Aldous (Guilford Press: New York and London).

Targ, D. (1981), 'Ideology and utopia in family studies since the Second World War', *Women's Studies International Quarterly*, **4**.

Taubin, S., and E. Mudd (1983), 'Contemporary traditional families', in *Contemporary Families and Alternative Lifestyles*, eds. E. Macklin and R. Rubin (Sage: Beverly Hills).

Thomas, D., and G. Henry, (1985), 'The religion and family connection', *Journal of Marriage and the Family*, **47**.

Thomas, D., and J. Wilcox (1987), 'The rise of family theory', in *Handbook of Marriage and the Family*, eds. M. Sussman and S. Steinmetz (Plenum: New York).

Thorne, B. (1982), 'Feminist rethinking of the family', in *Rethinking the Family*, eds. B. Thorne and M. Yalom (Longman: New York and London).

Thornton, A. (1989), 'Changing attitudes toward family issues in the United States', *Journal of Marriage and the Family*, **51**.

Thornton, A., and D. Camburn (1989), 'Religious participation and adolescent sexual behavior and attitudes', *Journal of Marriage and the Family*, **51**.

Tilly, L., and J. Scott (1978), *Women, Work, and Family* (Holt, Rinehart and Winston: New York).

Tiryakian, E. (1979), 'The significance of schools in the development of sociology', in *Contemporary Issues in Theory and Research*, eds. W. Snizek, E. Fuhrman and M. Miller (Greenwood: Westport, CO).

Tomm, K. (1980), 'Towards a cybernetic systems approach to family therapy at the University of Calgary', in *Perspectives on Family Therapy*, ed. D. Freeman, (Butterworth: Vancouver).

Touraine, A. (1977), *The Self-Production of Society* (University of Chicago Press: Chicago and London).

Touraine, A. (1984), 'The waning sociological image of social life', *International Journal of Comparative Sociology*, **25**.

Touraine, A. (1988), 'Modernity and cultural specificities', *International Social Science Journal*, **40**.

Trifiletti, R. (1989), 'The impact of social policies on the Italian family of the seventies', *Marriage and Family Review*, **14**.

Trost, J. (1977), 'The family life cycle: a problematic concept', in *The Family Life Cycle in European Societies*, ed. J. Cuisenier (Mouton: The Hague).

Trost, J. (1980), 'The concept of one-parent family', *Journal of Comparative Family Studies*, **11**.

Trost, J. (1988), 'Conceptualising the family', *International Sociology*, **3**.

Trost, J. (1990), 'Do we mean the same by the concept of family?', *Communication Research*, **17**.

Turner, B. (1989), 'Commentary: some reflections on cumulative theorizing in sociology', in *Theory Building in Sociology*, ed. J. Turner (Sage: Newbury Park).

Turner, J. (1989), 'Introduction: can sociology be a cumulative science?', in *Theory Building in Sociology*, ed. J. Turner (Sage: Newbury Park).

Turner, R. (1970), *Family Interaction* (Wiley: New York).

Uhlenberg, P. (1978), 'Changing configurations of the life course', in *Transitions*, ed. T. Hareven (Academic Press: New York).

Ungerson, C. (1983), 'Why do women care?', in *A Labour of Love*, eds. J. Finch and D. Groves (Routledge and Kegan Paul: London).

Ungerson, C. (1987), 'The life course and informal caring', in *Social Change and the Life Course*, ed. G. Cohen (Tavistock: London and New York).

Ursel, J. (1984), 'Toward a theory of reproduction', *Contemporary Crises*, **8**.

Ursel, J. (1986), 'The state and the maintenance of patriarchy', in *Family, Economy and State*, eds. J. Dickinson and B. Russell (St Martin's Press: New York).

Vanier Institute of the Family (1981), *A Mosaic of Family Studies* (The Vanier Institute of the Family, Ottawa).

Vannoy-Hiller, D., and W. Philliber (1989), *Equal Partners*, (Sage: Newbury Park).

Vattimo, G. (1988), *The End of Modernity* (Polity Press: Cambridge).

Veevers, J. (1980), *Childless By Choice*, (Butterworth: Toronto).

Vetere, A. (1987), 'General system theory and the family', in *Ecological Studies of Family Life*, eds. A. Vetere and A. Gale (Wiley: Chichester).

Vogel, L. (1983), *Marxism and the Oppression of Women* (Rutgers University Press: New Brunswick, NJ).

Voydanoff, P. (1988), 'Work and family', *Journal of Social Behavior and Personality*, **3**.

Voydanoff, P., and L. Majka, eds. (1988), *Families and Economic Distress* (Sage: Newbury Park).

Voysey, M. (1975), *A Constant Burden* (Routledge and Kegan Paul: London and Boston).

Wagner, P. (1989), 'Social science and the state in continental Western Europe', *International Social Science Journal*, **41**.

Walby, S. (1990), *Theorizing Patriarchy* (Blackwell: Oxford).

Wallace, C. (1987), *For Richer, For Poorer* (Tavistock: London and New York).

Wallerstein, I. (1988), 'Should we unthink nineteenth-century social science?', *International Social Science Journal*, **40**.

Walsh, F. (1982), 'Conceptualizations of normal family functioning', in *Normal Family Processes*, ed. F. Walsh (Guilford Press: New York and London).

Wayne, J. (1986), 'The function of social welfare in a capitalist economy', in *Family, Economy and State*, eds. J. Dickinson and B. Russell (St Martin's Press: New York).

Wearing, B. (1984), *The Ideology of Motherhood* (Allen and Unwin: Sydney).

Weber, M. (1968), *Economy and Society, vol. 3*, (Bedminster: New York).

Weigert, A., and D. Thomas, (1971), 'Family as a conditional universal', *Journal of Marriage and the Family*, **33**.

Wenger, G.C. (1984), *The Supportive Network* (Allen and Unwin: London).

Wicks, M. (1983), 'Does Britain need a family policy?', in *Family Matters*, ed. A. Franklin (Pergamon: Oxford).

Williams, C. (1988), *Examining the Nature of Domestic Labour* (Avebury: Aldershot).

Wilson, P., and R. Pahl (1988), 'The changing sociological construct of the family', *Sociological Review*, **36**.

Witkin, S. (1989), 'Scientific ideology and women: implications for marital research and therapy', *Journal of Family Psychology*, **2**.

Wittrock, B. (1989), 'Social science and state development', *International Social Science Journal*, **41**.

Yeatman, A. (1984), 'Gender and the differentiation of social life into public and domestic domains', *Social Analysis*, **15**.

Young, M., and P. Willmott (1974), *The Symmetrical Family* (Pantheon: New York).

Zaretsky, E. (1982) 'The place of the family in the origins of the welfare state', in *Rethinking the Family*, eds. B. Thorne and M. Yalom (Longman: New York and London).

Zaretsky, E. (1986a), *Capitalism, the Family, and Personal Life*, revised edn, (Harper and Row: New York [1973]).

Zaretsky, E. (1986b), 'Rethinking the welfare state: dependence, economic individualism and the family', in *Family, Economy and State*, eds. J. Dickinson and B. Russell (St Martin's Press: New York).

Zimmerman, S. (1988), *Understanding Family Policy*, (Sage: Newbury Park).

AUTHOR INDEX

Adams, B., 12, 14
Ahrons, C., 124, 131–2
Aldous, J., 71, 135
Alexander, J., 75
Allen, K., 124
Allen, S., 112
Anderson, M., 86
Andrews, M., 66
Askham, J., 51
Atwater, L., 139
Avis, J., 73

Backett, K., 138
Badham, R., 28
Bane, M.J., 56
Barrett, M., 6, 10, 13, 56, 90, 97–8, 102, 111, 117
Baudrillard, J., 147–8
Bauman, Z., 146, 150
Beaujot, R., 26
Beavers, W.R., 61
Becker, G., 117–18
Beechey, V., 6, 99, 102, 130
Bellah, R., 19–20, 42–7
Benn, S., 83
Bennholdt-Thomsen, V., 100, 117
Berardo, F., 23, 25
Berger, B., 12
Berger, P., 12, 133
Berman, M., 39, 143
Bernard, J., 16
Bernardes, J., 26, 57, 124, 126, 130–1, 140
Beutler, I., 12, 48, 85
Bimbi, F., 104
Bishop, L., 116
Blau, F., 118

Bograd, M., 77, 82
Boh, K., 26, 124–5, 133
Boris, E., 111
Boss, P., 25, 35, 62, 67, 69–70, 73, 163
Brannen, J., 118
Brenner, J., 82, 91, 119, 136
Briger, R., 39, 41
Broderick, C., 8, 14, 23, 49–50, 68
Bruegel, I., 103
Brym, R., 6
Buchmann, M., 133, 142
Burch, T., 37
Burgess, E., 136–7, 143–5
Burr, W., 7–8, 12, 15, 23, 48, 137
Burton, C., 90, 109

Camburn, D., 42
Cancian, F., 89
Carlson, A., 30
Carter, B., 70, 72
Chalmers, L., 83
Chappell, N., 64
Charles, N., 92
Cheal, D., 4, 48, 50, 88, 102, 111, 113, 126, 130, 133–4, 136, 138–40, 150
Chilman, C., 39
Christensen, H., 23
Close, P., 56, 100, 117
Cohen, S., 44
Collier, J., 9
Collins, R., 60
Constantine, L., 66
Coontz, S., 82
Cotton, S., 124
Cottrell, L., 137
Coward, R., 10, 84
Creighton, C., 102

Crow, G., 136
Currie, D., 17

Dahl, T.S., 83
Dahlström, E., 20–2, 36, 112
Dalla Costa, M., 99
Daniels, C., 112
Darling, C., 66
Daune-Richard, A.-M., 112
Davids, L., 6
Davis, K., 4, 26, 37
Delphy, C., 10, 90, 97
Dencik, L., 149–50
Denzin, N., 119, 146–8, 152, 165
Dhruvarajan, V., 26
Dickinson, J., 100, 117
DiIorio, J., 138
Donzelot, J., 54
Dornbusch, S., 48
Dumon, W., 56, 72
Durkheim, E., 160–2
Duvall, E., 70–1

Ebert, T., 148–9
Edelman, M., 26
Edgell, S., 6
Edwards, J., 18, 85
Ehrlich, C., 19
Eichler, M., 12–13, 16–18, 79, 89, 111, 139
Eisenstein, Z., 56
Elder, G., 25, 37, 139–40, 143
Elliot, F.R., 34, 86
Engels, F., 32, 91, 96–8

Fahmy-Eid, N., 109
Fararo, T., 46
Featherstone, M., 146
Ferber, M., 118
Ferguson, A., 10, 98, 111
Ferree, M., 114, 116
Fewer, W., 66
Finch, J., 102, 110–11, 115, 138, 150
Finn, G., 148
Fischer, C., 88
Fletcher, R., 31
Flitcraft, A., 55
Fogarty, M., 56
Folbre, N., 98, 118
Foucault, M., 52–5, 57–8, 60, 63
Fox, B., 6, 11, 100
Fox, G., 42
Franklin, A., 57, 61

Furstenberg, F., 123, 140

Gagnon, A.-G., 55
Gamarnikow, E., 90
Garbarino, J., 55, 66
Gardiner, J., 117
Gaus, G., 83
Gee, E., 122
Gelles, R., 82
Genov, N., 42
Gerson, J., 113
Gerson, K., 115–16, 141
Gerstel, N., 124
Giddens, A., 1, 7, 23, 24, 28–9, 46, 116
Giles-Sims, J., 77–8, 135
Gittins, D., 84
Glazer, N., 112
Glendinning, C., 11, 88
Glenn, E.N., 138, 150
Glennon, L., 46, 82
Glick, P., 6
Goldner, V., 73, 75–7
Goldthorpe, J.E., 3
Goode, W., 3–4, 15
Graham, H., 11
Gravenhorst, L., 72
Greenberg, J., 69
Gross, H., 124
Groves, D., 110
Gubrium, J., 63, 84, 130

Haavind, H., 113
Habermas, J., 31, 112–13, 152
Hadden, J., 41
Hall, C., 10
Hamilton, R., 8, 117
Hansen, D., 7, 23–4, 62
Hansen, K., 82
Harding, S., 154, 159, 162
Hare-Mustin, R., 73, 76
Hareven, T., 136, 139
Hargrove, B., 42
Harris, C., 4, 7–8, 100, 117, 131
Hartmann, H., 9–10, 96–7, 157
Hartsock, N., 17, 150
Hassan, I., 157
Henry, G., 41
Hernes, H., 108
Hertz, R., 124
Hill, R., 7–8, 15, 23–4, 48, 62, 65–6, 70–1, 151
Himmelstrand, U., 7
Himmelweit, S., 98

Hobart, C., 70
Hobsbawm, E., 48
Höhn, C., 26, 35, 37, 143, 151
Holman, T., 12, 23
Holstein, J., 63, 84, 130
Holter, H., 113
Humphries, J., 98, 116
Hunt, J., 150
Hunt, L., 150
Hutter, M., 137

Ihinger-Tallman, M., 69–70

Jacobson, N., 74, 76
Jallinoja, R., 119
James, K., 76–7, 82
Jargowsky, P., 56
Jehu, D., 53, 79
Jensen, A.-M., 104
Johnson, M., 166
Johnson, V., 62
Joshi, H., 26, 110
Jurich, J., 85

Kantor, D., 64
Kaslow, F., 47, 62
Katz, R., 39, 41
Katzenstein, M., 44
Kellner, D., 146
Kellner, H., 133
Kelly, R., 61
Kerber, U., 37
Kerr, M., 92
Kiernan, K., 26
Kitzinger, S., 60
Kobrin, F., 6
Kohli, M., 86, 124, 133
Komarovsky, M., 12
Kooistra, P., 30
Kuhn, A., 102

Lamphere, L., 86, 136
Land, H., 11, 110
Lapointe, J., 17–18
Lasch, C., 37, 116
Laslett, B., 82, 87, 91, 119, 136
Laurin-Frenette, N., 109
Laws, J.L., 6
Lawson, A., 39
Leavitt, R., 149
Lee, G., 34
Lehr, W., 64
Leigh, G., 48, 137

Leik, R., 56
Lenero-Otero, L., 34
Leonard, D., 97
Levinger, G., 135
Lewis, J., 60, 91
Lewis, R., 135, 151
Libby, R., 39
Libow, J., 74
Liljeström, R., 2, 35, 83, 86, 108, 112
Linton, R., 127
Locke, H., 144–5
Long, N., 117
Lopata, H., 141
Luhmann, N., 134
Lupri, E., 150
Lüscher, K., 26, 35, 37, 143
Luxton, M., 92, 104
Lynott, R., 63
Lyotard, J.-F., 157

Mace, D., 28
Macfarlane, A., 86
Mackie, M., 138
Mackintosh, M., 10, 102, 117
Maddock, J., 69
Majka, L., 37
Malos, E., 99
Marshall, B., 50
Marx, K., 32, 91, 94, 96–8
Mattessich, P., 48, 71, 151
Mayer, K., 133
McBride, B., 58
McDaniel, S., 41
McGoldrick, M., 70, 72
McIntosh, M., 6, 10, 13, 56, 90, 93, 107
McIntyre, D., 76–7, 82
McKinney, R., 157
McLain, R., 134
Menaghan, E., 85
Merton, R., 36
Meyer, J., 82, 108, 133
Meyer, P., 108
Miles, A., 103
Millar, J., 11, 88
Miller, B., 42, 71
Mitterauer, M., 23
Moch, L., 136
Modell, J., 136
Moen, P., 55–6
Molyneux, M., 106
Montgomery, J., 66
Morgan, D.H.J., 6, 9, 12, 36, 41, 47, 48, 62, 66, 84, 136, 160

Morgan, P., 55, 108
Morris, L., 118
Mortimer, J., 112
Mowrer, E., 14, 37–8
Mudd, E., 127
Mullins, N., 3, 6, 163
Münch, R., 19
Murphy, J., 146
Murphy, M., 139
Murphy, R., 166
Murphy-Lawless, J., 60
Murstein, B., 135

Nave-Herz, R., 35, 127
Nelson, M., 114–15
Nelson, R., 37
Nicholson, L., 10
Nissel, M., 37
Nock, S., 48
Nye, F.I., 15, 23, 134, 151

O'Barr, J., 154
O'Brien, M., 11, 97–8
O'Neill, J., 55
Oakley, A., 6, 16, 60
Oliker, S., 111
Olson, D., 67, 71
Oppenheimer, V., 79
Ory, M., 56
Osmond, M., 12, 50, 82
Owen, S., 118

Pahl, J., 82–3, 118
Pahl, R., 112, 131
Paolucci, B., 64, 66
Parpart, J., 100, 117
Parsons, T., 3, 5–7, 31–6, 44, 59, 76,
    79, 86, 101, 121–3, 133, 146, 153,
    161, 165–6
Pasley, K., 70
Pateman, C., 82
Paterson, F., 54, 109–10
Peiss, K., 113
Perlman, D., 37
Philliber, W., 151
Piotrkowski, C., 64
Pleck, J., 112
Popenoe, D., 40–1, 104
Power, M., 149
Price, M., 87
Purvis, J., 90

Rapoport, R., 119, 132

Rapoport, R.N., 119
Rapp, R., 13
Reiger, K., 122
Reiss, I., 4, 42, 50–1, 53
Reiter, R., 87
Renvoize, J., 124
Richards, L., 82, 84
Richardson, L., 39, 139
Riley, D., 58
Rindfuss, R., 140
Risman, B., 138
Ritzer, G., 164
Rodgers, B., 56
Rodgers, R., 48, 70–1, 124, 131
Rook, K., 37
Rose, H., 11
Rosenthal, C., 124
Roussel, L., 41
Rueschemeyer, M., 34
Russell, B., 100, 117
Russell, C., 61, 67
Ryant, J., 55

Sacks, K., 97
Sangren, S., 152
Saraceno, C., 112–13
Sauer, W., 84
Savage, M., 166
Sayers, J., 97
Scanzoni, J., 3, 22, 128–9, 135, 165
Schoepflin, U., 133
Schorr, A., 55–6
Schwartz, P., 138
Scott, J., 86
Seccombe, W., 92, 98, 100–3, 105–6
Sennett, R., 88
Sgritta, G., 119
Shanas, E., 64
Sharistanian, J., 116
Shehan, C., 25
Shera, W., 56
Shkilnyk, A., 26
Sieder, R., 23
Siltanen, J., 82
Skidmore, F., 37
Skolnick, A., 7
Slater, P., 57
Sluzki, C., 66
Smart, B., 10
Smart, C., 10
Smith, D., 8, 17, 90, 92–3
Smith, J., 51, 68
Smith, P., 83

Snare, A., 83
Sorensen, G., 112
Spanier, G., 123, 135, 151
Sprey, J., 2, 154
Stacey, J., 15
Stacey, M., 16–17, 87
Stanworth, M., 82
Stapleton, C., 151
Stark, E., 55
Stets, J., 138
Stichter, S., 100, 117
Stolcke, V., 97
Storrie, K., 82
Straus, M., 82
Strober, M., 48
Stryker, S., 137
Sussman, M., 64
Sydie, R., 17
Symons, G., 150
Szinovacz, M., 135

Taggart, M., 76–7
Tallman, I., 135
Targ, D., 19
Taubin, S., 127
Théry, I., 41
Thomas, D., 9, 14–15, 18, 41
Thorne, B., 6, 10, 12–13, 15, 35, 73
Thornton, A., 26, 42
Tilly, L., 86
Tiryakian, E., 163
Tomm, K., 74
Touraine, A., 119–20, 150
Trifiletti, R., 56
Trost, J., 124, 126, 132, 139
Turner, B., 30
Turner, J., 15
Turner, R., 137

Uhlenberg, P., 124
Ungerson, C., 111, 118, 141
Ursel, J., 107

Vanier Institute of the Family 8, 12
Vannoy-Hiller, D., 151
Vattimo, G., 147
Veevers, J., 124
Vetere, A., 66
Vogel, L., 97, 117
Voydanoff, P., 37, 112
Voysey, M., 158

Wagner, P., 55
Walby, S., 10
Wallace, C., 140
Wallerstein, I., 32
Walsh, F., 66
Wayne, J., 93
Wearing, B., 13
Weber, M., 13, 87
Weigert, A., 9, 134
Wenger, G.C., 84
Whitehurst, R., 39
Wicks, M., 56
Wilcox, J., 14–15, 18
Williams, C., 34, 117
Willmott, P., 121, 150
Willms, S., 56
Wilson, G., 118
Wilson, P., 131
Witkin, S., 72
Wittrock, B., 55

Yeatman, A., 82
Young, M., 121, 150

Zaretsky, E., 92–6, 108–9
Zimmerman, S., 55

SUBJECT INDEX

Abuse, 69, 83–4, 90
  see also family, violence; wifebeating
Adaptation, 4, 32, 65, 136
Adjustment, 70, 137, 151
Adolescents, 42, 140
Adulthood, 21, 84, 140
Agency, 83, 135
  and gender, 90
  as theoretical problem, 115–16, 119, 166
Alcoholism, 26, 67, 147
Alienation, 94, 109
Altruism, 85
  see also giving
Anthropology, 29, 127
Anti-modernism, 40–7
  versus modernism, 21, 39, 46, 52, 155
  and morality, 42
  and opposition to feminism, 45
  and post-modernism, 151–2
  and religion, 41
  in sociology, 42, 46
Attachment, 58
Australia, 84, 122
Autonomy, 27, 35, 44, 133
  family, 83, 109, 112
  individual, 110, 133, 144
  in the private sphere, 90
  see also liberation

Battered wives *see* wife-beating
Belgium, 56
Birth, 59–60, 72
  rates, 54, 58, 104
Body
  control over, 52–4, 60–1

female, 52, 60
performance criteria for, 57
  see also sex
Boundary (system), 64, 69, 76
  see also family, boundaries
Breadwinners, men as, 35, 93, 99, 110
Britain, 12, 36, 56, 60, 99, 117
  see also England; Scotland
Bureaucracy, 22, 64, 87, 152

Canada, 12, 41, 56, 99, 104, 117, 122
Capitalism, 92
  defined, 94
  division of labour in, 100–1, 103
  and domestic labour, 100–2
  and family, 92–3, 95, 100, 102, 112, 116
  and household, 105, 117
  and housewives, 100–2
  and patriarchy, 91, 99, 103, 157
  and power over life, 54
  and separation of spheres, 94–5, 100
Care, 36, 64, 84–5, 110, 118, 141
  health, 98, 107
  see also childcare; daycare; women, caring by
Careers *see* occupations, and careers
Catholics *see* Roman Catholics
Causality, 74–5, 81
  see also Marxism, and economic determinism
Change
  attitudes toward, 3, 27–8, 31, 37–9, 50, 147, 159–62
  cultural, 120, 127, 147–8
  demographic, 6
  effects of, 44, 142–4

Change (*continued*)
  and family, 37–9, 120–3, 139
  and modernity, 27, 29–31, 34, 39,
    120, 143
  as positive result of intervention, 62
  see also differentiation; diversifica-
    tion; individualization; moderniza-
    tion; post-modernization; social
    evolution; standardization
Childcare, 40, 98, 101, 108, 122
  see also daycare
Children
  attitudes toward, 85, 97, 123, 128,
    149–50
  development of, 70, 147, 149
  effects of on women's lives, 118, 141
  harmful environments for, 26, 69,
    146–7
  relations of with parents, 110, 151
Christians, 41–2, 44
Cities, 88, 144
Class, 97, 106, 121
  see also middle-class; working-class
Clinical model *see* medical model
Cohabitation, 123, 127–8
Communication
  familial, 65, 68, 113, 130–1, 137
  of love, 113, 134
  marital, 47
  and the mass media, 112, 147–8
  professional, 66
Communism, 105
Community, 40, 42, 44, 60, 108
Companionship family, 144
Concepts, 20, 129–30, 158
  abandoned, 128
  displaced, 130
  expanded, 131, 151
  specified, 126
  see also family theory, conceptual
    problems in
Conflict
  in families, 9, 36, 73–4, 135, 138
  theories, 50, 59
Conjugal family, 4–5, 112
Consensus, 7, 50, 65
Consumption, 100–3, 112, 118
Contradictions, 20–3, 36, 42, 51, 82,
    102, 107
  in modernity, 46, 49, 143, 161
  in post-modernity, 148
  see also family, and contradictions
Control
  over the body, 52–4, 60–1

cybernetic, 68, 73
  family, 40, 68–9, 109–10, 144
  male, 10–11, 52, 60, 73, 96–7
  over reproduction, 11, 52, 96–7
  over sexuality, 40, 52
  see also domination; patriarchy;
    power
Critical theory, 50, 112
Culture
  changes in, 39, 120, 127, 147–8
  effects on family preferences, 22, 83,
    121, 126–7
  and the mass media, 112, 147
  modern, 27–8, 50
  post-modern, 146–7
  and the social sciences, 19, 23, 25,
    28, 84, 128–9, 164

Daycare, 26, 114–15, 147, 149
Deconstruction, 13
De-differentiation, 148, 152
Demography, 6, 98
  see also fertility; marriage, trends in;
    mortality; population
Denmark, 149
Dependence, 60
  of wives, 72, 89, 93, 101, 110, 117
Deprivation, 93, 144
  see also poverty
Destandardization, 133
Development, 4, 70–1, 147, 149
Diagnosis, 29, 62, 76
Differentiation, 32, 59–60, 87
  and individualization, 35, 44, 133–4
  in modernity, 27, 86, 133
  of roles, 5, 10, 33
  see also de-differentiation
Discipline *see* control
Discourse, 20, 58
  family, 20, 63, 129–31
  and knowledge, 17, 58, 63
  medical, 59–61
  and the self, 148
  social scientific, 125, 164
Disfunctions, 36, 53, 61–2, 79
Diversification, 124–5, 133, 141, 151
  see also family, diversity; life-styles
Divided life, 114
Division of labour
  in capitalist societies, 100–1, 103
  and gender, 10, 87, 92–3, 101
  in the symmetrical family, 121
Divorce
  effects of, 70, 93, 118, 131–2, 140

Divorce (*continued*)
   increase in, 35, 105, 124, 132
Domesticity, 44, 88–9, 91, 95, 141
Domestic labour, 99
   and capitalism, 100–2, 104
   debate, 100–1, 105–6, 116–17
   of women, 90, 92, 101, 110
   see also housework
Domestic sciences, 122
   see also home economics; human
      ecology
Domination, 89–90
   see also control; patriarchy;
      submission; women, oppression of
Double burden, 34, 104, 114
Double presence, 104
Double standard, 52
Dualism, 82, 157
Dysfunctions *see* disfunctions

Economic theory, 117
Economy *see* capitalism; family, and
      industrial economy; family, and
      the market; industrial societies;
      markets; mode of production
Education, 107, 109
Elderly, 64, 141
Emancipation *see* liberation
Emotions
   and emotional needs, 4–5
   in families, 33, 35, 67, 84–5, 88
   and intimacy, 52, 88
   see also expressiveness; love
Empiricism, 29, 47–8
Employment
   and conflicting obligations, 33–4,
      114, 121, 141
   and gender, 5, 44, 104, 111
   see also homeworking; occupations;
      wage labour; wives, employment
      of; women, and careers; women,
      effects of employment of
England, 86, 121
Enlightenment, the, 28
Epistemology, 76, 154, 158
Equality *see* gender, and equality
Ethnicity, 124
Europe
   capitalism in, 54, 105
   communism in, 105
   family patterns in, 35, 125
   social policy in, 56, 72
   women in, 104

   see also Belgium; Britain; Denmark;
      England; France; Germany;
      Ireland; Italy; Norway;
      Scandinavia; Scotland; Sweden
Evolution *see* social evolution
Exchange
   in families, 10, 135
   in markets, 100, 117
Exchange theory, 134–5, 150–1
Expressiveness, 6, 43, 89, 134

Familism, 51, 145
Familogy, 48
Family
   adaptation, 4, 65
   autonomy, 83, 109, 112
   boundaries, 65, 69–70, 76–8, 82–4
   and contradictions, 20–3, 36, 114
   crises, 37, 40, 62, 67–8, 93
   criticisms of, 38, 90
   decline of, 40, 43
   definitions, 4, 9, 63–4, 126, 136, 140,
      147
   deinstitutionalization of, 40
   destandardization of, 133
   development of, 70–1
   discourse, 20, 63, 129–31
   disfunctions, 36, 61
   disorganization, 62, 69, 121, 144
   diversity, 6, 23, 123, 125
   functioning, 33, 35, 63, 68, 71, 84
   functions, 4, 40, 65, 95
   and gender, 82
   as haven, 116
   healthy, 62
   and ideology, 10–11, 13, 51, 93, 101, 130
   and income, 110, 117–18, 123–4
   and industrial economy, 4–5, 34, 86
   institution, 4, 144
   interior of, 84, 90
   life cycle, 48, 70–1, 139, 151
   love in, 44–5, 89, 112–13
   and the market, 104, 113
   and the mass media, 112, 147–8
   modern, 33
   neglect, 37
   normal, 5–6, 62, 82, 110, 123–4, 127,
      161
   norms, 65, 70–1, 106, 115, 123, 144
   obligations, 42, 115
   politics of, 11, 56–7, 98
   post-modern, 147
   private, 82–4, 88, 90–1, 96

Family (*continued*)
  problems, 26, 62, 65
  and property, 53, 96–7
  realm, 85
  reorganization, 62, 131, 144
  resources, 71, 79, 93
  rituals, 133
  roles, 65, 111, 123, 137–40
  rules, 68, 115
  and social evolution, 4, 31, 125
  and social policy, 11–12, 55–6,
    107–8, 110–11
  and society, 4, 40
  and the state, 55, 84, 106–11
  strengths, 67, 116
  supports, 37, 64, 84, 116
  tasks, 65, 70
  and time, 70, 139
  types *see* companionship family;
    conjugal family; nuclear family;
    private family; single-parent
    families; stepfamilies; symmetrical
    family
  unity, 136–7
  universality of, 4, 9, 126–7
  violence, 36, 77–8, 82, 138, 147
  wage, 93, 107, 109
  and the welfare state, 107–10
  see also capitalism, and family;
    communication, familial; conflict,
    in families; control, family;
    emotions, in families; individuals,
    or families; interaction, family;
    production, in families; stress,
    family; systems, family; tradition,
    and family; work, and family
Family life education, 66
Family policy, 55–7, 72, 79, 103
Family practitioners, 22, 63–4, 66,
    144–5
  interventions by, 122
  see also family life education; family
    therapy; home economics; human
    ecology; marriage, counselling;
    social work
Family science, 14, 49, 63, 84
Family studies *see* sociology, of the
    family, history of
Family theory
  conceptual frameworks in, 23
  conceptual problems in, 8–9, 13,
    126–32, 151
  diversity of, 18, 153–4

  unification of, 7–8, 15
  value-free, 14
  value-laden, 129
  see also familogy; feminist theory, of
    family; sociology, of the family;
    theoretical approaches
Family therapy
  criticisms of, 73–7
  goals of, 62
  and sociology, 47
  see also systems theory, in family
    therapy; therapy, marital
Family values
  and nostalgia, 3, 85
  and religion, 38, 41–2, 51
Fathers, 58, 97
  see also paternity
Feedback, 68–9, 74–5, 77–8
Feminism, 9–13
  and attitudes toward change, 9, 38,
    159
  and criticisms of family, 38, 90
  and criticisms of family studies, 9, 16, 72
  and criticisms of family therapy, 73–5
  and criticisms of marriage, 10
  and deconstruction, 13
  influence of, 2, 12, 17, 81, 99
  and marxism, 97–100
  marxist, 92, 106–7, 111
  materialist, 98, 107
  and modernity, 46
  opposition to, 12, 45
  radical, 22, 111
  socialist, 111, 117
  see also feminist theory
Feminist theory
  of family, 13, 90
  of knowledge, 16–17, 159, 162
  of medicine, 59–60
  of separate spheres, 87, 89–90, 110
  of the state, 109–10
  of work, 111–12, 114
  see also feminism; patriarchy
Fertility, 93, 104
Food, 91–2
France, 41, 56, 112
Freedom *see* autonomy; liberation
Functions *see* family, functioning;
    family, functions; marxism,
    functionalist logic in; nuclear
    family, and functional specializa-
    tion; structural functionalism
Future, 27, 38, 159, 161–2

Gender, 12–13
  differences, 10, 16, 75, 138
  divisions, 44, 60, 100, 110
  and domination, 89–90, 148
  and equality, 52, 97
  and family, 82, 110
  and inequality, 10, 73, 88, 101
  and power, 60, 73
  and the private sphere, 87, 89
  relationships, 6, 10
  roles, 5, 10, 34–5
  and sex, 96–7
  and social theory, 16–17
  see also division of labour, and
    gender; employment, and gender;
    men; women
General systems theory *see* systems
  theory
Germany, 34, 37, 114, 116, 127, 133,
  143
Gerontology, 64
Giving, 10
Government *see* state, the
Growth
  in marriage, 28, 62
  and modernity, 39
  personal, 4, 43

Health
  of families, 61–2
  and modernity, 54
  and social support, 64
  see also home, health care in;
    hospitals; therapy
Heterosexuality, 10, 148
Historicism, 120
History *see* social history
Home
  domestic labour in, 92, 98–9,
    101
  health care in, 60, 98, 110
  management of, 122
  ownership, 84
  and separate spheres, 87, 95
  women in, 87, 89, 114
  see also homeworking
Home economics, 64
Homemakers *see* housewives
Homeworking, 111
Hospitals, 60
  and families, 63, 66
Household
  in capitalism, 105, 116–17

  and family, 105–6
  poverty in, 88
Housewives
  in capitalism, 100–2
  dependent, 89, 101, 110
  women as, 92–3, 99, 101, 110,
    117–18
  see also domestic labour; housework
Housework
  ignored, 16
  unpaid, 95, 99, 101
  see also domestic labour
Human ecology, 64
Human services, 63–4, 66, 122, 145
  see also family practitioners; social
    policy; support, by the state;
    welfare state
Husbands, 5–6, 82, 89, 101, 121
  and their wives, 77, 90, 96, 111
  see also wife-beating

Identity, 51, 104, 137–8, 149
Ideology
  in family life, 10–11, 13, 51, 93, 101,
    130, 148
  and science, 154
  and social theory, 19, 22, 50–1, 132
Income
  family, 110, 118, 123–4
  and personal dependence or
    independence, 89
  supports, 107, 110
Independence *see* autonomy
India, 26
Individualism
  and decline of the family unit, 40,
    43
  and expressiveness, 43, 134
  and interpersonal ties, 133–4
  and loss of attachment, 37
  and men, 44
  and modernization, 39–40, 44, 86,
    133
  see also individualization;
    individuals, or families
Individualization
  and destandardization, 133
  and differentiation, 35, 44, 132–4
  in the female life course, 141
  see also individualism
Individuals, or families, 134, 136,
  138–9
  see also individualism

Industrial societies
  children in, 151
  family in, 4–5, 86–7, 109
  and modernization, 34, 143
  see also capitalism
Inequality *see* class; gender, and
  inequality; inheritance
Inheritance, 96–7
Instability
  of knowledge, 149–50, 155–7, 162
  in social life, 88, 139, 146, 148
Instrumental tasks, 6, 35
Integration, 32–3, 44, 137
Interaction
  family, 67, 74, 123, 133, 136–8
  intimate, 35, 134
  in marriage, 6, 43, 47, 77, 135,
    137
  rituals, 138, 144
Intimacy
  and communication, 134
  emotional, 52, 88
  in family and marriage, 51, 130
  non-family, 138
Ireland, 60
Israel, 40
Italy, 56, 99, 104

Kinship, 5, 53, 87, 115, 136
Knowledge
  and culture, 19, 25, 28, 129, 164
  and discourse, 17, 58
  in everyday life, 130
  expert, 26, 61, 144, 149–50
  instability of, 157, 162
  and modernity, 28–9
  post-modern, 156–8, 164
  and power, 55, 57–8, 63
  social scientific, 14–17, 128–9
  sociological, 41–2, 158

Labour, 100–1
  see also division of labour; domestic
    labour; production; wage labour;
    work
Law, 53, 87, 144
  see also Napoleonic Code
Leisure, 103, 113
Liberalism, 83, 89
Liberation
  of women, 72, 97, 145
Life, 54, 91–2
  see also body; food; pro-life

Life course, 139–41
  see also life cycle; transitions
Life cycle
  family, 48, 71, 139, 151
  see also life course
Life-styles, 39, 124, 132–3
  see also family, diversity
Love
  and communication, 113, 134
  feminization of, 89
  as an ideal in family life, 44–5,
    112
  and sex, 96–7

Markets
  commodity, 100
  effects of, 107, 112–13
  and families, 104
  and individualism, 43
  labour, 100, 102
  and modernity, 27, 86
  see also capitalism; value
Marriage
  adjustment in, 137, 151
  and children, 96–7, 123, 127–8
  and choice of partner, 135
  commitment to, 77–8
  commuter, 124
  conflict in, 73–4, 135
  and the conjugal family, 4–5
  counselling, 22, 145
  and economic conditions, 122
  enrichment, 28
  feminist criticism of, 10
  versus identity, 51
  inequality in, 88, 101
  integration in, 137
  medicalization of, 62
  norms, 123
  power in, 10, 16, 75, 96–7
  quality of, 135, 151
  rape in, 83
  and respectability, 138
  roles, 118, 121
  and sex, 53, 96–7
  and therapy, 47, 73
  timing of, 136
  as transition, 140
  trends in, 122, 124
  women in, 6, 10, 77–8, 93
  see also divorce; husbands;
    interaction, in marriage;
    monogamy; remarriage; wives

Marxism
  and the capitalist mode of
    production, 94, 100
  and the domestic labour debate,
    100–6, 116–17
  and economic determinism, 91–3, 98
  and family strengths, 116
  and feminism, 92, 97–100, 106–7,
    111
  functionalist logic in, 102–3
Mass media, 27, 112, 147–8
Materialism, 91–2, 98
  see also marxism
Maternity, 58, 107
  see also birth; pro-life; pro-natalism
Medical model, 60–2
  see also diagnosis; pathology;
    prognosis; symptoms
Men
  and agency, 90
  and care, 141
  and children, 96–7
  and control, 10–11, 52, 60, 144
  differences among, 160
  domination by, 17
  and family therapy, 73, 82
  and individualism, 44
  and instrumental tasks, 6
  and the life course, 140–1
  and marriage, 96
  and parental competence, 58
  and the public sphere, 87, 90
  and wage labour, 101
  see also breadwinners, men as;
    gender; patriarchy
Methodology, 17, 84, 138, 160
Middle-class, 5, 84, 92, 121
Mode of production, 92
  see also Marxism, and the capitalist
    mode of production
Models
  in family therapy, 74
  folk, 20
  in mass media simulations, 148
  in social theory, 13, 18, 131, 151
Modernism, 31
  versus anti-modernism, 21, 39–42,
    45–7
  and attitudes toward evolution,
    31–2, 34
  versus post-modernism, 22–3, 142,
    157
  see also modernity

Modernity, 26–30
  and change, 26–32, 39, 120, 143
  crisis of, 120
  criticism of, 43–4
  culture of, 27–8, 50
  and feminism, 46
  and health, 54
  and individualism, 39, 43, 133
  and knowledge, 28
  and markets, 27, 86
  and mass media, 27
  and modernization, 120
  and permissiveness, 39, 42
  and power, 57
  and progress, 27
  and reason, 27–8
  and science, 27
  and the social sciences, 26, 28–30,
    50, 55
  in sociology, 28–9, 46, 49, 120
  and the state, 27
  see also family, modern; modernism;
    modernization; progress
Modernization, 26
  and differentiation, 44, 86
  and family, 40–1, 127
  and individualization, 35, 133
  and modernity, 120
  and rationalization, 122, 142
  and secularization, 28, 39, 108
  and standardization, 120–1
  and the state, 107–8
  see also modernity; social evolution
Monogamy, 96–8, 123
Morality
  and anti-modernism, 42
  and anxiety, 39, 45
  Christian, 41–2
  and social organization, 113, 166
  of women, 45, 95
  see also altruism
Moral Majority, 41
Mormonism, 51
Morphogenesis, 69
Mortality, 122
Motherhood, 58, 141
  see also maternity; mothers
Mothers
  adolescent, 123, 147
  and children, 6, 82, 151
  daycare use by, 114–15
  idealized, 95
  see also maternity; motherhood

Napoleonic Code, 41
National Council on Family Relations, 49
Negotiation, 115, 138
Networks, 84, 111, 163
Normality
  in family theory, 36, 121, 161
  in therapeutic intervention, 58, 76
  see also family, normal
Norway, 104, 113
Nuclear family, 4–5
  and capitalism, 103, 105
  decline of, 147
  in family therapy, 76
  and functional specialization, 5, 32–3
  golden age of, 3, 76
  and industrial societies, 4–5, 86, 109
  isolated, 5, 76, 83
  tension management in, 5, 82

Occupations
  and careers, 118, 121, 141
  and status, 5, 79
  see also employment; professions
Ontology, 76
Organizations, 63–4, 87

Paralogy, 157
Parenthood *see* fathers; motherhood; mothers; parents
Parents
  and children, 109–10, 151
  single, 6, 124, 128, 147, 151
  see also fathers; mothers
Past, 27, 38, 47
  see also social history; tradition
Paternity, 11, 97
Pathology, 58, 61, 69, 161
Patriarchy, 10
  and capitalism, 99, 103, 157
  and control, 11, 60
  and marriage and the family, 72, 91, 96
Permissiveness, 39, 42
Personal relationships, 94–5, 108, 133–4, 144
Phenomenology, 134
Pluralism
  and post-modernism, 146, 157–9
  social, 119, 139, 140
  in sociology, 158
Pluralization, 158

Politics
  of the body, 54, 60
  of the family, 11, 56–7, 98
  of housework, 99
  of reproduction, 57–8
  and the state, 106–8
  see also feminism; liberalism; marxism; socialism
Population, 54–5, 104
Positivism, 14–15
  criticisms of, 16–18, 129, 154
  and general laws, 14, 160
  imitation of natural sciences in, 14, 29
  units of analysis defined in, 125
  see also science
Post-modernism, 146
  and anti-modernism, 151–2
  versus modernism, 22–3, 142
  and pluralism, 157–8
  see also post-modernity
Post-modernity, 150
  culture of, 147–8
  family in, 143, 147–8
  instability of, 146, 148–9, 164
  knowledge in, 156–8
  and the mass media, 147–8
  and social theory, 145–6, 148, 156–9
  see also post-modernism; post-modernization
Post-modernization
  and de-differentiation, 148, 152
  and social acceleration, 149
  see also post-modernity
Post-positivism, 18, 130–1
Poverty
  children in, 26, 146
  women in, 88
Power
  in capitalism, 54, 106–7
  criticisms of, 50, 57, 109–10
  and gender, 60, 73, 75
  and knowledge, 55, 58, 63
  in marriage, 10, 16, 75, 96–7
  and modernity, 39, 57
  see also control; domination; patriarchy
Pre-modern societies, 25–6
Present, 27, 43, 161
Primary relationships, 6, 22, 128–9, 137
Private family, 86–91
  see also family, private

Private property *see* property
Private sphere
  and autonomy, 83–4, 90
  and gender, 87, 89–91
  invasion of, 112, 148
  non-intervention in, 83
  primary relationships in, 129
  and the public sphere, 82–4, 87,
    89–90, 94, 108, 111–13, 116
  and isolation, 82–3
  and the stàte, 87, 108, 110
  see also women, in the private
    sphere
Problems
  behavioural, 140, 145
  family, 26, 118
  financial, 93
  particularized, 76–7
  as private troubles, 83
  as public issues, 108
  as stressor events, 62
  as symptoms, 61–2
Production
  capitalist, 22, 54, 92, 94, 100
  in families, 33, 65, 87–8, 98–9, 101,
    109
  and reproduction, 22, 91, 98–9, 101,
    107
  see also domestic labour; labour;
    wage labour
Professions, 60–1, 63, 66
Prognosis, 29, 62
Progress, 27, 31
  end of, 146–7
  family, 36–7, 70
  and knowledge, 55
  and modernity, 27
  and self-fulfilment, 40
  and social evolution, 31–2, 161
  and social theory, 28–9, 41–2, 49
  and the state, 107
  see also modernity;
    modernization
Pro-life, 41
Pro-natalism, 58, 104, 107
Property, 96–7, 105
Protestants, 41
Psychiatry, 145
Psychology, 58, 70, 75, 134, 145
Psychotherapy, 62
Public
  policy, 108
  sphere, 22, 82–4, 87, 89–90, 94,
    107–8

Racism, 116
Rape, 83
Rational choice, 135
  see also reason
Rationalization, 87, 122, 142
  see also reason
Reason
  and modernity, 27–8
  and social theory, 28, 146
Relationships, 114–15
  see also personal relationships;
    primary relationships
Religion
  and anti-modernism, 41–2
  and divine power, 26, 28
  and family, 38, 44
  influence of in the social sciences,
    19, 41–2, 46, 51
  and tradition, 44
Remarriage, 135
Reproduction, 4, 65
  control over, 11, 52, 96–7, 106–7
  effects of economy on, 93, 107
  politics of, 58, 60
  and production, 22, 91, 98–9, 101, 107
Ritual, 133, 138, 144
Roles
  and dependence, 59–60, 117–18
  differentiation of, 5, 10, 33
  in family, 5, 65, 111, 123, 137–40
  and gender, 5, 10, 34–5
  marital, 118, 121
  set of, 104, 114, 140
Roman Catholics, 41
Romance, 148

Scandinavia, 104, 108
  see also Denmark; Norway; Sweden
School *see* education
Science
  critical rethinking of, 17, 154, 157,
    159
  and hypothesis testing, 14–15, 125,
    160
  and modernity, 27
  and objectivity, 14, 16
  and scientific management, 122
  and sociology, 160–1
  see also family science; positivism
Scotland, 51, 109
Secularization, 28, 39
Self
  fulfilment, 40, 43
  production, 29, 50

Self (*continued*)
  sense of, 10, 137, 148–9
  see also identity
Separation
  marital, 97, 135
  and maternal deprivation, 58
  of spheres, 87, 89
Sex
  abuse, 69
  adolescent, 42
  control of in the family, 40, 52
  and domination, 96–7
  and the double standard, 52
  disfunctions, 53
  and love, 97
  in marriage, 53, 96
  outside marriage, 39, 42, 96, 138–9,
    159
  and religion, 42
  and reproduction, 11
  and satisfaction, 98
  and therapeutic intervention, 53, 57,
    79
  see also heterosexuality; sexuality
Sexuality, 52–3, 95
  see also permissiveness
Single-parent families, 6, 105, 124,
    128, 147, 151
Social change *see* change
Social construction, of
  commitment, 78
  desire, 11
  meaning, 115, 138, 144
  reality, 10, 68, 148
  relationships, 114, 133
Social contradictions *see* contradictions
Social control *see* control
Social evolution, 161
  and family, 4, 32–3
  see also modernization;
    post-modernization
Social history, 23, 86, 135–6, 139
Socialism, 22, 34, 38
  and feminism, 111, 117
Socialization, 4–5, 10, 40, 65, 138, 149
Social movements, 38, 41–2
Social policy, 56, 72, 108
  and the social sciences, 26
  see also family, and social policy;
    family policy; welfare state
Social sciences
  and culture, 19, 25, 28, 84, 128–9,
    164
  feminist criticism of, 15–17

knowledge in, 17, 41–2, 58, 119
  and modernity, 26, 28, 50, 55
  and objectivity, 14, 16
  religious influence on, 19, 41–2, 46,
    51
  and secularization, 28
  social influences on, 19–20, 37–9,
    63–4
  and the state, 55
  see also anthropology; demography;
    economic theory; familogy; family
    science; gerontology; psychology;
    sociology
Social services *see* human services;
    social policy; social work; support,
    by the state; welfare state
Social status, 5, 79, 121
Social support *see* support
Social theory
  conceptual dualism in, 82, 113
  diversity of, 12, 17, 45–6, 153–4
  effects of gender on, 17
  and ideology, 19, 22, 41, 50
  influence of social history on, 23, 86,
    135–6, 139
  instability of, 155–7
  and modernity, 39
  pluralization of, 158
  polarization of, 50
  post-modern rethinking of, 146
  and progress, 28–9, 49–50
  and reason, 28
  and schools of thought, 163–5
  see also family theory; feminist
    theory; theoretical approaches
Social work, 63
Sociology
  in crisis, 2, 119–20
  of the family, criticisms of, 72, 119
  of the family, history of, 3–4, 7–9,
    12, 37–9, 99–100, 119, 130–1, 140,
    153–4
  and modernity, 28–30, 46, 49–50,
    120, 142–3
  as a science, 160–1
Space, 24, 84, 88
Stability, 21, 51
Standardization, 120–2, 124, 142
Standard sociological theory, 3–4,
    126–7, 157
  criticisms of, 6, 8–9, 12–13, 123, 130
  and structural functionalism, 4–5
  and symbolic interactionism, 137
  and systems theory, 66–7

State, the, 106
    and family, 84, 106–11
    and family policy, 55
    increased power of, 40, 86, 108, 133, 143
    and modernity, 27, 107–8
    and public/private spheres, 87, 108
    and the social sciences, 55
    see also law; support, by the state; welfare state
Status *see* social status
Stepfamilies, 70
Strategies, 62, 79, 118, 135–6
Stratification *see* class; gender, and inequality; inheritance; power, and gender; social status
Stress
    causes of, 58, 71–2
    family, 69
    response to, 62–3, 65, 67–8
    see also tension management
Structural analysis
    macro, 11, 115–16
    micro, 138
Structural functionalism, 4–5
    criticisms of, 8–9, 35–6, 79, 86, 101–2
Submission, 78, 89
Suburbs, 84
Support
    emotional, 35
    by the family, 37, 63–4, 84, 116
    for the family, 66, 107
    financial, 89, 110
    and health, 64
    by kin, 115
    by the state, 34, 107, 110
Sweden, 20, 40, 56, 104, 108
Symbolic interactionism
    criticism of, 138
    and family, 136–7
    and the life course, 139
    and standard sociological theory, 137
Symmetrical family, 121, 150
Symptoms, 61–2, 67, 82
System, 64
    closed, 69, 71, 78
    control in, 68, 73
    family, 65
    morphogenesis in, 69
    open, 69
    support, 37, 64
Systems theory, 64
    criticisms of, 72–9

of family, 65–8
in family therapy, 64, 67, 74–7, 81–2
in home economics, in human ecology, 64
of wife-beating, 77–8
see also boundary; feedback

Teenagers *see* adolescents
Television *see* mass media
Tension management, 5, 82
Theoretical approaches, 18–19, 125
    diversification of, 153–4
    see also critical theory; exchange theory; feminism, marxist; feminist theory; marxism; materialism; phenomenology; standard sociological theory; structural analysis; structural functionalism; symbolic interactionism; systems theory
Theoreticism, 166
Theory groups, 163
Therapy
    feminist, 74–5, 145
    and gender, 73–5
    marital, 47
    and the medical model, 61–2
    sexual, 53
    and therapeutic intervention, 58
    see also family therapy; systems theory, in family therapy
Time, 24
    family in, 70, 73, 139–40
    management of, 122
    modern attitude toward, 43
    shortage of, 150
    see also future; past; present
Tradition
    and family, 25–6, 39–41, 48, 127
    loss of, 27, 39, 43, 52
    and religion, 42, 44
    in social science, 19, 46
    see also past
Trajectories, 140–1
Transitions, 71, 122–3, 140, 142
Trust, 88

United Kingdom *see* Britain; England; Scotland
United States of America
    anti-modernism in, 41–2
    family in, 40, 43, 51–2, 58, 121–3, 147
    family studies in, 3, 7, 12, 14–15, 23,

United States of America (*continued*)
family studies in,
42, 48, 65, 70, 143–4, 151
and modern attitude toward time, 43
positivism in, 14–15
and standard sociological theory, 3–4
theory unification in, 7
see also Utah
Urban life *see* cities; suburbs
Utah, 51, 75, 85

Value, 114, 117
Value generalization, 32, 166
Value-judgments, 19
Violence *see* family, violence;
wife-beating

Wage labour
and domestic labour, 100–2
and the family wage, 93, 107, 109–10
performed at home, 111, 114
see also capitalism; employment;
value; wives, employment of
Welfare state, 107–10
see also social policy; support, by the
state
Wife-beating
causes of, 72, 77–8
invisibility of, and family privacy,
82–3
Wives
dependence of, 72, 89, 93, 101, 110,
117–18
and domestic labour, 101
employment of, 79, 99, 104, 121
and their husbands, 77, 90, 96, 111
see also housewives; wife-beating
Women
and agency, 90, 115–16, 119
and careers, 118, 141
caring by, 11, 36, 110, 118, 141
and children, 118, 141, 151
and class, 97
differences among, 116, 140–1

effects of employment of, 34, 39,
104, 107, 114, 141
and expressiveness, 6, 35, 89
and family therapy, 73, 82
and the female body, 52, 59–60
friendship networks of, 111
as homemakers/housewives, 93,
99–102, 110, 118
invisible, 16, 72, 82, 88
and kinship, 87
liberation of, 97, 145
and the life course, 140–1
and love, 89
and morality, 44, 95
and motherhood, 58, 141
oppression of, 10, 16, 73, 90, 109,
111
and poverty, 88
in the private sphere, 82–3, 87,
89–91, 95
and/as property, 97, 105
and reproduction, 98
and sexuality, 52
social isolation among, 83, 90
in the social sciences, 17
and woman's sphere, 44
and work, 92, 95, 101, 104, 111–12,
114–15
see also double burden; double
presence; feminism; feminist
theory; gender; home, women in;
housewives, women as; marriage,
women in; wives
Work, in capitalist production, 94
differentiation of, 33
and education, 109
and family, 82, 87–8, 92, 109–10,
112, 136
in the home, 95, 100, 111–12, 114–15
see also domestic labour; double
burden; employment; housework;
occupations; women, and work
Working-class, 93, 97–9, 101–2, 107,
116